Bread Machine Cookboo

Unlock the Full Potential of Your Bread Machine

Follow Recipes for Beginners to Always Have Fresh, Delicious

Homemade Bread

By

ELOISE BOURN

Introduction

The bread that one makes at home is nutritious and delicious, but making it from scratch requires tremendous work. It requires a lot of effort, time, and patience to combine the ingredients, knead the dough, wait for it to rise, knead it again, and then bake it, but it does not have to be always this way.

The bread maker can do all the hard work, and you have only to taste and appreciate the excellent taste of homemade bread. If one is not yet persuaded and wonders if it is wise to invest in such an appliance, all the recipes in this book can reassure you of its merit. The bread-making process is slow and labor-intensive, and as many people do not have the patience to go through the entire process in this time, bread machines have become a requirement.

Although a person can still buy bread from markets, it would always be a better choice to bake bread at home, as bread can be optimized as per the tastes and health needs of the individual/family.

A home machine for baking bread is a bread machine that transforms all the ingredients into tasty bread. The wonderful thing about an automated bread maker is that all these steps are completed for you. A bread-making appliance is a portable electric oven that contains a single wide bread tin. The tin is still a little unique; it has a bottom axle that attaches to the electric motor below it. Within the tin, a small metal paddle spins on the axle. A waterproof seal holds the axle, so the bread mixture cannot leak. Bread has always been eaten along with all sorts of food, rendering it mandatory for all occasions, whether it be lunch, brunch, or dinner. Using a bread maker is better than purchasing the bread at a store.

Store-bought bread is full of synthetic chemicals, but you only need natural ingredients at home with a bread machine. You may even include specific ingredients, including grains or seeds, to make it much better; apart from flour, you will need yeast and water. Homemade bread is even tastier because you must always use fresh ingredients, and you can personalize ingredients according to the particular preference. Even if that's not enough, after traditional bread-making, many dishes have to be washed too. One has to put in the ingredients with a bread machine, and after the bread is baked, clean the tin.

Current bread machines bring a lot of unique controls that allow several bread specialties to be prepared. For individuals who are intolerant or sensitive to such foods, such as Gluten, a bread machine may be handy.

This book will provide you with all sorts of recipes. These devices can also be used for recipes other than bread, such as jelly, fruit jam, scrambled eggs, tomato sauce, and casseroles, and even some desserts, with a couple of ingredients variations. All you have to do is use fresh ingredients and walk away

Chapter 1-Bread machine and Baking

Since the beginning of baking, freshly made bread is the best thing ever. The only trouble is, time and commitment are required. Many individuals have never baked bread in their lives and will never think of doing so, but much of that has begun to shift with the new advent of automated bread-making machines. Today millions convert their homes into bakeries, and every day one can enjoy their own freshly made bread at a fraction of the price they might spend in a shop. There are different explanations for why an individual should suggest using a bread maker instead of any other choices that he has access to. Bread machines in cafes, households, workplaces, etc., have often been more comfortable people's choice. The majority of available bread makers on the market are automatic.

Bread machines reduce effort and time by helping their customers. An ingredient may be added to it by a baker, homemaker, or any other user. It completes its work automatically, without any control on the part of its consumer. Bread machines allow consumers to do other required things, such as preparing the main course, dinner, etc., while reducing the workload. It is necessary to remember, though, that not all bread machines are automated. Many Pricey bread makers only give automatic functions. To finish the bread-making method, you just need all the necessary ingredients.

Bread makers are often simple to use and manage, much like ovens for bread makers. Assume an individual doesn't know how to bake or doesn't even want to bake; bread machines are the ideal substitute for those people. Besides, it is often likely that individuals wish to bake a specific form of bread at home, like French bread, but does not know how to use an oven for baking one. A bread maker allows us to produce such bread in these situations, while alternate cycles or settings also come with it.

The dough must go through 5 phases if you make bread the conventional way, primarily as mixing, kneading, rising, punching down, proving, and baking, but it's all in one move with the bread maker. All ingredients you have to add to the system, adjust the cycles, and let it do its thing. Each time, you'll get accurate outcomes.

Chapter 2-Criteria For Selecting The Right Bread Machine

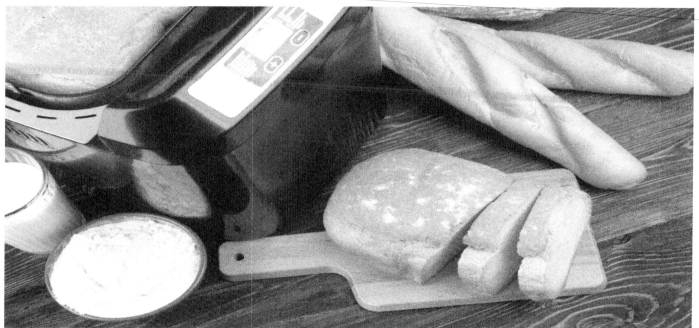

Think of yourself what the criteria will be before selecting the right kind of bread machine for yourself.

Timer: You can manually determine when to set the timer for a baking cycle. Then you have to come at the right time, to take the bread out of the maker. Otherwise, the bread would be preheated and cooked, or choose a one where the machine will calculate the time.

Size: Get the bread machine that carries a recipe comprising 3 cups of flour if one has a big family. Some can hold flour cups of up to 4 to 5-1/2.

Blades: Blades in horizontal pans do not often knead the dough too well, leaving the pan's corners with flour. A significant negative is incomplete blending. However, the upright settings do a better job of mixing. Many new machines are made vertically, but some horizontal pans also offer two blades, so choose carefully.

Chapter 3-Bread in Five Easy Steps

Bread machines are effortless and straightforward to use. Add in ingredients specifically in an order, following the bread machine's manufacturer suggested order. In most machines, add liquids first, then in dry ingredients, or as your machine specifies. All ingredients that are to be used should be at room temperature or specified otherwise.

1. Measure the ingredients and add them to the bread pan.

Before adding the ingredients, remove the bread pan from the unit (otherwise, it is easy to spill them onto the heating elements where they will burn)

Until the ingredients are applied, the kneading blade should be in place (on its mounting shaft). It is necessary to accurately calculate the ingredients using weighing scales and the measuring cups and spoons that your bread machine comes with.

In the right order for your specific unit, apply the ingredients to the pan (follow the manufacturer's instructions).

2. Fit the bread pan into the bread machine and close the lid.

It should be surely locked into position with the handle folded down.

3. Select the appropriate program.

Of course, at the risk of sounding obvious, you would need to first turn on the bread machine at the mains!

Pick the appropriate size of the loaf and the color of the crust. Set the delay timer when necessary, too.

4. Press start.

The bread machine starts its mixing, kneading, growing, and baking cycle, alerting you when it is time to add additional ingredients such as seeds or nuts (with a beeping sound).

A beeping sound will announce at the end of the program that the program has ended, and the bread is baked.

5. Turn the loaf out onto a wire rack and leave to cool.

The baked loaf would be kept warm by most bread machines for up to one hour. If the curriculum has ended, though, it is best to turn out the loaf as quickly as possible.

Remove the bread pan from the machine by using oven gloves to open the lid.

Turn the pan upside down and shake it until the loaf is released several times.

Using a heat-resistant utensil that will not scrape the non-stick surface, such as a wooden spatula or spoon, you will need to remove the kneading blade from the dough.

Switch the loaf up appropriately and leave to cool for at least 30 minutes before slicing (and ideally longer).

Chapter 4-Cycles involved in bread making

Like in any other bread making, the bread machine also goes through cycles to make you the flavorful bread. The cycles involved in making the bread are described as under: -

- ## Kneading Cycle

The first cycle is kneading, and perhaps the most significant step in baking bread that includes yeast. Kneading combines all the ingredients well and is probably the bread machine's noisiest period. It will also take anywhere between 15 to 45minutes for this cycle. The time it takes depends on the bread machine and the sort of bread one is making. In most machines at the bottom of the baking tin, kneading propellers combines almost everything.

- ## Rest Cycle

The rest cycle makes the dough rest until it begins kneading again. Autolyzing is the scientific baking word for this. Essentially, it helps the moisture surrounding the dough to soak in the starch and Gluten thoroughly. It can take this process from only a couple of minutes to over 35 minutes.

- ## Rise Cycle

It would require this cycle if the flour has Gluten in it, so it will rise and make the bread airy and soft. It is a fermentation. Depending on the bread machine, this cycle can generally take about 40 to 50 minutes. It can take considerably longer occasionally, particularly if you're making French bread.

- ## Punch Cycle

The next cycle is Punch Cycle, after the dough has finished the rising cycle. In this cycle, the bread machine continues to knead the dough yet again. The distinction is that it is performed even more lightly at this point, and the goal is to remove the small air pockets produced in the growing period by the fermentation of the yeast.

Usually, the Punch cycle, often referred to as the shape-forming cycle, is a short cycle that takes only seconds to complete, and it is still necessary.

- **Baking Cycle**

The Baking cycle is the most important. It is in this step that the bread maker bakes the bread. Depending on the bread maker and the kind of bread you are making, this cycle will take anywhere from half an hour to more than 90 minutes.

Other important baking modes of the bread machine are

- Basic Bread
- Sweet Bread
- Whole-Wheat Cycle
- Gluten-Free Bread
- Rapid Bake
- Cake & Jam—yes, you can make Jellies and Jam and sauces.

Chapter 5-Basic Ingredients Required To Make Your Bread

- **Baking powder**

Baking powder, produced from starch and tartar cream, is a fermenting agent that allows the batter to grow. It has an acidic ingredient incorporated into it, so one does not need to integrate something else for raising the flour. A bitter-tasting food can result from too much baking powder, whereas too little results in a hard cake with minimal volume.

- **Baking soda**

Baking soda is a simple sodium bicarbonate, which has to be mixed with yogurt, honey, or cocoa, as an acidic ingredient. It's a fermenting product much like baking soda. Using baking soda too much will make the cake rough in texture.

Baking soda and baking powder can lose their strength more quickly than you would know. If the packages are not fresh, inspect them before using them. Place a couple of teaspoons of white vinegar in a tiny bowl to test the baking soda and put a teaspoon of baking soda. It can vigorously foam out, and it will take some moments for the frothing to subside. The more bubbles, the stronger the baking soda would be. You should substitute the baking soda for fresh baking soda if there is no action, or it just ends up with a couple of tiny bubbles. To check the baking powder, add a spoon full of baking powder into a cup. Fill the bowl with hot water to cover the baking powder; if it continues to burst furiously, it's safe to include it in the recipes. When weighing, do not add a wet spoon into the baking powder bag for better results. The water can trigger the baking powder left unused in the can, and each time, it will not be as pleasant to use. If you can see lumps in the baking soda, it's typically a warning that humidity has made its way in the baking soda.

- **Butter**

Butter, as a stable fat, butter is ideally used for baking than any other fat material. Butter adds taste, with a melting point only below body temperature. Hence certain cookies and bakery items appear to "melt in the mouth."

- **Cornstarch**

Cornstarch has many uses based on the kind of recipe it's being incorporated. Cornstarch is commonly either a binder or thickener, although it may be an anti-caking agent as well. It's perfect to use to thicken custards sauces or in gluten-free cooking.

- **Eggs**

Eggs have many uses, but most significantly, they add volume to foods and are a binding agent, ensuring they hold together the final product. For glazing, flavor, thickening, and binding, you can use the entire egg or just use the egg yolks and egg whites for different reasons. Egg whites, providing moisture and strength. Egg yolks contribute to Shape and flavor.

- **Flour**

Flour has a very crucial part of making bread. Its paramount quality is that it binds all the products together. It transforms into Gluten as flour protein is mixed with heat and moisture. Different flour varieties have different protein amounts and are ideal for various bakery products.

- **Milk**

Milk provides softness, moisture, taste and lightens color to baked goods. It provides a double function since it adds structure and strength to the batter or dough and provides tenderness, flavor, and moisture.

- **Sugar**

Sugar, in every particular recipe, sugar is executing a variety of functions. It provides texture, moisture and holds the form. Although operating in combination with eggs, fat, and liquid materials, it is also just another rising agent. Sugar gives "crunch" to certain cookies and cakes

Chapter 6-How to measure ingredients to make Bread

The bread machine can label a 1-pound, 1.5 pounds, or 2-pound loaf. What it means is the "flour capacity." Review the manufacturer's booklet of the bread machine to calculate any individual bread machine's flour capability. You can check if the manufacturer's brochure calls for 3-4 cups of flour regularly, then it is your bread machine's capacity. Now you can convert oven recipes to bread machine recipes. These are general flour capacities that yield a specific pound of bread loaf:

- The bread machine that yields 1-pound uses 2 or 2-3/4 cups of flour
- Bread machine that yields 1.5 pound uses 3-4 cups of flour
- Bread machine that yields 2-pound use 4 to 5 and a half cups of flour

Here are some measurements to help you convert the oven to bread machine recipes:

1. Reduce the amount of yeast to 1 teaspoon for a 1.5-pound bread machine and 1 and 1/4 teaspoon for a two-pound device.
2. Reduce the flour to three cups for a 1.5-pound bread machine and 4 cups for a 2-pound Bread machine.
3. Reduce the other ingredients as well, along with flour and yeast.
4. If a recipe calls for two or different kinds of flour, add the flour quantities and use it to decrease the formula. The total amount of flour used can be either 3 -4 cups based on the bread's size.
5. Use 1-3 tablespoons of gluten flour in a bread machine with all-purpose flour, or only use bread flour, which is a better option. If you are using any rye flour, combine it with one tablespoon of gluten flour, if even the base is bread flour.
6. All ingredients should be at room temperature and added to the bread machine in the manufacturer's suggested order.
7. Add any nuts, raisins, dried fruits to the ingredient signal, or as the manufacturer's booklet specifies.
8. If you are using only dough cycle, try to handle the dough with a little more flour after making the machine easy to handle.
9. Use the whole-grain cycle if the bread machine has one, for whole-wheat, rye, and any grain flour.
10. Always try to keep the recipe or any additional changes made to the recipe safe for future references.
11. Use the sweet bread cycle with a light crust for rich and sweet bread.

Conversion Tables

Here are some conversion tables to help you measure recipes accurately

CUPS	TBSP	TSP	ML
1	16	48	250
3/4	12	36	175
2/3	11	32	150
1/2	8	24	125
1/3	5	16	70
1/4	4	12	60
1/8	2	6	30
1/16	1	3	15

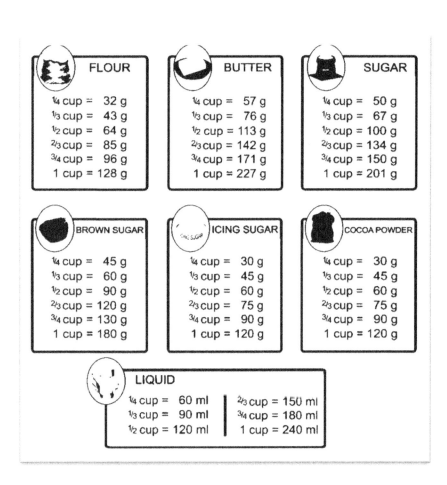

FLOUR
¼ cup = 32 g
⅓ cup = 43 g
½ cup = 64 g
⅔ cup = 85 g
¾ cup = 96 g
1 cup = 128 g

BUTTER
¼ cup = 57 g
⅓ cup = 76 g
½ cup = 113 g
⅔ cup = 142 g
¾ cup = 171 g
1 cup = 227 g

SUGAR
¼ cup = 50 g
⅓ cup = 67 g
½ cup = 100 g
⅔ cup = 134 g
¾ cup = 150 g
1 cup = 201 g

BROWN SUGAR
¼ cup = 45 g
⅓ cup = 60 g
½ cup = 90 g
⅔ cup = 120 g
¾ cup = 130 g
1 cup = 180 g

ICING SUGAR
¼ cup = 30 g
⅓ cup = 45 g
½ cup = 60 g
⅔ cup = 75 g
¾ cup = 90 g
1 cup = 120 g

COCOA POWDER
¼ cup = 30 g
⅓ cup = 45 g
½ cup = 60 g
⅔ cup = 75 g
¾ cup = 90 g
1 cup = 120 g

LIQUID
¼ cup = 60 ml
⅓ cup = 90 ml
½ cup = 120 ml
⅔ cup = 150 ml
¾ cup = 180 ml
1 cup = 240 ml

If you want to double the recipes:

Original Recipe   Double Recipe

1/8 tsp	1/4 tsp
1/4 tsp	1/2 tsp
1/2 tsp	1 tsp
3/4 tsp	1 1/2 tsp
1 tsp	2 tsp
1 Tbsp	2 Tbsp
2 Tbsp	4 Tbsp or 1/4
1/8 cup	1/4 cup
1/4 cup	1/2 cup
1/3 cup	2/3 cup
1/2 cup	1 cup
2/3 cup	1 1/3 cups
3/4 cup	1 1/2 cups
1 cup	2 cups
1 1/4 cup	2 1/2 cups
1 1/3 cup	2 2/3 cups
1 1/2 cup	3 cups
1 2/3 cup	3 1/3 cups
1 3/4 cup	3 1/2 cups

Cups to Grams Conversions (Metric)

Butter Measurements

Cups	Sticks	Pounds	Tablespoons	Grams
1/4	1/2	1/8	4	55 g
1/2	1	1/4	8	112 g
1/3	1/2+1 & 1/Three tablespoons	n/a	5 & 1/3	75 g
2/3	1 + 2 & 2/Three tablespoons	n/a	10 & 2/3	150 g
3/4	1 & 1/2	3/8	12	170 g
1	2	1/2	16	225 g
2	4	1	32	450 g

All-Purpose Flour, Icing or Powdered Sugar

Cup	Grams
1/8 cup	15 grams
1/4 cup	30 grams
1/3 cup	40 grams
3/8 cup	45 grams
1/2 cup	60 grams
5/8 cup	70 grams
2/3 cup	75 grams
3/4 cup	85 grams
7/8 cup	100 grams

1 cup	110 grams

Cake Flour

Cup	Grams
1/8 cup	10 grams
1/4 cup	20 grams
1/3 cup	25 grams
3/8 cup	30 grams
1/2 cup	50 grams
5/8 cup	60 grams
2/3 cup	65 grams
3/4 cup	70 grams
7/8 cup	85 grams
1 cup	95 grams

Granulated Sugar

Cup	Grams
1/8 cup	30 grams
1/4 cup	55 grams
1/3 cup	75 grams
3/8 cup	85 grams
1/2 cup	115 grams
5/8 cup	140 grams
2/3 cup	150 grams
3/4 cup	170 grams
7/8 cup	200 grams
1 cup	225 grams

Brown Sugar

Cup	Grams
1/8 cup	25 grams
1/4 cup	50 grams
1/3 cup	65 grams
3/8 cup	75 grams
1/2 cup	100 grams
5/8 cup	125 grams
2/3 cup	135 grams
3/4 cup	150 grams
7/8 cup	175 grams
1 cup	200 grams

Sliced Almonds

Cup	Grams
1/8 cup	10 grams
1/4 cup	20 grams
1/3 cup	25 grams
3/8 cup	30 grams
1/2 cup	40 grams
5/8 cup	50 grams
2/3 cup	55 grams
3/4 cup	60 grams
7/8 cup	70 grams
1 cup	80 grams

Ground Almonds

Cup	Grams
1/8 cup	25 grams
1/4 cup	50 grams
1/3 cup	65 grams
3/8 cup	75 grams
1/2 cup	100 grams
5/8 cup	125 grams
2/3 cup	135 grams
3/4 cup	150 grams
7/8 cup	175 grams
1 cup	200 grams

Flaked Coconut

Cup	Grams
1/8 cup	10 grams
1/4 cup	20 grams
1/3 cup	25 grams
3/8 cup	30 grams
1/2 cup	40 grams
5/8 cup	45 grams
2/3 cup	50 grams
3/4 cup	60 grams
7/8 cup	65 grams
1 cup	75 grams

Grated Coconut

Cup	Grams
1/8 cup	10 grams
1/4 cup	25 grams

1/3 cup	35 grams
3/8 cup	40 grams
1/2 cup	50 grams
5/8 cup	60 grams
2/3 cup	65 grams
3/4 cup	75 grams
7/8 cup	85 grams
1 cup	100 grams

Unsweetened Cocoa Powder

Cup	Grams
1/8 cup	15 grams
1/4 cup	30 grams
1/3 cup	40 grams
3/8 cup	45 grams
1/2 cup	60 grams
5/8 cup	70 grams
2/3 cup	75 grams
3/4 cup	85 grams
7/8 cup	100 grams
1 cup	125 grams

Baking Measurements

If a recipe calls for this amount	You can also measure it this way
Dash	2 or 3 drops (liquid) or less than 1/8 teaspoon (dry)
1 tablespoon	3 teaspoons or 1/2 ounce
2 tablespoons	1 ounce
1/4 cup	4 tablespoons or 2 ounces
1/3 cup	5 tablespoons plus 1 teaspoon
1/2 cup	8 tablespoons or 4 ounces
3/4 cup	12 tablespoons or 6 ounces
1 cup	16 tablespoons or 8 ounces
1 pint	2 cups or 16 ounces or 1 pound
1 quart	4 cups or 2 pints
1 gallon	4 quarts
1 pound	16 ounces

Volume Measurements

US Units	Canadian Units	Australian Units
1/4 teaspoon	1 ml	1 ml
1/2 teaspoon	2 ml	2 ml
1 teaspoon	5 ml	5 ml
1 tablespoon	15 ml	20 ml
1/4 cup	50 ml	60 ml
1/3 cup	75 ml	80 ml
1/2 cup	125 ml	125 ml
2/3 cup	150 ml	170 ml
3/4 cup	175 ml	190 ml
1 cup	250 ml	250 ml
1 quart	1 liter	1 liter
1 and 1/2 quarts	1.5 liters	1.5 liters
2 quarts	2 liters	2 liters
2 and 1/2 quarts	2.5 liters	2.5 liters
3 quarts	3 liters	3 liters
4 quarts	4 liters	4 liters

Weight Measurements

US Units	Canadian Metric	Australian Metric
1 ounce	30 grams	30 grams
2 ounces	55 grams	60 grams
3 ounces	85 grams	90 grams
4 ounces (1/4 pound)	115 grams	125 grams
8 ounces (1/2 pound)	225 grams	225 grams
16 ounces (1 pound)	455 grams	500 grams (1/2 kilogram)

Temperature Conversions

Fahrenheit	Celsius
32	0
212	100
250	120
275	140
300	150
325	160
350	180
375	190
400	200
425	220
450	230
475	240
500	260

Chapter 7-Advantages and Disadvantages of using a Bread machine

• Advantages of Bread machine

1. It is easier to bake bread in a bread machine.
2. The process is cleaner and more straightforward than traditional bread baking.
3. Every time the bread machine produces the same consistency & exceptional taste.
4. The benefit of Jam and jelly making.
5. You don't need to do the kneading.
6. Make your fresh bread, at home, for the sandwiches.
7. You can add many ingredients to make the bread to your taste.
8. It is convenient for busy people.
9. It saves long-term resources and money.

• Disadvantages of Bread machine

1. The paddle of the machine often gets stuck in the bread, and when it is removed, a hole is caused at the end of the bread, which is a nightmare for trying to make sandwiches.
2. Some machines are limited to their pre-set program.
3. Bread makers can be fiddly to clean
4. They use a lot of electricity.
5. Most bread makers last for a limited number of loaves.

Chapter 8-How to store Bread

- ## Freezing the bread

The best way to maintain that crusty loaf for the longest possible time is to freeze bread. Wrap tightly, either whole or sliced, in a freezer bag.

The best way is to defrost an entire frozen loaf overnight in the refrigerator; it can get soggy on the counter, and while it will toast just fine, it makes for a better loaf in the refrigerator. Also, when defrosting, don't forget to unwrap the freezer bag. While it defrosts, this prevents any water from pooling. And not to worry, if defrosting seems daunting: you can always reheat bread straight from the freezer. Try to bake at 325 degrees for 25 to 30 minutes for a whole loaf, while slices can be popped right inside the toaster.

- ## Store in the paper, never plastic

Within two to three days, a fresh loaf of bread is best eaten. If you plan on promptly devouring it, it should be kept on the counter in a paper bag. While the correct idea seems to be stored in plastic, this actually encourages mold growth, resulting in the bread going bad much faster.

- ## Bread boxes

Bread boxes are a great way to store bread and a fun way to make your kitchen more stylish. They have small holes in them that make it possible to circulate just a little air, keeping the bread from molding. Try to toss in a slice of bread with your loaf if you have pest concerns and prefer to keep bread in an airtight container. Water will be attracted by the slice with more surface area and help control the moisture content in your container.

- ## The place to store bread

Where your loaf is stored can be as important as how you store it. Keeping bread in the fridge will dry out paper-bagged bread and mold it more quickly with plastic bagged bread. This comes from all the heat put out by your refrigerator. Same for storage near a dishwasher; it is not bread-friendly to store the excess heat and moisture these appliances give off. Always store in a cool and dry area of your kitchen. Most probably try to store it in a deep drawer or cabinet.

- ## Reusable bread bags

Try a reusable bread bag if you are looking for a more versatile or eco-friendly way to conserve your bread. These days, there are more on the market, and many are washable by machine and work great in the freezer. Take them to the store with you and toss that fresh loaf right in. This can be a nice alternative to a torn paper bag that always seems to let crumbs escape onto the counter. Reusable bags are made from breathable materials, so without waste, they act like a paper bag.

Chapter 9-Frequently made errors

Dough errors

1   Dough too 'soft': it must be corrected immediately, adding more flour, identical to the one used. Add a little at a time, letting the machine work. If the dough is too soft, the result will be practically nil. Make a note of the new quantity for the next bread making.
2   Too hard and lumpy dough. Add lukewarm water, a little at a time, until you reach the optimal consistency. Make a note of the new quantity for the next bread making
3   Dough that does not rise: rethink the doses of brewer's yeast or mother yeast, increasing it. Check that the dough is not too soft. Adding a pinch of a teaspoon of baking soda can help.

Cooking errors

1   It only cooks underneath and, on the side, not inside: the dough is too watery. Use more flour or less water before leavening; it must be a soft but very elastic ball of dough
2   Above remains white: it is one of the most common and least solvable problems. The cooking time can be extended, but hardly any machine cooks on all four sides; the top part with the inspection glass does not give off heat.
3   The crust is not crunchy: add a little wheat malt or honey to the dough. A tablespoon is enough. In this case, the salt must be increased.
4   The bread cooks well, but when cut, it crumbles and falls into a thousand pieces: the dough is too dry. Better to add water and extend the cooking time.

Chapter 10-Tips and Suggestions

Following are some tips that will help you to avoid making mistakes while using a bread machine

Prior to baking

1. Many new owners know within a week that their bread machine is one of those unusual things... A cooking unit that will stay and be used regularly on the countertop; it will not be banished to any back corner of the pantry. Thus, you should keep all the products used while baking in one place.
2. Small pots and jars of flour, rice, palm sugar, non-fat dried milk, oats, oil, honey, etc., used while baking should be at your arm's reach. The molasses, salt, raisins, potato flakes, cornmeal, herbs, spices, and measuring utensils should be near your bread machine only.
3. Whole-grain flours, wheat germ, bran, nuts, and seeds (including sesame and poppy seeds) are all that you need, and therefore, it is quite beneficial to keep a whole cabinet dedicated to keeping them. A second freezer is also a good option.

While baking the bread

1. Use the freshest ingredients for the finest bread.
2. If your well-used bread pan seems to have lost its nonstick ability, before adding ingredients, spraying it gently with a nonstick cooking spray will ease the process of extracting the baked bread later on.
3. When baking bread for the first time, check your dough from time to time; it is a tiny measure you should take that will always stop disappointed outcomes four hours later.
4. If the recipe states otherwise, use big eggs.
5. Unless the guidance manual says otherwise, use room-temperature ingredients for the best performance. It is necessary to heat liquids to 80°F. Use a dry measuring cup to measure the dry ingredients and a glass or plastic liquid measuring cup to measure the liquids.
6. Do not use the measuring cup to scoop up the flour and then pack it in and level it off; it is the most common cause of small loaves. With that procedure, you should add 1 to 2 teaspoons more flour to the recipe with each cup. You can also scoop the flour carefully into a dry measuring cup from your canister and then level it with a straight-edged knife or spatula.
7. When attempting to measure the ingredients for your next bread, stop answering or communicating on the phone. That way, we have spoiled many loaves!
8. Before adding them one by one to the bread pan, we find it convenient to gather all the ingredients on the counter; there seems to be less likelihood of omitting one of them. Yeast bread made without yeast is a monstrosity that will snub even the family cat.

9. Follow the instructions of the manufacturer as to the order in which you put the ingredients into the bread pan.

10. However, unless there is a yeast dispenser on your machine that divides the yeast from the liquid ingredients, consider adding the liquids first and the yeast last while using the Delayed-Bake timer. Making a well for the yeast in the dry ingredients keeps it from getting into contact too easily with the liquids.

11. The more you add spices to your dough, the thicker it'll be. If it is a hesitant riser with an enhancer such as extra gluten, ascorbic acid, or a commercial dough enhancer, you will have to either decrease the number of additions or give the dough a lift.

12. Exceeding 1/4, 1/3, or 1/2 cup of fat and/or sugar respectively in 1-, 1 1/2-, and 2-pound loaves can significantly hinder the capacity of gluten to properly grow.

13. Break it into little pieces or melt it first in the microwave by using butter straight from the refrigerator.

14. Break the shortening into smaller bits first if you add more than two tablespoons of butter or margarine to a recipe.

15. Whole-grain bread is not going to rise as fast as all-white bread flour bread.

16. If you choose to use foods that have the ability to scrape the coated surface of your bread pan, such as grape nuts or granola, apply the liquid and let it soak for a few minutes to soften.

17. Gluten consumes water, but the more liquid you use to make a smooth, silky dough, the higher the amount of gluten in your flour.

18. When baking bread that is high in fat or sugar or contains cheese, eggs, or whole-grain flours, choose the Light Crust setting.

19. Be careful to cool the cooked ingredients at room temperature before adding them to the rest of the ingredients.

20. Heat it up in the microwave for 5 to 10 seconds to get the last little bit of honey or molasses out of the glass.

21. Near the end of the rising time, pay a glance at the dough. Simply deflate it marginally by poking it once or twice with a toothpick if it tries to burst the pan.

After the bread is baked

1. Rap the corner of the bread pan on a wooden cutting board or padded surface multiple times if you have trouble separating the bread from the pan. To release it, stop inserting a knife or metal spatula into the pan; you'll scratch the coating.

2. A decent knife with serrated bread is priceless. We've discovered that an electric knife can create more consistent cuts if you're not happy with your slicing abilities. And if anything else fails, there are some really small electric food slicers that each time can yield perfect slices! In kitchen specialty shops and catalogs, you'll find them.

3. We know the moment you turn it out of the bread pan, it's tempting to break it into the freshly baked loaf of bread. To give it a chance to set up enough to be sliceable, aim to wait at least 15 minutes. When you try to slice it too fast, a hot loaf of bread will crumble or compress.

4. Few pieces of bread are much softer to prepare than others. Wait until the next day, if you can, to slice some softies.

5. Get in the habit of holding your bread pan together with all the little bits and sections. Without a handmade well, a mixing blade lost down the disposal will mean weeks and see this one coming, you would be smart to buy a spare or two right now whilst you're dreaming about it.

Chapter 11-Frequently asked questions

- **How expensive is a bread machine?**

Some automated control machines are a bit pricey since they do not need your supervision, but some machines require your full-time attention, so keep that fact in mind.

- **How is a bread machine different from an oven?**

An oven is like a box that helps you to cook the bread or any other food you like. With the technical advancements, various ovens come with different configurations and help you to cook various complex food items very efficiently. Whereas a bread machine is a machine specially designed to make bread. All one has to do is put all the ingredients of the bread-making in the device, and after two to three hours, one will get a perfectly baked bread.

- **Can one wash the bread machine in a dishwasher?**

The pan or the container of the bread machine can be easily washed in the dishwasher.

- **How to set the bread machine at home?**

When you buy a bread machine, a user's manual will bo provided to you with step-by-step instructions on how to set up the bread machine and even how to use the machine on your own.

Chapter 12-Classic Bread Recipes

Bread is the staple food of many in the world and is one of the universal food items that is being eaten by people around the whole world. This chapter provides the recipes of classic, timeless bread that is eaten everywhere. You can also have this classic bread at home, made out of your own bread machine.

Traditional White Bread

(Ready in about 2 hours 30 minutes I Servings- one loafl Difficulty-Moderate)

Ingredients

- 3 and 3/4 cups of flour
- One cup of lukewarm water
- Three tablespoons of butter
- 1/3 cup of lukewarm milk
- Two teaspoons of Bread machine Yeast
- Three tablespoons of sugar
- One teaspoon of salt

Instructions

1. In the bread machine, add all the ingredients according to your machine's order.
2. Select 2 pounds' loaf, and basic setting, medium crust. Click on start.
3. After it's baked, let it cool down before slicing.

Honey Whole-Wheat Bread

(Ready in about 3 hours 30 minutesl Servings-one loafl Difficulty-Moderate)

Ingredients

- ⅓ cup of olive oil
- Four and a half cups of whole wheat flour
- One and a half cups of warm water
- ⅓ cup of honey
- One tablespoon of yeast
- Two teaspoons of Kosher Salt
- One teaspoon of Gluten (optional)

Instructions

1. In the machine, add water, then oil, and then honey. Add half flour, Salt, Gluten, and the rest of the flour.
2. Make a well in the center, and then add the yeast.
3. Select whole wheat and light crust. Press the start button.
4. Serve fresh bread.

Molasses Wheat Bread

(Ready in about 4 hours 10 minutesl Servings-one loaf I Difficulty-Moderate)

Ingredients

- One and ¾ cups Whole wheat flour
- ¾ cup of water
- Three tablespoons of melted butter
- 1⅓ cup of milk
- Two tablespoons of sugar

- Three tablespoons of molasses
- Two and 1/4 teaspoons of fast-rising yeast
- Two cups of bread flour
- One teaspoon of salt

Instructions

1. Add all the ingredients to the machine according to your suggested machine's order. Make sure the ingredients are at room temperature
2. Use light crust, basic setting.
3. Serve fresh.

100 Percent Whole-Wheat Bread

(Ready in about 4 hours 10 minutesI Servings-one loafI Difficulty-Moderate)

Ingredients

- Three and 1/Three cups of whole wheat flour
- Two tablespoons of powdered milk
- One and a half cups of water
- Two tablespoons of honey
- Two tablespoons of molasses
- Two tablespoons of margarine
- One and a half teaspoons of salt
- One and a half teaspoons of yeast

Instructions

1. Add liquid ingredients before dry ingredients or as per your machine's order.
2. Mix the powdered milk and water. Heat in microwave for 30 seconds, then adds in the bread machine followed by rest of the ingredients.
3. Select 2 lb. loaf and whole wheat bread. Press the start button.
4. Serve fresh.

Crusty French Bread

(Ready in about 3 hours 35 minutesI Servings-one loafI Difficulty-Moderate)

Ingredients

- One teaspoon of instant yeast
- One and a half teaspoons of sugar
- One cup of lukewarm water
- One and a half teaspoons salt
- One and a half teaspoons of butter
- Three cups of bread flour

Glaze:

- One teaspoon of water
- One egg white

Instructions

1. Add all the ingredients required to the bread machine as per your machine's suggested order.
2. Select the dough cycle. Adjust the dough's consistency after 5 to 10 minutes by adding one tablespoon of water at a time for very dry dough or one tablespoon of flour if it's too sticky.
3. It should pull away after sticking to the sides.
4. When the machine beeps and the dough is done, take it out on a clean, floured surface. Shape into cylinder shape loaves. Shape into French bread.
5. Place the loaves in oiled baking pans. Cover with a towel and let it rise in a warm place.

6. Let the oven preheat to 425 F. make the glaze by mixing water with egg.
7. Coat the loaf's surface with a glaze.
8. Make cuts onto the dough surface.
9. Bake in the oven for 20 minutes.
10. Lower the oven's temperature to 350 F, bake for 5 to 10 minutes more or until golden brown.
11. Check the bread's internal temperature. It should be 195 F.
12. Cool slightly and Serve fresh.

Pumpernickel Bread

(Ready in about 3 hours 45 minutesI Servings-one loafI Difficulty-Moderate)

Ingredients

- One and a half tablespoons of vegetable oil
- One and 1/8 cups of warm water
- Three tablespoons of Cocoa
- One tablespoon of caraway seed
- 1/3 cup of Molasses
- One and a half cups of bread flour
- One cup of Whole wheat flour
- One and a half teaspoons of salt
- Two and a half teaspoons of bread machine yeast
- One cup of Rye flour
- One and a half tablespoons of wheat gluten

Instructions

1. Add all ingredients in the bread machine in the suggested order by the manufacturer.
2. Select the basic cycle and Press the start button.
3. Serve fresh bread.

Lovely Oatmeal Bread

(Ready in about 3 hours 15 minutesI Servings-one loafI Difficulty-Moderate)

Ingredients

- Three Tablespoons of sliced Unsalted Butter
- One cup of lukewarm milk
- One and a half teaspoons of Bread Machine Yeast
- 3/4 Cup of Old-Fashioned Oatmeal
- Two and 1/4 Cups of Bread Flour
- One and a half Teaspoons of Salt
- Brown Sugar (packed) 1/4 Cup for sweet and One tablespoon for non-sweet

Instructions

1. Add all ingredients in the bread machine in the suggested order by the manufacturer.
2. Select 1.5 lb. loaf. Light crust and basic setting. Press the start button.
3. Before the baking cycle begins, add some oatmeal to the top.
4. Serve fresh bread.

Oat Bran Molasses Bread

(Ready in about 3 hours 20 minutesI Servings-One loafI Difficulty-Moderate)

Ingredients

- Three cups of Whole-wheat flour
- One cup of warm water
- ¼ cup of molasses
- Two tablespoons of melted margarine
- Two and a 1/4 teaspoon of yeast
- Half teaspoon of salt
- One cup of oat bran

Instructions

1. Add all ingredients in the bread machine in the suggested order by the manufacturer.
2. Click one lb. loaf, whole wheat, and Press the start button.

Whole-Wheat Buttermilk Bread

(Ready in about3 hours 10 minutesl Servings-One loafl Difficulty-Moderate)

Ingredients

- Two cups of bread flour
- Two cups of Whole-wheat flour
- Two tablespoons olive oil (or other oil)
- One and a half teaspoons of sesame seeds
- One and ¾ teaspoons of salt
- Six tablespoons water
- One cup buttermilk
- Three tablespoons of sugar
- One and a half teaspoons of caraway seeds
- One and a half teaspoons of celery seeds
- Two teaspoons of bread machine yeast
- Half teaspoon of mustard seeds

Instructions

1. Add all ingredients mentioned to the machine in the manufacturer's suggested order.
2. Add the yeast on top after making a well.
3. Select basic cycle, light crust. Press the start button
4. Serve fresh.

Soft Egg Bread

(Ready in about 2 hours 10 minutesl Servings-One loafl Difficulty-Moderate)

Ingredients

- Three cups of Bread machine flour
- ⅔ cup of milk
- Two tablespoons Softened butter
- Two tablespoons of sugar
- Two teaspoons of Bread machine yeast
- Two whole eggs
- One teaspoon of salt

Instructions

1. Add all ingredients required to the bread machine's container in the suggested order by the manufacturer.
2. Select white bread, light crust. Press the start button.
3. Serve fresh.

Healthy Bran Bread

(Ready in about 3 hours 45 minutesl Servings-One loafl Difficulty-Moderate)

Ingredients

- One egg beaten mixed with enough water to make one cup
- One and a half teaspoons of Kosher Salt
- One tablespoon of honey
- One tablespoon of olive oil
- Half teaspoon of bread machine yeast
- Five and a half tablespoons of unprocessed wheat bran
- Three cups of bread flour

Instructions

1. Add all ingredients required in the container of the bread machine in the suggested order by the manufacturer.
2. Select the basic cycle—Press the start button.
3. Serve fresh.

Dark Rye Bread

(Ready in about 3 hours 10 minutesl Servings-One loafl Difficulty-Moderate)

Ingredients

- One and ¼ cups of warm water
- Two and ¼ teaspoons Yeast
- One cup of rye flour
- Two and a half cups of bread flour
- ⅓ cup of molasses
- Half teaspoon of salt
- One tablespoon of Caraway seed
- ⅛ cup of Vegetable oil
- ⅛ cup of Cocoa powder

Instructions

1. Place all the ingredients in the machine in the suggested order by the manufacturer.
2. Select white bread—Press the start button.
3. Serve fresh.

Golden Raisin Bread

(Ready in about3 hours 10 minutesl Servings-One loafl Difficulty-Moderate)

Ingredients

- One Cup of quick Oatmeal
- One and 1/Three cups of warm milk
- Two Teaspoons of Bread Machine Yeast
- Three cups of Bread Flour
- Half cup of Brown Sugar
- Two teaspoons of molasses
- Four Tablespoons of sliced butter
- One cup of Golden Raisins
- Two Teaspoons of salt

Instructions

1. Place all ingredients except raisins in the bread machine in the suggested order by the manufacturer.

2. Select basic, light crust, and 2 lb. loaf.
3. Press the start button.
4. After the machine completes its first cycle of kneading, add raisins.
5. Serve fresh.

Golden Corn Bread

(Ready in about3 hours 10 minutes| Servings-One loaf| Difficulty-Moderate)

Ingredients

- One cup of cornmeal
- Two eggs, lightly beaten
- 1/4 cup of melted butter
- One and a 1/4 cup of bread flour
- One cup of milk
- Four teaspoons of baking powder
- One teaspoon of Vanilla
- 1/4 cup of sugar
- One teaspoon of salt

Instructions

1. Place all ingredients in the machine in the suggested order by the manufacturer.
2. Select light crust and cake setting if available, or quick setting.
3. Press the start button.
4. Serve fresh.

English Muffin Bread

(Ready in about 3 hours 40 minutes| Servings-One loaf| Difficulty-Moderate)

Ingredients

- One cup of Lukewarm milk
- One teaspoon of vinegar
- Two tablespoons of butter
- 1/3 to 1/4 cup of water
- One and a half teaspoons of salt
- Two and 1/4 teaspoons of instant yeast
- Three and a half cups of all-purpose flour
- One and a half teaspoons of sugar
- Half teaspoon of baking powder

Instructions

1. In the tin of bread machine, add all ingredients. Use less water in a humid environment and more water in a dry or colder environment.
2. Select basic and light crust. Press the start button. Adjust dough consistency by adding more flour if too sticky and add water if too dry.
3. Serve fresh.

Traditional Italian Bread

(Ready in about3 hours 10 minutes| Servings-One loaf| Difficulty-Moderate)

Ingredients

- One tablespoon of sugar
- 3/4 cup of cold water
- One teaspoon of salt
- Two cups of bread flour
- One teaspoon of Aotivo dry yeast
- One tablespoon of olive oil

Instructions

1. Add all ingredients in the pan of the bread machine in the suggested order by the manufacturer.
2. Select Italian cycle or basic cycle. Light crust. Press the start button.
3. Serve fresh.

Cocoa Bread

(Ready in about3 hours 5 minutes| Servings-One loaf| Difficulty-Moderate)

Ingredients

- One whole egg
- One cup of milk
- One yolk only
- One teaspoon of salt
- Three tablespoons of canola oil
- One teaspoon of vanilla extract
- One tablespoon of wheat gluten
- Three cups of bread flour
- Half cup of brown sugar
- Two and a half teaspoons of bread machine yeast
- 1/3 cup of cocoa powder

Instructions

1. Add all the ingredients in the bread machine in the suggested order by the manufacturer.
2. Select the white bread, medium crust. Press the start button.
3. Serve fresh.

Light whole wheat bread

(Ready in about3 hours 5 minutes| Servings-One loaf| Difficulty-Moderate)

Ingredients

- One cup of water
- One large egg
- Two tablespoons vegetable or nut oil
- Two and a half cups bread flour
- Half cup whole wheat flour
- Three tablespoons dry buttermilk powder
- Two tablespoons dark brown sugar
- One tablespoon gluten
- One and a half teaspoons salt
- Two and a half teaspoons bread machine yeast

Instructions

1. Add all the ingredients to the machine according to the order in the manufacturer's instructions.
2. Set the setting for the medium crust and Basic cycle; press Start.
3. When the baking cycle ends, immediately remove the pan's bread and place it on a rack. Let cool to room temperature before slicing.

Buttermilk whole wheat bread

(Ready in about3 hours 5 minutes| Servings-One loaf| Difficulty-Moderate)

Ingredients

- One and 1/8 cups buttermilk
- Two tablespoons canola oil
- Two tablespoons maple syrup
- One and a half cups whole wheat flour
- One and a half cups bread flour
- One tablespoon plus one teaspoon gluten
- One and a half teaspoons salt
- Two and a half teaspoons bread machine yeast

Instructions

1. Add all the ingredients to the machine as per the manufacturer's instructions.
2. Set the setting for the medium crust and the Basic or Whole Wheat cycle; press Start.
3. When the baking cycle ends, remove the pan's bread and place it on a rack. Let cool to room temperature before slicing.

Lou's Daily Bread

(Ready in about3 hours 5 minutesl Servings-One loafl Difficulty-Moderate)

Ingredients

- Zest of two oranges, cut into very thin strips
- One and 1/4 cups fat-free milk
- Two tablespoons olive or walnut oil
- Two tablespoons honey
- One and 5/8 cups whole wheat flour
- One and a half cups bread flour
- One tablespoon gluten
- One and 1/4 teaspoons salt
- Two and 1/4 teaspoons bread machine yeast

Instructions

1. Chop the orange peel finely, either with a knife or in a food processor.
2. Place all the ingredients in the pan as per the instructions of the manufacturer.
3. Set the crust settings on medium and program for the Whole Wheat cycle; press Start. When the baking cycle ends, remove the pan's bread and place it on a rack. Let cool to room temperature before slicing.

Healthy whole wheat challah

(Ready in about3 hours 5 minutesl Servings-One loafl Difficulty-Moderate)

Ingredients

- 2/3 cup water
- Three large eggs
- Three tablespoons vegetable oil
- Two tablespoons honey
- One and a half cups whole wheat flour
- One and a half cup bread flour
- One and a half tablespoons gluten
- One tablespoon instant potato flake
- One and a half teaspoons salt
- Two and a half teaspoons bread machine yeast

Instructions

1. According to the order suggested by the manufacturer, place all ingredients in the pan. Set the medium or dark crust and the Basic or Whole Wheat cycle program; press Start. The dough's going to be moist. During kneading, do not add more flour, or the bread will dry.
2. Press Pause and then open the lid to check the dough by lifting it out of the pan when Rise 2 ends. Split the dough into two equal pieces. Roll each portion with the palms of your hands into a flat oblong sausage, about 10 inches in length.
3. Side by side, place the two pieces. Holding each end, wrapping one around the other, and simultaneously twisting each one to create a fat twist effect. Tuck the ends underneath and replace them in the machine pan. In the machine, the twisted form will bake.
4. Remove the bread from the pan when the baking cycle ends, and then place it on a rack to cool it on a rack before slicing.

Dakota Bread

(Ready in about3 hours 5 minutesl Servings-One loafl Difficulty-Moderate)

Ingredients

- One and ¼ cups of water
- Two tablespoons canola oil
- Two tablespoons honey
- Two and ¼ cups of bread flour
- Half cup whole wheat flour
- 1/4 cup raw bulgur cracked wheat
- Two teaspoons gluten
- One and a half teaspoons salt
- 1/4 cup raw sunflower seeds
- 1/4 cup raw pumpkin seeds, chopped
- Two teaspoons sesame seeds
- One and a half teaspoons poppy seeds
- Two and a half teaspoons bread machine yeast

Instructions

1. Place all the ingredients in the machine as per the directions mentioned in the manufacturer's instructions. Set the crust settings on dark and program for the Basic cycle; press Start.
2. When the baking cycle ends, remove the pan's bread and place it on a rack. Let cool to room temperature before slicing.

Butter Bread

(Ready in about3 hours 5 minutesl Servings-One loafl Difficulty-Moderate)

Ingredients

- 7/8 cup water
- One large egg
- Five tablespoons unsalted butter or margarine, cut into pieces
- Three cups bread flour
- One tablespoon gluten
- One and a half teaspoons salt

- Two and a half teaspoons bread machine yeast

Instructions

1. According to the directions mentioned in the manufacturer's instructions, place all ingredients in the pan. For the Basic or Variety cycle, set crust on medium and program; press Start.
2. Press Pause after Rise 1 ends, remove the bread from the machine and close the lid if you are using the Basic cycle. Delete the pan when Shape appears on the display if you are using the Variety cycle.
3. Lift out the dough and divide it into two equal portions on a clean work surface. Flatten each part into a small rectangle and roll up to form 2 fat squares of dough from a short side. Place the two separate pieces in the pan side-by-side. Bring the pan back to the machine.
4. To continue to rise and bake as scheduled, press Start. If the baking cycle ends, remove the bread from the pan immediately and then place it on a rack to cool down before slicing.

Olive Oil Bread

(Ready in about3 hours 5 minutesl Servings-One loafl Difficulty-Moderate)

Ingredients

For the biga starter:

- 3/4 cup water
- One and a half cups bread flour
- Half teaspoon SAF yeast or bread machine yeast

For the dough

- 1/4 cup water
- Three tablespoons olive oil
- One and a half cups bread flour
- Two teaspoons sugar
- One teaspoon gluten
- One and a half teaspoons salt
- One and 3/4 teaspoons bread machine yeast

Instructions

1. Place starter ingredients in the pan to prepare the biga starter. Dough Cycle Program and set a timer for 10 minutes. Press Stop and unplug the machine when the timer rings. For 12 to 18 hours, let the starter sit in the machine.
2. Make the starter break up into 6 or 8 pieces with a rubber spatula and leave it in the machine. Place the ingredients for all the dough in the pan. Set the dark crust and the program for the cycle of French Bread; press Start. The dough is going to be damp and smooth but flaccid.
3. If the baking cycle ends, remove the bread from the pan immediately and place it on a rack to cool down before slicing.

White Bread with Malted Grain

(Ready in about3 hours 5 minutesl Servings-One loafl Difficulty-Moderate)

Ingredients

- One and 1/4 teaspoon Easy bake yeast

- 1.4 cups of strong white bread flour
- 0.6 cups of malted grain or granary-style flour
- One and 1/4 teaspoon fine sea salt
- One tablespoon malt extract
- One and a half water

Instructions

1. Put all the ingredients in the container of the machine in the correct order.
2. Fit the pan into the bread machine and close the lid.
3. Select the basic white setting, medium crust, and the appropriate size. Press Start.
4. When the program has finished, lift the pan out of the machine, turn the bread out on to a wire rack

White Bread with Rye

(Ready in about3 hours 5 minutesl Servings-One loafl Difficulty-Moderate)

Ingredients

- One teaspoon Easy bake yeast
- 1.75 cups of extra strong or Canadian white bread flour
- Half rye flour
- One and a half teaspoon fine sea salt
- One and a half cup of water

Instructions

1. Add all the ingredients in the container in the correct order for your respective machine.
2. Fit the pan into the bread machine and close the lid.
3. Select the basic white rapid setting, dark crust, and the appropriate size. Press Start.
4. When the program has finished, lift the pan out of the machine, turn the bread out onto a wire rack and leave to cool completely.

Soft grain Loaf

(Ready in about3 hours 5 minutesl Servings-One loafl Difficulty-Moderate)

Ingredients

- One teaspoon Easy bake yeast
- Three cups of soft grain strong white bread flour
- One and 1/4 teaspoon fine sea salt
- One tablespoon malt extract
- 1.26 cups of water

Instructions

1. Add all the ingredients in the container in the correct order for your respective machine.
2. Fit the pan into the bread machine and close the lid.
3. Select the basic white setting, medium crust, and the appropriate size. Press Start.
4. When the program has finished, lift the pan out of the machine, turn the bread out onto a wire rack and leave to cool completely.

Oat Loaf

(Ready in about3 hours 5 minutesl Servings-One loafl Difficulty-Moderate)

Ingredients

- One and ¼ teaspoon Easy bake yeast
- Three cups of strong white bread flour
- One and ¼ cup of whole rolled porridge oats
- One teaspoon fine sea salt
- One and ¾ cup of water

Instructions

1. Add all the ingredients in the container in the correct order for your machine.
2. Fit the pan into the bread machine and close the lid.
3. Select the basic setting, medium crust, and the appropriate size. Press Start.
4. When the program has finished, lift the pan out of the machine, turn the bread out onto a wire rack and leave to cool completely.

Milk Loaf

(Ready in about 3 hours 5 minutes‖ Servings-One loaf‖ Difficulty-Moderate)

Ingredients

- One teaspoon Easy bake yeast
- Three cups of strong white bread flour
- One teaspoon fine sea salt
- Two tablespoons of butter cut into small pieces
- One teaspoon golden caster sugar
- Four tablespoons dried skimmed milk powder
- One and ¾ cups of water

Instructions

1. Put all the ingredients into the pan in the correct order as suggested by the manufacturer.
2. Fit the pan into the bread machine and close the lid.
3. Select the basic white setting, medium crust, and the appropriate size. Press Start.
4. When the program has finished, lift the pan out of the machine, turn the bread out onto a wire rack and leave to cool completely.

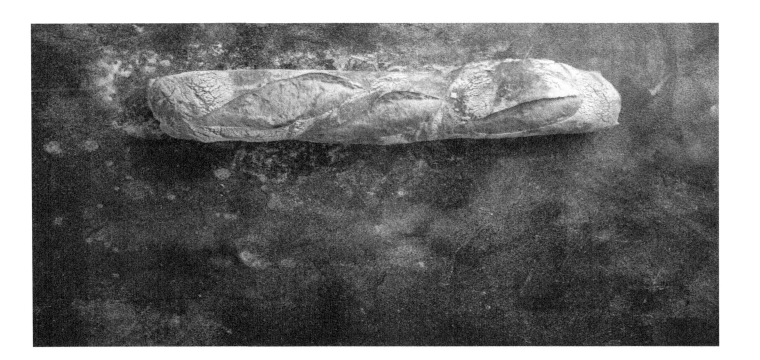

Chapter 13-Herby Bread Recipes

Herb is the heart of all the recipes, and you can make the herb-infused bread in your bread machine. In this chapter, various mouth-watering herb bread recipes are provided for you to make at home in your bread machines.

Fragrant Herb Bread

(Ready in about 3 hours 5 minutesI Servings-One loaf I Difficulty- Moderate)

Ingredients

- Two tablespoons of olive oil
- One cup of warm water
- One egg, lightly beaten
- Two teaspoons of dried rosemary leaves
- Two tablespoons of white sugar
- One teaspoon of salt
- One teaspoon of dried oregano
- Two teaspoons of Bread machine yeast
- One teaspoon of Dried basil
- Three cups and two tablespoons of All-purpose flour

Instructions

1. Add all ingredients in the pan of the bread machine, as per the suggested order.
2. Select a large loaf with a light crust. Press the start button.
3. Serve fresh

Rosemary Bread

(Ready in about 3 hours 15 minutes I Servings- One loaf I Difficulty- Moderate)

Ingredients

- One tablespoon of onion powder
- Four tablespoons of butter
- Three cups of bread Flour
- One and 1/3 cups of warm milk
- One cup of one-minute oatmeal
- One teaspoon of salt
- One and a half Teaspoons of Bread Machine Yeast
- Six teaspoons of White Granulated Sugar
- One tablespoon of Dried Rosemary

Instructions

1. Put all ingredients in the container of the bread machine in the order suggested by the manufacturer.
2. Select the settings for the light crust and the size, then press the start button.
3. Before the baking cycle begins, sprinkle some rosemary on top and let it bake.
4. Serve fresh.

Spicy Cajun Bread

(Ready in about 2 hours 20 minutes I Servings- One loaf I Difficulty- Moderate)

Ingredients

- Two cups of bread flour
- 1/4 cup of diced green bell pepper
- Half cup of water
- 1/4 cup of chopped onion
- Two teaspoons of soft butter
- Two teaspoons finely chopped garlic
- One teaspoon of Active dry yeast
- One tablespoon of Sugar
- One teaspoon of Cajun seasoning
- Half teaspoon of salt

Instructions

1. Place all ingredients in the container of the bread machine in the suggested order by the manufacturer.
2. Select white bread, dark or medium crust, and not the delay cycle.
3. Press the start button.
4. Serve fresh

Aromatic Lavender Bread

(Ready in about 2 hours 55 minutes I Servings- One loaf I Difficulty- Moderate)

Ingredients

- 1/3 cup of water
- 3/4 cup of buttermilk
- One teaspoon of fresh lavender flowers, finely chopped
- Three cups of bread flour
- Three tablespoons of olive oil
- Two tablespoons of Fresh lavender leaves, finely chopped
- One tablespoon of Gluten
- Zest of one lemon
- Two and a half teaspoon of bread machine yeast
- One and a half teaspoons of salt

Instructions

1. Add all ingredients in the container of the bread machine in the suggested order by the manufacturer.
2. Select dark crust, basic cycle, and press the start button.
3. Serve fresh.

Cracked Black Pepper Bread

(Ready in about 2 hours 45 minutes I Servings- One loaf I Difficulty- Moderate)

Ingredients

- Three tablespoons of minced chives
- Three tablespoons of olive oil
- Three tablespoons of sugar
- One and a half cups water
- One teaspoon of cracked black pepper
- Two teaspoons of salt

- Two minced garlic cloves
- One teaspoon of dried basil
- One teaspoon of garlic powder
- Two and a half teaspoons of active dry yeast
- 1/4 cup of grated parmesan cheese
- Four cups of bread flour

Instructions

1. Add all ingredients in the bread machine in the suggested order by the manufacturer.
2. Select basic, light crust. Do not use the time delay—Press the start button.
3. Serve fresh.

Herb & Garlic Cream Cheese Bread

(Ready in about 2 hours 15 minutes I Servings- One loaf I Difficulty- Moderate)

Ingredients

- Three cups of bread flour
- Two teaspoons of active dry yeast
- One cup of warm water
- One and a half teaspoons of salt
- One teaspoon of dry herbs
- One tablespoon of butter
- One tablespoon of sugar
- Two teaspoons of garlic powder
- One tablespoon of powdered milk

Instructions

1. Put all the required ingredients in the container of the bread machine in the suggested order by the manufacturer.
2. Select knead or mix cycle. After ten minutes, check dough consistency, adjust if too dry or too wet by adding one tablespoon of water or flour one at a time.
3. Select a basic setting, light crust. Press the start button.

Honey-Spice Egg Bread

(Ready in about 3 hours 25 minutes I Servings- One loaf I Difficulty- Moderate)

Ingredients

- Two Fresh eggs
- One cup of warm water
- One and a half Tablespoons of unsalted butter
- Two tablespoons of Honey
- One teaspoon of salt
- Three tablespoons of powdered milk
- Three cups of bread flour
- Two teaspoons of active dry yeast
- One teaspoon of cinnamon
- One teaspoon of cardamom
- One teaspoon of ginger
- One teaspoon of nutmeg

Instructions

1. Place all ingredients in the container of the bread machine in the suggested order by the manufacturer.

2. Select white bread, light crust. Press the start button.
3. Serve warm with honey or butter.

Cinnamon Swirl Bread

(Ready in about 3 hours 25 minutes I Servings- One loaf I Difficulty- Moderate)

Ingredients

- One and a half tablespoon of butter
- ¾ cup of warm milk
- One whole egg
- One tablespoon of brown sugar
- Half teaspoon of salt
- One and ¾ teaspoon of active yeast
- Two and a half cups of bread flour

For Cinnamon Swirl
- Half tablespoon of cinnamon
- Three tablespoons of white sugar
- One and ¼ cups of raisins

Instructions

1. Warm the milk to 110 F. Mix with butter and stir, so it melts.
2. Add to the bread machines. Add the rest of the ingredients as per the suggested order.
3. Select basic. Choose crust to your liking. Select knead. Meanwhile, combine the swirl ingredients.
4. After the second knead cycle's beeping, add the swirl ingredients.
5. After the third kneading cycle's beeping, remove paddles and place the dough back in the machine.
6. Serve fresh.

Simple Garlic Bread

(Ready in about 3 hours 15 minutes I Servings- One loaf I Difficulty- Moderate)

Ingredients

- One tablespoon of butter
- One cup of warm water
- One tablespoon of powdered milk
- One tablespoon of white sugar
- One and a half teaspoons of salt
- Two teaspoons of active dry yeast
- Three teaspoons of minced garlic
- One and a half tablespoons of dried parsley
- Three cups of bread flour

Instructions

1. Add all ingredients in the container of the bread machine in the suggested order by the manufacturer.
2. Select the basic cycle and Press the start button.
3. Serve fresh.

Herbed Pesto Bread

(Ready in about 2 hours 5 minutes I Servings- One loaf I Difficulty- Moderate)

Ingredients

- Three cups of bread flour
- One and a half teaspoons of sugar

- One cup of water
- One teaspoon salt
- ¼ cup of pesto sauce
- Two and a ¼ teaspoons of bread machine yeast
- One teaspoon of lemon juice

Instructions

1. Add all ingredients in the container of the bread machine in the suggested order by the manufacturer.
2. Select the basic cycle and size.
3. Press the start button and serve fresh.

Caraway Rye Bread

(Ready in about 4 hours 10 minutes I Servings- One loaf I Difficulty- Moderate)

Ingredients

- Two tablespoons of dry milk powder
- One and a ¼ cups of lukewarm water
- Two tablespoons of brown sugar
- One teaspoon of salt
- Two tablespoons of butter
- ¾ cup of rye flour
- ¾ cup of whole wheat flour
- Two tablespoons of molasses
- One and a ¾ teaspoons of active dry yeast
- One and a ¾ cups of bread flour
- One and a half tablespoons of caraway seeds

Instructions

1. Add all ingredients in the container of the bread machine in the suggested order by the manufacturer.
2. Select grain, the crust of your liking. Press the start button.
3. Serve fresh.

Anise Lemon Bread

(Ready in about 3 hours 5 minutes I Servings- One loaf I Difficulty- Moderate)

Ingredients

- Water
- Juice and zest of one lemon
- One tablespoon of olive oil
- Half cup of milk
- Two tablespoons of honey
- Three teaspoons of instant active dry yeast
- One tablespoon of anise seeds
- One teaspoon of salt
- Three cups of bread flour

Instructions

1. Add lemon juice to a cup and enough lukewarm water to make a half cup.
2. Heat this mixture to 110 F.
3. Add to the bread machine, then lemon zest and rest of the ingredients.
4. Select basic and crust to your liking—press the start button.

5. After 10 minutes, check the dough's consistency. Add more flour or water if required.
6. Serve fresh.

Fragrant Cardamom Bread

(Ready in about 1 hour 5 minutes | Servings- One loaf | Difficulty- Moderate)

Ingredients

- One whole egg
- Half cup of milk
- 1/4 cup of honey
- One teaspoon of ground cardamom
- 1/4 cup of unsweetened apple sauce
- Two teaspoons of active dry yeast
- One teaspoon of salt
- Two and a 3/4 cups of bread flour

Instructions

1. Put all the required ingredients in the container of the bread machine in the suggested order by the manufacturer.
2. Select basic, light crust—Press the start button.
3. Serve warm with butter.

Chocolate Mint Bread

(Ready in about 3 hours 5 minutes | Servings- One loaf | Difficulty- Moderate)

Ingredients

- Two tablespoons of softened butter
- One and a 1/4 cups and two tablespoons of water
- One and a 1/4 teaspoons of salt
- Four cups of bread flour
- Two and a half teaspoons of bread machine dry yeast
- 1/3 cup of sugar
- 2/3 cup of mint chocolate chips

Instructions

1. Carefully measure and place all ingredients in the pan as per the order suggested by the manufacturer.
2. Select the sweet cycle. Light crust. Press the start button.
3. Serve fresh.

Molasses Candied-Ginger Bread

(Ready in about 3 hours 10 minutes | Servings- One loaf | Difficulty- Moderate)

Ingredients

- 1/4 cup of molasses
- Three and 1/3 cups of bread flour
- One whole egg
- 3/4 cup of milk
- Three tablespoons of butter
- One tablespoon of brown sugar
- 3/4 teaspoon of ginger
- 1/3 cup of raisins
- 3/4 teaspoon of salt

- 3/4 teaspoon of cinnamon
- Two and a 1/4 teaspoons of active dry yeast

Instructions

1. Put all the required ingredients in the container of the bread machine in the suggested order by the manufacturer. Do not add raisins yet.
2. Select white bread and light crust—Press the start button.
3. Add raisins on ingredient beeping.
4. Serve warm.

Fresh Dill Bread

(Ready in about 3 hours 10 minutes | Servings- One loaf | Difficulty- Moderate)

Ingredients

- Half cup of water
- One large egg
- Four ounces of cream cheese, at room temperature and cut into pieces
- Three and 1/4 cups bread flour
- One tablespoon gluten
- 1/3 cup finely chopped yellow onion
- 1/4 cup chopped fresh dill
- One and a half teaspoon salt
- One tablespoon bread machine yeast

Instructions

1. Place all the ingredients in the container as per the order in the manufacturer's instructions. Set the crust setting on medium and program for the Basic cycle; press Start.
2. When the baking cycle ends, remove the pan's bread and place it on a rack. Let cool to room temperature before slicing.

Brooklyn Botanic Garden Herb Bread

(Ready in about 3 hours 10 minutes | Servings- One loaf | Difficulty- Moderate)

Ingredients

- 3/4 cup milk
- One large egg
- Two tablespoons unsalted butter, cut into pieces
- Three cups of bread flour
- One tablespoon gluten
- One tablespoon caraway seed, crushed
- One teaspoon dried sage
- One teaspoon fresh grated nutmeg
- One and 1/4teaspoons salt
- Two and a half teaspoons bread machine yeast

Instructions

1. Place all the ingredients in the pan according to the order in the manufacturer's instructions. Set crust on dark and program for the Basic cycle; press Start.
2. When the baking cycle ends, immediately remove the pan's bread and place it on a rack. Let cool to room temperature before slicing.

Rosemary-Lemon Bread

(Ready in about 3 hours 10 minutes I Servings- One loaf I Difficulty- Moderate)

Ingredients

For the dough:

- Two cups of water
- Three tablespoons baking soda
- Half cup (2 ounces) whole hazelnuts
- 2/3 cup milk
- One large egg
- Two tablespoons unsalted butter, cut into pieces
- Three tablespoons honey
- Two and 3/4 cups bread flour
- One and a half teaspoons chopped fresh rosemary
- Grated zest of one large lemon
- One tablespoon gluten
- One and 3/4 teaspoon salt
- One and 3/4 teaspoons salt
- Two and 1/4teaspoons bread machine yeast
- 3/4 cup golden raisins

For the lemon icing:

- 3/4 cup sifted confectioners' sugar
- Two tablespoons warm fresh lemon juice

Instructions

1. Preheat the oven to 350°F.
2. In a saucepan, bring two cups of water to a boil in order to peel the nuts. To it, add the baking soda and the nuts. Simmer for 3 to 5 minutes; the water turns black. Drain the nuts in a colander afterward and run them under a stream of cold water. Slip off each skin using your fingers, and place them on a clean dishtowel. Dry Pat and place her on a clean baking sheet. For 10 to 15 minutes, toast the nuts in the oven, stirring twice. On the baking sheet, cool. Have the nuts chopped and set aside?
3. To make the dough, according to the order in the manufacturer's instructions, put the dough ingredients, except the hazelnuts and raisins, in the pan. Set the medium crust and the Simple or Fruit and Nut Cycle Program; press Start.
4. Raisins and hazelnuts should be added when the machine beeps or between Knead 1 and Knead 2. If the dough ball seems dry, add an additional tablespoon or two of water.
5. If the baking cycle ends, remove the bread from the pan immediately and place it on a rack to let it cool down before slicing, or drizzle with lemon icing.
6. If you use it, mix in a small bowl, the sugar and the lemon juice with the lemon icing. Place the rack over a piece of waxed or parchment paper with the hot bread to catch the drips. Drizzle over the whole loaf with the glaze, letting the sides drip down some.
7. Let the loaf stand at room temperature until the glaze is set and it is totally cool.

Mountain Herb Bread

(Ready in about 3 hours 10 minutes I Servings- One loaf I Difficulty- Moderate)

Ingredients

- One and 1/4cups water
- Two tablespoons olive oil
- 1/4 cup wildflower honey
- Two cups of bread flour
- One cup of whole wheat flour
- Three tablespoons light brown sugar
- Three tablespoons nonfat dry milk
- One tablespoon gluten
- One and a half tablespoons minced fresh parsley
- One and a half teaspoons dried basil
- One teaspoon dried dill weed
- One teaspoon dried summer savory
- 3/4 teaspoon dried marjoram
- Half teaspoon dried tarragon
- 1/4 teaspoon dried thyme
- One and a half teaspoons salt
- Two and a half teaspoons bread machine yeast

Instructions

1. In accordance with the order in the manufacturer's instructions, place all the ingredients in the pan. Set the Dark Crust and the Basic Cycle Program; press Start.
2. When the baking cycle ends, remove the bread and place it on a rack. Before slicing, let the room temperature cool down.

Buttermilk Bread with Lavender

(Ready in about 3 hours 10 minutes I Servings- One loaf I Difficulty- Moderate)

Ingredients

- 1/3 cup water
- 3/4 cup buttermilk
- Three tablespoons olive oil
- Three cups of bread flour
- Two tablespoons finely chopped fresh lavender leaves
- One teaspoon finely chopped fresh lavender flowers
- Grated zest of one small lemon
- One tablespoon gluten
- One and a half teaspoons salt
- Two and a half teaspoons bread machine yeast

Instructions

1. Analogous to the order in the manufacturer's orders, put all ingredients in the pan. Set the Dark Crust and Simple Cycle Schedule; press Start.
2. When the baking period stops, take the bread from the pan instantly and put it on a rack. Until slicing, let it cool to room temperature.

Whole Wheat Bas Bread

(Ready in about 3 hours 10 minutes I Servings- One loaf I Difficulty- Moderate)

Ingredients

- 3/4 cup buttermilk
- 1/3 cup water
- Two tablespoons butter, cut into pieces
- Two tablespoons honey
- Three cups of white whole wheat flour
- 1/4 cup chopped fresh basil
- 1/4 cup pine nuts, chopped
- One tablespoon gluten
- One and a half teaspoons salt
- Two and a half teaspoons bread machine yeast

Instructions

1. Analogous to the order in the manufacturer's orders, put all ingredients in the pan. Set the Dark Crust and Simple Cycle Schedule; press Start.
2. When the baking period stops, take the bread from the pan instantly and put it on a rack. Until slicing, let it cool to room temperature.

Herb Light Rye Bread

(Ready in about 3 hours 10 minutes I Servings- One loaf I Difficulty- Moderate)

Ingredients

- Half teaspoon dill seeds
- Half teaspoon poppy seeds
- 1/4 teaspoon celery seeds
- 7/8 cup water
- One large egg
- 3/4 cup medium or dark rye flour
- One and a half tablespoons minced shallot
- One tablespoon molasses
- Two and 1/4cups bread flour
- One tablespoon gluten
- One and a half teaspoons caraway seed
- One and 3/4 teaspoons salt
- Two and a half teaspoons bread machine yeast

Instructions

1. Analogous to the order in the manufacturer's orders, put all ingredients in the pan. Set the Dark Crust and Simple Cycle Schedule; press Start.
2. When the baking period stops, take the bread from the pan instantly and put it on a rack. Until slicing, let it cool to room temperature.

Sour Cream Semolina Bread with Herb Swirl

(Ready in about 3 hours 10 minutes I Servings- One loaf I Difficulty- Moderate)

Ingredients

For the dough:

- 3/4 cup water
- One tablespoon olive oil
- Half cup sour cream
- One and a half cups bread flour
- One cup of semolina flour
- Two teaspoons sugar
- One tablespoon gluten
- One and a half teaspoons salt
- Two and a half teaspoons bread machine yeast

For the herb swirl:

- 1/3 cup chopped fresh flat-leaf parsley
- Three to Four tablespoons chopped fresh herbs, such as dill, basil, chervil, marjoram, or tarragon
- One and 1/4teaspoons dried herb mixture, such as Italian herbs

Instructions

1. In accordance with the order in the manufacturer's instructions, place all the dough ingredients in the pan.
2. For the Basic or Variety cycle, set crust on medium and program; press Start. Click Pause after Raise 2 of the Simple cycle has stopped, or delete the pan and close the lid when the monitor displays Form in the Variety cycle. Remove the dough immediately and place it on a lightly floured work surface; pat it into a rectangle of 12-by-8-inch fat. Brush with two tablespoons of olive oil. Sprinkle with parsley and the rest of the herbs, leaving the entire way around a 1-inch space.
3. Roll up jelly-roll style, starting at a brief edge. Tuck the ends under and pinch the seam at the rim. Using cooking spray to cover the bottom of the pastry. Remove the kneading blade and put the dough back in the pan; press Start to begin to rise and bake as programmed.
4. If the baking period stops, take the bread from the pan instantly and put it on a rack. Let cool to room temperature before slicing.

Sun-dried Tomato and Rosemary Loaf

(Ready in about 3 hours 10 minutes I Servings- One loaf I Difficulty- Moderate)

Ingredients

- One teaspoon Easy bake yeast
- 1.4 cups of strong white bread flour
- 0.6 cups granary-type or malted grain flour
- One teaspoon fine sea salt
- 1.35 cups of water
- ¼ cup of sun-dried tomatoes in oil, drained and finely chopped
- Two tablespoon tomato oil (from the jar of sun-dried tomatoes)
- One tablespoon finely chopped fresh rosemary

Instructions

1. Put all the ingredients into the pan in the correct order suggested by the manufacturer's instructions.
2. Fit the pan into the bread machine and close the lid.

3. Select the basic white setting, medium crust, and the appropriate size. Press Start.
4. When the program has finished, lift the pan out of the machine, turn the bread out onto a wire rack and leave to cool completely.

Minted Bread

(Ready in about 3 hours 10 minutes I Servings- One loaf I Difficulty- Moderate)

Ingredients

- One teaspoon Easy bake yeast
- One and 2/3 cups of strong white bread flour
- Half cup of strong whole meal bread flour
- Half teaspoon fine sea salt
- Two tablespoons finely chopped fresh mint or two teaspoons dried mint
- One and a half cup of apple juice

Instructions

1. Add all the ingredients in the container in the correct order for your machine.
2. Fit the container into the bread machine and close the lid.
3. Select the basic white setting, medium crust, and the appropriate size. Press Start.
4. When the program has finished, lift the pan out of the machine, turn the bread out onto a wire rack and leave to cool completely.

Coriander and Chili Bread

(Ready in about 3 hours 10 minutes I Servings- One loaf I Difficulty- Moderate)

Ingredients

- One teaspoon Easy bake yeast
- Two and 1/8 cups of strong white bread flour
- 3/4 teaspoon salt
- 2/3 cup of coconut milk and water each
- Two mild green chilies, seeds removed and finely chopped
- A handful of chopped fresh coriander

Instructions

1. Put all the ingredients, except for the chilies and coriander, into the pan in the correct order for your bread machine.
2. Fit the pan into the bread machine and close the lid.
3. Select the basic white raisin setting, medium crust, and the appropriate size. Press Start. When the machine indicates (with a beeping sound), add the chilies and coriander and close the lid again.
4. When the program has finished, lift the pan out of the machine, turn the bread out on to a wire rack and leave to cool completely

Chapter 14-Fruit and Vegetable Bread Recipes

Some of the fruit and vegetable bread recipes that you can make in your bread machine are provided in this chapter.

Yeasted Carrot Bread

(Ready in about 4 hours 10 minutes I Servings- One loaf I Difficulty- Moderate)

Ingredients

- 2/3 cup of whole wheat flour
- One and a 1/3 cup of rolled oats
- Two cups of bread flour
- One and a 1/3 teaspoon of salt
- One and a half tablespoons of vegetable oil
- One cup of water
- Two tablespoons of brown sugar
- 1/4 cup of dry milk powder
- Two and a half teaspoons of active dry yeast
- 2/3 cup of grated carrot

Instructions

1. Place all the required ingredients in the container of the bread machine in the suggested order by the manufacturer.
2. Select a basic setting, light crust. Press the start button.
3. Enjoy fresh bread.

Sauerkraut Rye Bread

(Ready in about 3 hours 50 minutes I Servings- One loaf I Difficulty- Moderate)

Ingredients

- Two cups of bread flour
- One cup of rinsed & drained sauerkraut
- One and a half tablespoons of butter
- ¾ cup of warm water
- One and a half tablespoons of brown sugar
- One and a half teaspoons of active dry yeast
- One and a half tablespoons of molasses
- One and a half teaspoons of salt
- One teaspoon of caraway seed
- One cup of rye flour

Instructions

1. Place all the required ingredients in the container of the bread machine in the suggested order by the manufacturer.
2. Use the Basic Cycle setting. Press the start button.
3. Serve fresh bread.

Savory Onion Bread

(Ready in about 3 hours 40 minutes I Servings- One loaf I Difficulty- Moderate)

Ingredients

For Caramelized Onions

- Two sliced onions
- One tablespoon of butter

For Bread

- One cup of water
- One tablespoon of olive oil
- Three cups of bread flour
- Two tablespoons of sugar
- One teaspoon of salt
- One and a ¼ teaspoons of bread machine

Instructions

1. In a skillet, sauté onions over medium flame in butter until caramelized and brown. Turn off the heat.
2. Put all the required ingredients in the container of the bread machine in the manufacturer's suggested order, except for caramelized onion.
3. Select Basic cycle, Press the start button. Do not use the delay feature. Add half a cup of onions at nut signal.
4. Serve fresh bread.

Tomato Herb Bread

(Ready in about 4 hours 10 minutes I Servings- One loaf I Difficulty- Moderate)

Ingredients

- One whole egg
- Two tablespoons of olive oil
- Two teaspoons of dried minced onion
- Half cup and two tablespoons of warm milk
- Half teaspoon of salt
- Two tablespoons of minced fresh parsley
- One tablespoon of sugar
- Two and a 1/4 teaspoons of active dry yeast
- Half teaspoon of garlic powder
- One can of (6 ounces) tomato paste
- Half teaspoon of dried tarragon
- Three cups of bread flour

Instructions

1. Put all the required ingredients in the container of the bread machine in the suggested order by the manufacturer.
2. Use basic bread setting, crust to your liking.
3. After five minutes, check the dough add flour if it's too wet and sticky.
4. Add one tablespoon of flour if required. Serve fresh bread.

Mashed Potato Bread

(Ready in about 3 hours 15 minutes I Servings- One loaf I Difficulty- Moderate)

Ingredients

- One tablespoon of dry milk powder
- One and a half teaspoons of dried yeast
- Two tablespoons of sugar
- Two tablespoons of sunflower oil
- Three and ¼ cups of white bread flour
- One teaspoon of salt
- 0.8 cup of potato cooking water at room temperature
- One and a half cups of mashed potatoes

Instructions

1. Put all the required ingredients in the container of the bread machine in the suggested order by the manufacturer.
2. Select a basic setting, medium crust. Press the start button.
3. Glaze the bread with milk with a brush at the start of cooking time.

Confetti Bread

(Ready in about 3 hours 10 minutes I Servings- One loaf I Difficulty- Moderate)

Ingredients

- Two teaspoons of instant skim-milk powder
- 3/4 cup of roughly chopped old cheddar cheese
- 3/4 teaspoon of salt
- One teaspoon of sugar
- 3/4 cup of water
- Half cup of shredded carrot
- Three cups of white flour
- One and a 1/4 teaspoon of bread machine yeast
- 1/3 cup of diced sweet mix bell pepper
- Two teaspoons of dried Italian seasoning

Instructions

1. Place all ingredients, except cheese, into the bread machine in the manufacturer's suggested order.
2. Select white bread cycle—Press the start button. Add cheese at the ingredients signal.
3. Serve fresh bread.

Pretty Borscht Bread

(Ready in about 3 hours 10 minutes I Servings- One loaf I Difficulty- Moderate)

Ingredients

- One package of onion soup mix (dry)
- 2/3 cup of tomato juice
- 1/4 teaspoon of ground ginger
- Two and a 1/4 teaspoons of active dry yeast
- Three cups of all-purpose flour
- 1/3 cup of grated carrot
- One tablespoon of wheat germ
- Two tablespoons of vegetable oil
- 3/4 cup of cooked & chopped beet
- Half cup of sour cream
- 1/4 teaspoon of granulated sugar:

Instructions

1. Put all the required ingredients in the container of the bread machine in the suggested order by the manufacturer.
2. Select the dough cycle. Take the dough out and let it rise for one and a half hours.
3. Punch the dough, let it rise again for 60 minutes.
4. Let the oven preheat to 350 F.
5. Bake for 20-25 minutes.
6. Serve fresh bread.

Yeasted Pumpkin Bread

(Ready in about 3 hours 5 minutes I Servings- One loaf I Difficulty- Moderate)

Ingredients

- One cup of mashed pumpkin puree
- One and a 1/4 teaspoons of salt
- Two tablespoons of sugar
- Four cups of bread flour
- Half cup and two tablespoons of milk
- Two and a 1/4 teaspoons active dry yeast
- Two tablespoons of vegetable oil

Instructions

1. Place all ingredients in the container of the bread machine, as per the manufacturer's suggested order.
2. Select white bread and light crust—Press the start button.
3. Enjoy fresh bread.

Oatmeal Zucchini Bread

(Ready in about 2 hours 10 minutes I Servings- One loaf I Difficulty- Moderate)

Ingredients

- Two whole eggs
- 1/3 cup of packed brown sugar
- 3/4 cup of shredded zucchini
- Three tablespoons of granulated sugar
- One and a half cups of all-purpose flour
- 1/3 cup of vegetable oil
- 3/4 teaspoon of ground cinnamon
- Half teaspoon of baking powder
- 3/4 teaspoon of salt
- 1/4 teaspoon of ground allspice
- 1/3 cup of raisins
- Half teaspoon of baking soda
- 1/3 cup of oatmeal

Instructions

1. Put all the required ingredients in the container of the bread machine in the suggested order by the manufacturer.
2. All ingredients should be at room temperature.
3. Select Cake/Quick bread. Press the start button.
4. After 5 minutes, clean the pan's surface with a rubber spatula and let the cycle continue.
5. Serve fresh bread.

Hot Red Pepper Bread

(Ready in about 3 hours 10 minutes I Servings- One loaf I Difficulty- Moderate)

Ingredients

- One tablespoon of butter
- Two tablespoons of unsweetened yogurt
- Two cloves of garlic
- Three cups of bread flour
- Three tablespoons of parmesan cheese
- 1/4 cup of chopped roasted red pepper
- One and a half teaspoons of dried basil
- 3/4 cup of water
- Two tablespoons of sugar
- Two teaspoons bread machine yeast
- One and a half teaspoons of salt

Instructions

1. Put all the required ingredients in the container of the bread machine in the suggested order by the manufacturer.
2. Set basic setting, Light crust. Press the start button.
3. Serve fresh bread.

French Onion Bread

(Ready in about 3 hours 10 minutes I Servings- One loaf I Difficulty- Moderate)

Ingredients

- Four tablespoons of softened unsalted butter
- Half onion diced and fried
- One tablespoon of onion Powder
- Three cups of bread Flour
- One and a half Teaspoons of Bread Machine Yeast
- One cup of lukewarm Milk
- One tablespoon of white Sugar
- One and a half teaspoons of salt

Instructions

1. Put all the required ingredients in the container of the bread machine in the suggested order by the manufacturer.
2. Select a basic setting. Light crust. Press the start button.
3. Enjoy fresh bread.

Golden Butternut Squash Raisin Bread

(Ready in about 3 hours 10 minutes I Servings- One loaf I Difficulty- Moderate)

Ingredients

- Three cups of bread flour
- Three tablespoons of Nonfat milk powder
- Four teaspoons of active dry yeast
- Three tablespoons of wheat germ
- Three tablespoons of Gluten four
- One and a half teaspoon of salt
- Three tablespoons of butter
- One cup of butternut puree
- 2/3 cup of water
- Half cup of raisins
- Four tablespoons of sugar

- Half teaspoon of ground ginger
- ¾ teaspoon ground cinnamon

Instructions

1. Put all the required ingredients in the container of the bread machine in the suggested order by the
2. manufacturer.
3. Select basic and crust to your liking—press the start button.
4. Serve fresh bread.

Sweet Potato Bread

(Ready in about 3 hours 10 minutes I Servings- One loaf I Difficulty- Moderate)

Ingredients

- Half teaspoon of cinnamon
- Half cup of Luke warm water
- Four cups of flour
- One teaspoon of vanilla extract
- ⅓ cup of packed brown sugar
- Two tablespoons of softened butter
- One and a half teaspoons of salt
- One cup of mashed sweet potatoes
- Two tablespoons of powdered milk
- Two teaspoons of yeast

Instructions

1. Put all the required ingredients in the container of the bread machine in the suggested order by the manufacturer.
2. Select white bread, light crust. Press the start button.
3. Serve fresh bread.

Potato Thyme Bread

(Ready in about 3 hours 10 minutes I Servings- One loaf I Difficulty- Moderate)

Ingredients

- One and a half teaspoon of salt
- Two tablespoons of butter softened
- One tablespoon of sugar
- 1.25 cups of lukewarm water
- Two teaspoons of bread machine yeast
- Half cup of instant potato flakes
- Three cups of bread flour
- Two tablespoons of dried thyme leaves

Instructions

1. Put all the required ingredients in the container of the bread machine in the suggested order by the manufacturer.
2. Select the white cycle and dark crust if you like.
3. Press the start button.
4. Serve fresh bread.

Light Corn Bread

(Ready in about 3 hours 10 minutes I Servings- One loaf I Difficulty- Moderate)

Ingredients

- One cup of milk
- 1/4 cup of sugar
- Two whole eggs – lightly mixed

- One and a 1/4 cup of bread flour
- Four teaspoons of baking powder
- One cup of cornmeal
- 1/4 cup of melted butter
- One teaspoon of salt
- One teaspoon of vanilla

Instructions

1. Put all the required ingredients in the container of the bread machine in the suggested order by the manufacturer.
2. Use cake cycle/quick cycle and a light crust. Press the start button.
3. Serve fresh bread

Pineapple Coconut Bread

(Ready in about 3 hours 10 minutes I Servings- One loaf I Difficulty- Moderate)

Ingredients

- Half cup of pineapple (crushed with juice)
- ¼ cup of milk
- ¼ cup of margarine
- ⅓ cup of sugar
- One teaspoon of coconut extract
- One whole egg, beaten
- Half cup of mashed banana
- Three cups of flour
- Half teaspoon of salt
- One and a half teaspoons of bread machine yeast
- Half cup of instant potato flakes

Instructions

1. Put all the required ingredients in the container of the bread machine in the suggested order by the manufacturer.
2. Select sweet bread and light crust—Press the start button.
3. Serve fresh.

Warm Spiced Pumpkin Bread

(Ready in about 3 hours 10 minutes I Servings- One loaf I Difficulty- Moderate)

Ingredients

- Half cup white sugar
- One cup, not pie filling of canned pumpkin
- 1/4 teaspoon of salt
- Half cup of brown sugar
- Two whole eggs
- One teaspoon of vanilla
- One and a half cups of all-purpose flour
- One and a half teaspoon of pumpkin pie spice
- Half cup of chopped walnuts
- 1/3 cup of canola oil
- Two teaspoons of baking powder

Instructions

1. Spray the bread machine pan with cooking oil.

2. Put all the required ingredients in the container of the bread machine in the suggested order by the manufacturer.
3. Select the Quick cycle, medium crust.
4. After three minutes, clean the sides of the pan with a spatula.
5. Start again, and serve fresh.

Black Olive Bread

(Ready in about 2 hours 10 minutes | Servings- One loaf | Difficulty- Moderate)

Ingredients

- One cup and half cup brine warm water
- Half cup of brine (from olives)
- Three cups of bread flour
- Two tablespoons of olive oil
- Two teaspoons of active dry yeast
- One and a half teaspoons of salt
- One and 2/3 cups of whole-wheat flour
- Two tablespoons of sugar
- Half to 2/3 cup of finely chopped olives
- One and a half teaspoons of dried basil

Instructions

1. Mix water with brine.
2. Add all ingredients, except for olives, to the bread machine in the manufacturer's suggested order.
3. Select wheat or basic setting. Press the start button.
4. Add the chopped olives to the ingredient signal.
5. Serve fresh bread, and brush with olive oil.

Robust Date Bread

(Ready in about 2 hours 10 minutes | Servings- One loaf | Difficulty- Moderate)

Ingredients

- 3/4 cup of boiling water
- Three tablespoons cut into half-inch pieces of unsalted butter
- 2/3 cup of granulated sugar
- One teaspoon of baking powder
- One and a 1/3 cup of all-purpose flour
- One teaspoon of vanilla extract
- 3/4 cup of chopped dates
- One teaspoon of baking soda
- 1/3 cup of chopped walnuts
- Half teaspoon of salt

Instructions

1. Put all the required ingredients in the container of the bread machine in the suggested order by the manufacturer.
2. Select basic and light crust.
3. After 4 minutes, scrape the sides of the pan with a rubber spatula.
4. Before baking starts, remove paddles.
5. Enjoy fresh.

Apple Spice Bread

(Ready in about 3 hours 35 minutes | Servings- One loaf | Difficulty- Moderate)

Ingredients

- 1/4 cup of vegetable oil
- One cup of milk
- Half teaspoon of cinnamon
- One and a half teaspoons of salt
- One and a 1/3 cup of diced apples (peeled)
- Two tablespoons of sugar
- Two and a half teaspoons of yeast
- Three cups bread flour

Instructions

1. Add all ingredients in the container of the bread machine, except for apples, in the manufacturer's suggested order.
2. Select medium crust. Press the start button.
3. Add apples to the ingredients signal.
4. Serve fresh

Lemon-Lime Blueberry Bread

(Ready in about 3 hours 10 minutes | Servings- One loaf | Difficulty- Moderate)

Ingredients

- 1/4 cup of lukewarm heavy cream
- One teaspoon of salt
- 1/3 cup of diced butter
- Three whole eggs
- One and a half cup and three tablespoons of All-purpose flour:
- One and a half cup of bread flour
- One and a half cup of blueberries
- Four tablespoons and two tablespoons of sugar
- Two teaspoons of bread machine yeast
- 1/4 cup of lukewarm water
- Two tablespoons of each of lime and lemon juice

Instructions

1. Add all ingredients in the container of the bread machine, except blueberries, in the manufacturer's suggested order.
2. Select basic cycle, crust to your liking. Press the start button.
3. Add blueberries to the ingredient signal.
4. Serve fresh bread with sugar on top of the loaf.

Banana Whole-Wheat Bread

(Ready in about 3 hours 10 minutes | Servings- One loaf | Difficulty- Moderate)

Ingredients

- One whole egg
- One tablespoon of softened butter
- One and a half teaspoons of bread machine yeast
- 1/3 cup of ripe bananas, mashed
- Three tablespoons of sugar
- 1/4 cup of warm (80 F) water
- Half teaspoon of salt
- 1 and 1/4 cups of bread flour
- Toasted chopped pecans: 1/3 cup

- 3/4 cup of whole wheat flour

Instructions

1. Add all ingredients, except nuts, to the bread machine in the suggested
2. order by the manufacturer. Add banana with water.
3. Select white bread cycle. Light crust. Press the start button. Add nuts at the ingredient signal. Do not use the delay feature.
4. Enjoy fresh.

Orange Cranberry Bread

(Ready in about 3 hours 5 minutes I Servings- One loaf I Difficulty- Moderate)

Ingredients

- One cup of dried cranberries
- Three cups of all-purpose flour
- Half cup of warm water
- Two teaspoons of active dry yeast
- Three tablespoons of honey
- ¾ cup of plain yogurt
- One tablespoon of melted butter
- One teaspoon of orange oil
- One and a half teaspoons of salt

Instructions

1. Put all the required ingredients in the container of the bread machine in the suggested order by the manufacturer.
2. Select basic and light crust. Press the start button.
3. Serve fresh bread

Plum Orange Bread

(Ready in about 3 hours 10 minutes I Servings- One loaf I Difficulty- Moderate)

Ingredient

- One and 1/4 cups of warm water
- 1/4 cup of packed brown sugar
- One and a half teaspoons of bread machine yeast
- Three and a 3/4 cup of bread flour
- Two tablespoons of orange juice
- 3/4 cups of plums
- Two tablespoons of vegetable oil
- One teaspoon of salt

Instructions

1. Place all ingredients in the container of the bread machine in the suggested order by the manufacturer.
2. Select basic with medium crust.
3. Press the start button. Enjoy fresh bread.

Peaches & Cream Bread

(Ready in about 3 hours 10 minutes I Servings- One loaf I Difficulty- Moderate)

Ingredients

- One whole egg, beaten
- One and a half teaspoon of salt
- One and a half cups of chopped peaches

- One and a half tablespoons of vegetable oil
- Three tablespoons of sugar
- ½ teaspoon of cinnamon
- Three and a half cups of bread flour
- One and a half teaspoons of active dry yeast
- 1/4 cup of heavy cream
- 1/4 teaspoon of nutmeg
- Half cup of rolled oats

Instructions

1. Add all ingredients in the container of the bread machine in suggested order by the manufacturer
2. Select a basic setting. Press the start button.
3. Enjoy fresh bread.

Fresh Blueberry Bread

(Ready in about 3 hours 10 minutes I Servings- One loaf I Difficulty- Moderate)

Instructions

- Eight tablespoons of melted Butter
- Two Eggs mixed
- One teaspoon of Vanilla Extract
- Three ripe bananas mashed
- One cup of Packed Light Brown Sugar
- Two cups of all-purpose flour
- Half teaspoon of Salt
- One teaspoon of baking Powder
- One teaspoon of baking Soda
- One cup of blueberries

Instructions

1. All ingredients should be at room temperature.
2. Add all ingredients, except blueberries, to the bread machine in the manufacturer's suggested order.
3. Select Quick bread, light crust—Press the start button.
4. After the first kneading, add blueberries.
5. Enjoy.

Blueberry Oatmeal Bread

(Ready in about 3 hours 10 minutes I Servings- One loaf I Difficulty- Moderate)

Ingredients

- Two cups of all-purpose flour
- One cup of quick-cooking Oatmeal
- One teaspoon of grated lemon
- Half teaspoon of salt
- Half teaspoon of baking soda
- 1/3 cup of vegetable oil
- Two teaspoons of baking Powder
- Two teaspoons of vanilla
- 3/4 cup of sugar
- One cup of thawed blueberries
- One and a 1/4 cup of Skim milk
- Two Eggs, lightly mixed

Instructions

1. Dust lightly the thawed blueberries with flour.
2. With cooking oil, spray the pan.

3. Add already mixed ingredients to the bread machine.
4. Select quick or cake cycle—Press the start button.
5. Serve fresh bread.

Fragrant Orange Bread

(Ready in about 3 hours 45 minutes I Servings- One loaf I Difficulty- Moderate)

Ingredients

- Half teaspoon of grated orange
- Three tablespoons of orange juice concentrate
- One whole egg
- Three cups of bread flour
- One and a ¼ teaspoons of salt
- Half cup and one tablespoon of water
- ¼ cup of granulated sugar
- Two tablespoons of instant dry milk
- One and a half tablespoons of softened butter
- Two teaspoons of bread machine yeast

For Orange Glaze

- One tablespoon of orange juice
- ¾ cup of powdered sugar

Instructions

1. Put all the required ingredients in the container of the bread machine in the suggested order by the manufacturer.
2. Select the white cycle. Do not use the delay feature. Select Light crust—Press the start button.
3. Meanwhile, mix the glaze ingredients.
4. Drizzle the glaze over fresh bread.

Moist Oatmeal Apple Bread

(Ready in about 3 hours 10 minutes I Servings- One loaf I Difficulty- Moderate)

Ingredients

- ⅓ cup of unsweetened apple sauce
- ⅓ cup of water
- ⅔ cup of unsweetened apple juice
- Three tablespoons of honey
- ¼ cup of oat bran
- Two tablespoons of vegetable oil
- ⅓ cup of quick-cooking oats
- One and a half teaspoons of salt
- Three cups of bread flour
- Two and a ¼ teaspoons of bread machine yeast
- One and a half teaspoons of ground cinnamon

Instructions

1. Put all the required ingredients in the container of the bread machine in the suggested order by the manufacturer.
2. Select basic cycle, light crust. Press the start button.

3. Serve fresh bread.

Strawberry Shortcake Bread

(Ready in about 3 hours 10 minutes I Servings- One loaf I Difficulty- Moderate)

Ingredients

- Two and a half teaspoons of bread machine yeast
- One teaspoon of vanilla extract
- 1/4 cup of warm heavy whipping cream
- Three cups of bread machine flour
- 1/4 cup of warm water
- One tablespoon of sugar
- 1/8 teaspoon of baking powder
- Two cups of fresh strawberries with 1/4 cup sugar
- One teaspoon of salt

Instructions

1. Add water, cream to the pan of the bread maker, mix with yeast and sugar. Let it rest for 15 minutes.
2. Coat the sliced strawberries with ¼ cup of sugar.
3. Add all ingredients, except for strawberries, to the bread machine in the manufacturer's suggested order.
4. Add strawberries to the fruit hopper or add at the ingredients signal.
5. Select basic, medium crust. Press the start button.
6. Slice and serve fresh bread.

Pain D'ail

(Ready in about 3 hours 10 minutes I Servings- One loaf I Difficulty- Moderate)

Ingredients

- Three cloves garlic
- Two tablespoons unsalted butter softened
- One and 1/4cups water
- Three and 1/8 cups bread flour
- One tablespoon gluten
- One tablespoon sugar
- One and a half teaspoons salt
- Two and a half teaspoons bread machine yeast

Instructions

1. The cloves of garlic firstly are to be sliced and pressed into the butter and mashed.
2. Similar to the order in the manufacturer's orders, put all ingredients in the pan. For the liquid ingredients, add garlic butter. Set the middle crust and the French Bread period program; click Start.
3. If the baking period stops, take the bread from the pan instantly and put it on a rack. Let cool to room temperature before slicing.

Balsamic—Caramelized Onion Bread

(Ready in about 3 hours 10 minutes I Servings- One loaf I Difficulty- Moderate)

Ingredients

For the onions:

- Three tablespoons olive oil
- Two tablespoons balsamic vinegar
- One large onion (about 3/4 pound) thinly sliced

For the dough:

- 3/4 cup water
- One tablespoon sugar
- Two and a half cups bread flour
- Half cup light or medium rye flour
- One tablespoon gluten
- One and a half teaspoons salt
- Two and a half teaspoons bread machine yeast

Instructions

1. Place the olive oil and the vinegar in a medium saucepan to cook the onions. Only add the onions. Cook steadily for about 20 minutes over low heat, stirring periodically, until the onions are soft and limp; do not burn. In a measuring cup, drain out the extra liquid and apply water to make the liquid measurement of the dough; you might have one or two tablespoons or none. To cool to room temperature, set the onions aside. You're going to have almost a whole cup of onions.
2. To make the dough, according to the manufacturer's instructions, place the dough ingredients in the pan. Set the medium or dark crust and the Simple or Fruit and Nut cycle program; press Start.
3. Caramelized onions are to be inserted as the system beeps or between Knead 1 and Knead 2. Initially, the dough will appear stiff, so don't be tempted to add liquid; the onions will have plenty to sell. If 3 minutes after adding the onions, the dough is too warm, apply a tablespoon of more flour in increments.
4. If the baking period stops, take the bread from the pan instantly and put it on a rack. Until slicing, let it cool to room temperature.

Cherry—Wheat Berry Bread

(Ready in about 3 hours 10 minutes I Servings- One loaf I Difficulty- Moderate)

Ingredients

- 1/3 cup wheat berries
- One cup of water
- One cup of water
- One large egg white
- Two tablespoons canola oil
- 1/4 cup honey
- Three cups of bread flour
- Two teaspoons gluten
- One and a half teaspoons salt
- One tablespoon bread machine yeast
- Half cup tart dried cherries tossed with one tablespoon flour

Instructions

1. In a saucepan, mix the wheat berries and one cup of water. Just get it to a boil. Reduce the heat, cover it partly, and simmer until chewy and tender

for about 45 minutes. Drain the excess water out and let it cool to warm up.
2. In compliance with the manufacturer's directions, add the ingredients, except the wheat berries and the cherries, to the jar. Set the Dark Crust and Simple Cycle Schedule; press Start.
3. Attach the wheat berries and the cherries while the system beeps, or at the break between Kneads 1 and 2. The ball of dough would be very fluffy and nubby.
4. If the baking period stops, take the bread from the pan instantly and put it on a rack. Until slicing, let it cool to room temperature.

Prune Bread

(Ready in about 3 hours 10 minutes I Servings- One loaf I Difficulty- Moderate)

Ingredients

- One and 1/8 cups water
- Three tablespoons unsalted butter, cut into pieces
- Two and 1/4cups bread flour
- 3/4 cup whole wheat flour
- Two tablespoons light brown sugar
- One tablespoon gluten
- One and 1/4teaspoons salt
- One teaspoon ground cinnamon
- 1/4 teaspoon fresh-ground nutmeg
- Two and a half teaspoons bread machine yeast
- Nine pitted prunes (about 3 ounces), chopped

Instructions

1. Place the ingredients in the pan according to the order in the manufacturer's instructions, without the prunes. For the Simple or Fruit and Nut loop, set the crust dark and program; press Start.
2. Attach the plums as the system beeps or between Knead 1 and Knead 2. Click Pause at the start of Raise 1 to cut the dough, pat it into a square, and sprinkle it with the prunes if you want large chunks of prunes. To spread the prunes, roll the dough up and knead it softly a couple of times. To restart the rising, return the dough ball to the machine and press Start.
3. If the baking period stops, take the bread from the pan instantly and put it on a rack. Until slicing, let it cool to room temperature.

Rosemary—Golden Raisin Bread

(Ready in about 3 hours 10 minutes I Servings- One loaf I Difficulty- Moderate)

Ingredients

- Three cups of bread flour
- One teaspoon dried rosemary
- 2/3 cup water
- 1/4 cup extra-virgin olive oil
- Two large eggs
- 1/3 cup nonfat dry milk
- 1/4 cup sugar
- One and a half teaspoons salt

- Two teaspoons SAF yeast or Two and a half teaspoons bread machine yeast
- Half cup golden raisins

Instructions

1. Combine one cup of the flour with the rosemary in the operating bowl of a food processor. Pulse for the rosemary to be pulverized.
2. In compliance with the order in the manufacturer's instructions, add the ingredients, including the rosemary flour but not the raisins, in the pan. Dough Cycle Program; Click Start.
3. Line the parchment paper with a baking sheet. Turn the dough out on a clean work surface as the unit beeps at the end of the loop, using a dough scraper. Pat into the irregular shape of the oval loaf. Sprinkle and fold in half with the raisins. To spread uniformly, knead softly. And smooth the dough out too. Shape around into a close one. Place it on the baking sheet and spray the roof with olive oil. Cover loosely with plastic wrap and grow until doubled in bulk, around 1 hour, at room temperature.
4. Preheat the oven to 350°F twenty minutes prior to baking. Brush the loaf surface again with olive oil, and, using a sharp knife, slash an X on the top, no deeper than Half-inch. Bake in the oven center for 30 to 35 minutes, until dark brown and the bottom, sounds hollow when tapped. Place the loaf on a rack. Let cool to room temperature before slicing.

Carrot Bread with Crystallized Ginger

(Ready in about 3 hours 10 minutes I Servings- One loaf I Difficulty- Moderate)

Ingredients

- Three tablespoons fat-free milk
- 3/4 cup pureed carrots
- Two large eggs
- Two tablespoons unsalted butter, cut into pieces
- Three cups of bread flour
- 1/4 cup chopped crystallized ginger
- One tablespoon gluten
- One and a half teaspoons salt
- Two and 1/4 teaspoons bread machine yeast

Instructions

1. Similar to the order in the manufacturer's orders, put all ingredients in the pan. Set the Dark Crust and Simple Cycle Schedule; press Start.
2. When the baking period stops, take the bread from the pan instantly and put it on a rack. Until slicing, let it cool to room temperature.

Applesauce Bread

(Ready in about 3 hours 10 minutes I Servings- One loaf I Difficulty- Moderate)

Ingredients

- 1/4 cup apple juice
- Half cup unsweetened applesauce

- One large egg
- Two tablespoons unsalted butter, cut into pieces
- Three cups of bread flour
- Three tablespoons light brown sugar, optional
- One tablespoon gluten
- One and a half teaspoons salt
- One teaspoon ground cinnamon or apple pie spice
- 1/3 teaspoon baking soda
- Two and a half teaspoons bread machine yeast

Instructions

1. Similar to the order in the manufacturer's orders, put all ingredients in the pan. In the manufacturer's manuals, set the crust to order. Set the medium crust and the medium schedule, and the Simple or Sweet Bread cycle program; press Start.
2. If the baking period stops, take the bread from the pan instantly and put it on a rack. Until slicing, let it cool to room temperature.

Sage and Onion Loaf

(Ready in about 3 hours 10 minutes I Servings- One loaf I Difficulty- Moderate)

Ingredients

- 1/3 cup of butter
- One large onion, finely chopped
- One teaspoon Easy bake yeast
- One and ¾ cups of strong white bread flour
- One and ¾ cups of strong whole meal flour
- One teaspoon fine sea salt
- ¼ teaspoon freshly ground black pepper
- One and 2/3 cups of water
- Two tablespoons chopped fresh sage or one tablespoon dried

Instructions

1. Melt the butter in a pan, add the onion and cook gently for about 10 minutes, occasionally stirring, until very soft but not browned. Alternatively, put the butter and onion into a casserole, cover, and microwave on high for 5 minutes, stirring once, until very soft. Leave to cool.
2. Put the remaining ingredients into the pan in the correct order for your machine. Add the buttery onion mixture.
3. Fit the pan into the bread machine and close the lid. Select the basic white setting, medium crust, and the appropriate size. Press Start.
4. When the program has finished, lift the pan out of the machine, turn the bread out onto a wire rack and leave to cool completely.

Chapter 15-Cake Bread Recipes

Cakes can easily be made in the bread machines. Some of the cakes that can be made with the bread machine are provided in this chapter.

Cinna bun Coffee Cake

(Ready in about 3 hours 10 minutes I Servings- 6I Difficulty- Moderate)

Ingredients

For the dough:

- 7/8 cup milk
- One and a half teaspoons vanilla extract
- One large egg yolk
- Two tablespoons unsalted butter, cut into pieces
- Two and 1/4cups unbleached all-purpose flour
- 1/4 cup sugar
- One teaspoon salt
- Two and a half teaspoons bread machine yeast

For the oat crumb topping:

- 3/4 cup unbleached all-purpose flour
- 3/4 cup light brown sugar
- Half cup rolled oats
- Half cup chopped pecans
- One and a half teaspoons ground cinnamon or apple pie spice
- Half cup (1 stick) unsalted butter, at room temperature
- Confectioners' Sugar Icing

Instructions

1. In order to make the dough, according to the manufacturer's directions, put all the dough ingredients in the tub.
2. Set the Dough Cycle Program; Press start. Like a thick batter, the dough would be moist and sticky. Don't add extra flour at all.
3. Make the topping ready when the dough cycle is operating. In a shallow cup, combine the rice, sugar, peas, pecans, and cinnamon together. To produce clumped crumbs, rub the butter in with your fingers. In a food processor, you can even easily do this.
4. Oil a baking dish of 13-by-9-inch metal or Pyrex. Click Pause and unplug the machine if the machine beeps at the end of the loop. Scrap the batter into the pan with a large rubber spatula. To fill the pan to the edges, distribute the batter equally using floured fingers. Sprinkle the topping with it. Cover loosely with a plastic wrap and allow them time to cool for 30 minutes.
5. In the meantime, preheat the oven to 375oF. Bake for about 20 to 25 minutes, or until the sides are goldon brown and the middle comes out clean with a cake tester inserted. On a wire rack,

position the pan and prepare the icing. Drizzle the top in a back-and-forth pattern with a large spoon.

6. Serve in the skillet warmly.

Sweet Babka with Chocolate Swirl

(Ready in about 3 hours 10 minutes I Servings- 2 loavesI Difficulty- Moderate)

Ingredients

For the dough:

- One and 1/4cups water
- Two tablespoons unsalted butter, cut into pieces
- Three cups of bread flour
- 1/3 cup nonfat dry milk
- Two tablespoons sugar
- One and a half teaspoons salt
- Two and a half teaspoons bread machine yeast

For the chocolate prune swirl:

- 3/4 cup semisweet chocolate chips
- 3/4 cup snipped dried prunes
- 1/4 cup chopped walnuts

For the chocolate spice swirl:

- 2/3 cup sugar
- Two and a half tablespoons unsweetened Dutch-process cocoa powder
- Two teaspoons ground cinnamon
- Plain or vanilla confectioners' sugar, for dusting, optional.

Instructions

1. In compliance with the order in the manufacturer's directions, put all the dough ingredients in the tub. Set the Dough Cycle Program; Click Start. The ball of the dough would be fluffy. Two 7-by-3-inch loaf pans with oil. In a small tub, mix the dry ingredients for the swirl filling you have picked.

2. Click Pause and unplug the machine if the machine beeps at the end of the loop. On a lightly floured work surface, roll out the dough. Divide half the dough. Pat into a 10-by-14-inch rectangle with each piece. Lightly clean each one with some melted butter. Sprinkle half of the filling with each, leaving a 1-inch room all the way around. Roll up jelly-roll style, beginning at a brief tip. Tuck the ends under and pinch the seams at the rim.

3. In the bowls, put the loaves seam side down. Lightly coat the tops with cooking spray, then lightly cover them with plastic wrap. Let it increase until doubled in bulk at room temperature, around 45 minutes.

4. Preheat the oven to 350oF for twenty minutes before baking.

5. Bake for 30 to 40 minutes, or until the loaves are golden brown and the sides are partially taken out of the plate. Cool on a rack and brush with plain or vanilla powdered sugar, if needed.

Alsatian Kugelhopf

(Ready in about 3 hours 10 minutes I Servings- 1 to 2 small tube cakesI Difficulty- Moderate)

Ingredients

- Half cup currants
- Two tablespoons golden raisins
- 1/4 cup Gewürztraminer wine
- 2/3 cup whole milk
- 1/4 cup water
- Two large eggs
- Three cups of unbleached all-purpose flour
- 1/4 cup sugar or vanilla sugar
- Grated zest of one small lemon
- One teaspoon salt
- Half cup unsalted butter, cut into pieces
- Two and a half teaspoons bread machine yeast
- 1/3 cup sliced almonds
- Three tablespoons confectioners' sugar for dusting

Instructions

1. In a small cup, put the currants and raisins and cover them with the wine. At room temperature, macerate for a period of an hour. Drain the fruit and save some liquid for it.

2. Place the ingredients in the container of the bread machine according to the order in the manufacturer's instructions, minus the currants, raisins, and almonds. Dough Cycle Program; Click Start.

3. Click Stop for five minutes into the kneading section and add the currants and raisins and the almonds. To restart the loop, Press Start.

4. Generously oil a nine-cup fluted tube pan or two kugelhopf molds of four and ½ cups. Click Pause and unplug the machine if the machine beeps at the end of the loop. For 1 hour, set a kitchen timer and let the dough rest in the machine. Remove the dough and scrape it into the tube pan with a rubber spatula as the timer sounds, filling it no more than two-thirds full. Cover with plastic wrap and place a tea towel on top. Let it rise at room temperature until the dough is almost to the mold's top, about 1 hour.

5. Preheat the oven to 350oF for 20 minutes before baking.

6. Remove the towel and wrap from the mold and bake for around 35 to 40 minutes (bake for 28 to 32 minutes in the small pans), until browned and taken out of the pan on the edges. It will come out clean with a cake tester placed into the middle. Onto a shelf, invert. Pour the stored soaking liquid into the middle of the cake when it is still warm. Allow it to cool completely. Wrap in foil for space storage temperature for 1 to 2 days. Dust with confectioners' sugar before serving.

Apple Challah

(Ready in about 3 hours 10 minutes I Servings- one braided loafI Difficulty- Moderate)

Ingredients

For the dough:

- 3/4 cup water
- Two large eggs
- Three tablespoons vegetable oil

- Three cups of bread flour
- Three tablespoons sugar
- Half teaspoon salt
- Two and a half teaspoons bread machine yeast

For the apple filling:

- Three medium tart baking apples, peeled, cored, and diced
- Juice of one lemon
- Two tablespoons honey
- Half teaspoon ground cinnamon
- Two tablespoons granulated or pearl sugar for sprinkling

Instructions

1. In order to make the dough, according to the manufacturer's directions, put all the dough ingredients in the tub.
2. Dough Cycle Program; Click Start.
3. Combine the apples with the lemon juice, sugar, and cinnamon in a medium bowl to make the filling. To cover uniformly, toss. Cover and cool with plastic wrap until the dough is filled. Before using, rinse.
4. Click Pause and unplug the machine if the machine beeps at the end of the loop. On a lightly floured work surface, roll out the dough. Break it into three equal parts. Roll into a 12-by-3-inch rectangle for each section. Brush and put 1/3 of the filling down the middle of each strip with some melted butter. Roll up every rectangular jelly-roll pattern, starting from a long side, and pinch the seam to seal.
5. Line the parchment paper with a baking sheet. Place the three ropes parallel to each other and start braiding, alternating the outside ropes of the middle. On the baking sheet, put the challah. Sprinkle sugar on end and gently cover it with plastic wrap. Let it increase until doubled in bulk, 45 minutes to 1 hour at room temperature.
6. Preheat the oven to 350oF fifteen minutes before baking.
7. Bake until golden brown or 35 to 40 minutes. On a shelf, cool.

Blueberry Crumb Cake

(Ready in about 3 hours 10 minutes I Servings- 16I Difficulty- Moderate)

Ingredients

For the dough:

- 3/4 cup sour cream
- One large egg plus two egg yolks
- 1/4 cup water
- Four cups unbleached all-purpose flour
- Grated zest of one large orange
- 1/4 cup sugar
- One and a half teaspoons salt
- One tablespoon plus one teaspoon bread machine yeast
- 3/4 cup (One and a half sticks) unsalted butter, cut into pieces

For the streusel topping:

- One and 1/3 cups of unbleached all-purpose flour
- 2/3 cup sugar
- One tablespoon ground cinnamon or apple pie spice
- One and a half teaspoons vanilla extract or Two and a half teaspoons vanilla powder
- Half cup (1 stick) plus three tablespoons unsalted butter, chilled and cut into pieces
- Three cups of fresh blueberries, rinsed and picked over, or frozen unsweetened blueberries, unthawed
- Half cup confectioners' sugar, for dusting

Instructions

1. Create the dough the night prior to baking. In compliance with the order in the manufacturer's instructions, put the dough ingredients, except the butter, in the pan. Dough Cycle Program; Click Start. Set a 10-minute kitchen timer. The dough would be strong but springy.
2. Open the lid as the timer sounds. Add a part or two of the butter at a time when the process is working, allowing the butter to be incorporated before inserting more parts. Adding both of the pieces will take a minute or two. Get the cover closed.
3. Set the timer for 30 minutes when the Knead 2 stage stops and let the dough rise in the unit. Click Pause, then unplug the computer. Remove the dough, cover it with plastic wrap, and refrigerate overnight in an oiled 4-quart plastic bucket.
4. In the working bowl of a food processor, combine the flour, sugar, and cinnamon to create the topping. Dribble in the vanilla with the motor going, then stop and apply the butter bits.
5. Do not overregulate. Place it in a sealed jar made of plastic. If you prepare it the day before, refrigerate it overnight or make it in the morning.
6. Line an 18-by-12-by-1-inch jelly roll sheet with parchment paper in the morning. Spray with butter-flavored cooking spray on the sides and bottom. Turn out the dough onto a work surface that is gently floured; it will be cold and rigid. Roll out into a square with a rolling pin that will complement the pan. Shift to the pan by pushing on the bottom to suit. Cover it with a plastic wrap and set aside to grow until doubled in bulk, around 3 hours, at room temperature.
7. Preheat the 350 degrees F
8. Uncover the pan and spread the blueberries on the top, pushing them into the dough gently. With a fork, remove the topping and brush over the whole pan in a dense layer, covering all the dough and berries.
9. Bake it for 30 to 35 minutes, or until the top and around the sides are golden brown and a cake tester inserted into the cake comes out clean. Let it cool down on the rack, then serve after slicing down.

Petits Pains Au Chocolate

(Ready in about 3 hours 10 minutes I Servings- 15I Difficulty- Moderate)

Ingredients

- 2/3 cup milk
- Two large eggs
- Four tablespoons unsalted butter, cut into pieces and softened
- Two and a half cups unbleached all-purpose flour
- Two tablespoons light brown sugar
- One teaspoon salt
- Two and a half teaspoons bread machine yeast
- One cup of semisweet chocolate, chopped or broken into 12-ounce pieces
- One egg beat with one teaspoon milk for glaze

Instructions

1. In compliance with the order in the manufacturer's instructions, add the ingredients, except the chocolate, to the pan.
2. Set the settings for Dough Cycle Program; Click Start. The dough's going to be sticky. The Deep Bowl Gasoline. Click Pause and unplug the machine if the machine beeps at the end of the loop. Transform the dough into the bowl using a dough card, scrape the sides of the pan and support the dough as it comes out. Cover and refrigerate for 4 hours to overnight with two coats of plastic wrap.
3. Line 2 wide parchment paper baking sheets and dust them with melted butter. Turn the frozen dough out onto a flour-dusted work surface. Divide it into 15 equal parts using a metal bench knife. Roll out any section to a 4-inch square about 1/4 inch thick with a floured rolling pin.
4. In the middle of each square, put half a cup of chocolate in the center. To enclose the chocolate, fold each corner into the middle. To seal, pinch. Place it on the baking sheet, about 1-inch apart, seam side down. Cover it loosely with plastic wrap and let rise until puffy, around 1 hour at room temperature.
5. Preheat the oven to 350oF for twenty minutes before baking.
6. Brush some egg glaze with each pastry. Bake for 15 to 18 minutes, one pan at a time, until soft golden brown and crisp to the touch. Though these are fine eaten wet, move to a rack to cool.

Sweet Cheese Puff Croissants

(Ready in about 3 hours 10 minutes I Servings- 24I Difficulty- Moderate)

Ingredients

- Four cups of natural, preferably, or packaged cream cheese
- 2/3 cup sugar
- One large egg
- One and a half teaspoons vanilla extract or grated zest of 1 large orange

- Half recipe Bread Machine French Butter Croissant dough, chilled overnight
- Sifted confectioners' sugar or vanilla confectioners' sugar for dusting

Instructions

1. Cream the cheese and sugar until creamy using an electric mixer or food processor; add the egg and the vanilla or zest.
2. Chill for an hour.
3. On a lightly floured work surface, roll out the chilled croissant dough to a 1/4 inch thick 16-by-16-inch rectangle.
4. Sprinkle on top of some flour so that the rolling pin won't stick. Trim the dough using a pastry wheel into 3-inch squares with a ruler. You'll have about 24 squares.
5. In the center of each rectangle, put a tablespoon of the cream cheese filling. To close and form a square puff, pull the four corners together into the middle and pinch in a knot. Set the puffs in uncoiled muffin cups of two and 1/4-inch diameter. Let it grow, exposed, until puffy, about 30 minutes at room temperature.
6. Preheat the oven to 375oF for twenty minutes before baking.
7. Bake the puffs for about 15 to 18 minutes or until the filling is set and golden brown. In the tub, cool for 10 minutes, and then switch to a cooling rack. Dust of sugar from confectioners prior to serving.

Coffee Cake

(Ready in about 3 hours 15 minutes I Servings- One loaf I Difficulty- Moderate)

Ingredients

- One and a half teaspoons of salt
- 3/4 cup of raisins
- One cup of strong brewed coffee
- Three tablespoons of canola oil
- Three cups and one tablespoon of bread flour
- One whole egg mixed
- 1/4 teaspoon of ground cloves
- One teaspoon of ground cinnamon
- 1/4 teaspoon of ground allspice
- Three tablespoons of sugar
- Two and a half teaspoons of active dry yeast

Instructions

1. Coat raisins with one tablespoon of flour and set it aside.
2. Add all ingredients, except raisins, to the bread machine in the suggested order by the manufacturer.
3. Select the basic cycle. Crust color to your liking. Press the start button.
4. Add raisins at the ingredient signal.
5. Serve fresh bread.

Chapter 16-Rolls, Pizza, and Bun Bread Recipes

Pizza is fun, and you can make this fun food at home with the help of your bread machine. This chapter provides you with the recipes of various pizzas, rolls, and buns you can make while at home using your bread machine.

Thin Crust Pizza Dough

(Ready in about one hour and 15 minutes I Servings- 8 I Difficulty-Moderate)

Ingredients

- ¾ cup of warm water
- Two cups of all-purpose flour
- ½ teaspoon salt
- ¼ teaspoon white sugar
- One teaspoon active dry yeast
- Two teaspoons olive oil

Instructions

1. Pour the hot water into the bread maker's pan and put the flour on top of the water. Sprinkle with sugar and salt, and apply the yeast to the tip. Set the computer to the setting for the dough and press the start button. Transfer to a well-floured work surface as the computer indicates that the dough is finished.
2. Preheat the oven to 425°F (220 degrees C).
3. Roll the dough into a thin crust about 14 inches wide or spread it out. Keep the edge of the dough thick. On a 14-inch pizza baking dish, place the dough and spray the dough with olive oil.
4. Bake in a preheated oven for 5 minutes before extracting the desired final baking ingredients.

Easy pizza dough

(Ready in about 3 hours 15 minutes I Servings- 2 pizzas I Difficulty- Moderate)

Ingredients

- Two teaspoons dried granulated yeast

- Three cups of bread flour
- One teaspoon salt
- Two tablespoons sugar
- Two tablespoons olive oil
- One cup water, plus
- Two tablespoons water

Instructions

1. Place all the above ingredients in the order listed into the bread machine.
2. Select the dough cycle and Press the start button.
3. When the dough cycle is complete, take the dough out of the machine, place it in a well-oiled bowl, and roll the dough around (in the bowl), thus 'coating' it in oil.
4. Cover and leave to rise in a warm place for about Half an hour.
5. Knead the risen dough lightly.
6. To shape and bake: roll the dough into a circle.
7. Place on a well-oiled baking tray or pizza pan.
8. Then add a topping of your choice and bake at 225 degrees Celsius.

Easy cheese pizza dough

(Ready in about 30 minutes I Servings- 16 I Difficulty- Easy)

Ingredients

- One and Half cups of water
- One and Half tablespoons of vegetable oil (or olive oil)
- Three and 3/4 cups of bread flour
- Half cup of grated cheese of your choice
- One tablespoon plus one teaspoon sugar (granulated)
- One and Half teaspoons of salt
- One and Half teaspoons of active dry yeast

Instructions

1. In the order recommended by the maker, apply ingredients to your bread machine. Pick the cycle of the dough.
2. Remove the dough and stretch it out, making a 1-inch-thick lip to fit into pizza pans.
3. Preheat the oven to 400 F.
4. Brush the crust with a small amount of olive oil or vegetable oil and let it rise for 10 to 15 minutes. Spread with tomato sauce or extra toppings.
5. Bake it for 20 to 25 minutes in the oven, or until the crust is browned and the cheese is melted and sparkling.
6. Enjoy and serve.

Basil Pizza Dough

(Ready in about 30 minutes I Servings- 16 I Difficulty- Easy)

Ingredients

- One and Half cups of water
- One and Half tablespoons of vegetable oil (or olive oil)
- Three and 3/4 cups of bread flour
- Two tablespoons of dried leaf basil
- One tablespoon plus one teaspoon sugar (granulated)
- One and Half teaspoons of salt

- One and Half teaspoons of active dry yeast

Instructions

1. In the order prescribed by the manufacturer, add ingredients to your bread machine. Choose the duration of the dough.
2. To fit into pizza pans, remove the dough and stretch it out, creating a 1-inch-thick lip.
3. Preheat the oven to 400 F
4. Brush the crust with a small amount of olive oil or vegetable oil, and let it rise for 10-15 minutes. Spread with tomato sauce or your choice of toppings.
5. Bake for 20 to 25 minutes in the oven or until the crust is browned and the cheese is melted and sparkling.
6. Serve and enjoy.

Whole Wheat Pizza Dough

(Ready in about 30 minutes I Servings- 16 I Difficulty- Easy)

Ingredients

- One and Half cups of water
- One and Half tablespoons of vegetable oil (or olive oil)
- Three and 3/4 cups of whole wheat flour
- One tablespoon plus one teaspoon sugar (granulated)
- One and Half teaspoons of salt
- One and Half teaspoons of active dry yeast

Instructions

1. In the order recommended by the maker, apply ingredients to your bread machine. Select the settings of the dough.
2. Remove the dough and stretch it out, making a 1-inch-thick lip to fit into pizza pans.
3. Preheat the oven to 400 F.
4. Brush the crust with a small amount of olive oil or vegetable oil and let it rise for 10 to 15 minutes. Spread with tomato sauce or extra toppings.
5. Bake for 20 to 25 minutes in the oven, or until the crust is browned and the cheese is melted and sparkling.
6. Enjoy and serve.

Parmesan and Herb Pizza Dough

(Ready in about 30 minutes I Servings- 16 I Difficulty- Easy)

Ingredients

- One and Half cups of water
- One and Half tablespoons of vegetable oil (or olive oil)
- Three and 3/4 cups of bread flour
- One teaspoon of Italian herb blend
- 1/4 cup of grated Parmesan cheese
- One tablespoon plus one teaspoon sugar (granulated)
- One and Half teaspoons of salt
- One and Half teaspoons of active dry yeast

Instructions

1. In the order recommended by the maker, apply ingredients to your bread machine. Select the duration of the dough.
2. Remove the dough and stretch it out, making a 1-inch-thick lip to fit into pizza pans.
3. Preheat the oven to 400 F.

4. Brush the crust with a small amount of olive oil or vegetable oil and let it rise for 10 to 15 minutes. Spread with tomato sauce or extra toppings.
5. Bake for 20 to 25 minutes in the oven, or until the crust is browned and the cheese is melted and sparkling.
6. Serve and enjoy.

Garlic Pizza Dough

(Ready in about 30 minutes I Servings- 16 I Difficulty- Easy)

Ingredients

- One and Half cups of water
- Three minced garlic cloves
- One and Half tablespoons of vegetable oil (or olive oil)
- Three and 3/4 cups of bread flour
- Half cup of grated cheese of your choice
- One tablespoon plus one teaspoon sugar (granulated)
- One and Half teaspoons of salt
- One and Half teaspoons of active dry yeast

Instructions

1. In the order prescribed by the manufacturer, add ingredients to your bread machine. Choose the duration of the dough.
2. To fit into pizza pans, remove the dough and stretch it out, creating a 1-inch-thick lip.
3. Preheat the oven to 400 F
4. Brush the crust with a small amount of olive oil or vegetable oil, and let it rise for 10-15 minutes. Spread with tomato sauce or your choice of toppings.
5. Bake for 20 to 25 minutes in the oven or until the crust is browned and the cheese is melted and sparkling. Serve and enjoy.

American homemade Pizza

(Ready in about one hour and 35 minutes I Servings-8 I Difficulty- Moderate)

Ingredients

- 3/4 teaspoon of salt
- Four cups of all-purpose flour
- Two teaspoons of active dry yeast
- One and 3/8 cup water
- Three tablespoons of olive oil
- One tablespoon of garlic powder
- Two tablespoons of Italian seasoning

Instructions

1. Combine all ingredients except toppings in a pan.
2. Select dough setting and Press the start button
3. When the unit is done, remove dough from the pan and place it on a lightly floured counter
4. Knead a few times to work the dough together
5. Roll out on pizza stone
6. Preheat oven to 400F
7. Spread sauce and other toppings over pizza
8. Bake, 15-20 minutes or until crust, is golden brown and cheese is melted

Soft whole wheat diner rolls

(Ready in about one hour and 35 minutes I Servings-16 I Difficulty- Moderate)

Ingredients

- 2/3 cup milk
- Half cup sour cream
- 1/4 cup honey
- Two large eggs
- Four tablespoons butter or margarine, cut into pieces
- Three cups of unbleached all-purpose flour
- One cup of whole wheat flour
- Half cup toasted wheat germ
- One and a half teaspoons salt
- Two and a half teaspoons bread machine yeast

Instructions

1. Similar to the order in the manufacturer's orders, put all ingredients in the pan. Dough Cycle Software, then press Start.
2. Turn the dough onto a gently floured surface after the kneading process. Roll each half into a 2-3-inch cylinder, then split the dough in half. Trim the cylinder into eight pieces using a metal dough scraper or a chef's knife.
3. For the second cylinder, replicate, producing 16 equivalent parts in all. By patting it into a rectangle, shape each part like a miniature bread, then rolling up from a short side to create a slim, compact cylinder about 4 inches long. With their long sides touching, put the rolls in two rows of 8. Brush the tops of the rolls with some molten butter. Cover loosely with plastic wrap and rise until doubled in bulk, around 45 minutes, at room temperature.
4. Preheat the oven to 375°F twenty minutes before baking. Place the baking sheet in the middle of the oven and bake until golden brown, for 25 minutes.
5. Take the pans from the rolls and let them cool on a rack.
6. Until eating, serve warm or cool to room temperature and reheat.

Whole Wheat Crescent Dinner Rolls

(Ready in about one hour and 35 minutes I Servings-16 I Difficulty- Moderate)

Ingredients

- 1/4 cup slivered blanched almonds
- Two cups of whole wheat flour
- One cup of water
- Two large eggs
- Four tablespoons unsalted butter, cut into pieces
- Half cup sour cream
- Two and 1/4cups bread flour
- Two tablespoons light brown sugar
- One tablespoon gluten
- Two teaspoons salt
- Two and 3/4 teaspoons bread machine yeast

Instructions

1. Place them in a dry skillet with the almonds. Lightly toast over medium heat, stirring continuously, for 2 minutes or so. Combine the almonds in a food processor with two teaspoons of whole wheat flour. Grind it for a decent dinner.
2. As per the order in the manufacturer's instructions, put all ingredients, including tho almond meal, in the pan.

3. Set the settings of the Dough Cycle Program; Click Start.

4. Top the parchment paper with two baking sheets. Turn the dough out directly on a lightly floured work surface as the computer beeps at the end of the cycle; split it into two separate parts. Roll each section into a 10-inch round with a rolling pin. Slice each round into eight pie-shaped wedges using a pastry wheel. At the base of the triangle, roll up each wedge from the broad edge and position the crescents 1-inch apart on the baking sheet, point-side down. Cover gently with plastic wrap and grow until almost doubled in bulk, about 30 minutes, at room temperature.

5. Preheat the oven to 375°F twenty minutes before baking.

6. Bake the rolls for 15 to 18 minutes, one pan at a time, or until lightly browned. Let it partly cool on a shelf. Eat the rolls warmly.

Rose Rolls with Rose Buttercream

(Ready in about one hour and 35 minutes I Servings-16 I Difficulty- Moderate)

Ingredients

For the dough:
- 3/4 cup milk
- Half cup of water
- One large egg
- Half cup (1 stick) unsalted butter, cut into pieces
- 4 cups unbleached all-purpose flour
- Half cup sugars
- Two teaspoons salt
- One tablespoon bread machine yeast

For the filling:
- Two and ¾ cup of cherry pie filling

For the rose buttercream:
- One cup of sifted confectioners' sugar
- Pinch of salt
- Two tablespoons warm milk
- Half teaspoon vanilla extract or One and 1/4teaspoons vanilla powder added to the sugar
- Half teaspoon rose water, optional
- One and a half tablespoons unsalted butter, room temperature

Instructions

1. In order to make the dough, according to the manufacturer's directions, put all the dough ingredients in the tub.

2. Select the Dough Cycle Program; Click Start. The ball of dough would be soft. Click Pause and unplug the machine if the machine beeps at the end of the loop. Turn out the dough and mold it into a thick square that will fit into a 4-quart plastic bucket that is oiled. Cover with plastic tape, and refrigerate overnight or for 2 hours.

3. Line 2 parchment paper baking sheets. In order to deflate it, softly press the dough and place it on a lightly floured work surface. Roll out the dough into a 12-by-16-by-14-inch rectangle. Break the dough lengthwise with a sharp knife or pastry wheel into 16 one-inch-wide strips. Twist one in the opposite direction from the other at the same time by placing your hands on either end of a strip. Wrap the whole

strip to create a coiled pinwheel at one end. Tuck beneath the tail. For the other strips of dough, repeat.

4. Place the pinwheels on the baking sheets at least 2 inches apart (8 per pan). Do not crowd. Cover with plastic wrap and set aside to rise at room temperature until doubled in bulk, One to One and a half hours.

5. Preheat the oven to 400oF.

6. Using your fingertips, gently press to the bottom of each coil's center to form an indentation for the filling. Place about two tablespoons of the pie filling into the center. Be careful not to use too much filling, or it will bubble over during baking. You want filling surrounded by dough.

7. Place a second baking sheet of the same dimensions under one of the pans holding pastries to double pan and prevent the bottoms from burning. Bake for 13 to 16 minutes. Remove the pan from the oven and place it on a wire rack. Double pan and place the second batch of rolls in the oven.

8. As the second batch bakes, frost the first batch. Make the buttercream frosting by mixing all the frosting ingredients together in a small bowl; beat until smooth and thick, yet pourable. Glaze the pastries while still warm and on the baking sheet, drizzling the glaze back and forth with the end of a spoon, a pastry bag fitted with a small plain tip, or the tips of your fingers. Move the pastries from the baking pan to a wire rack to cool. The frosting will set as it cools. When the second batch of rolls is finished, frost the same way. Let the pastries cool on the racks for 15 minutes before eating

Maritozzi Romani

(Ready in about one hour and 35 minutes I Servings-8 I Difficulty- Moderate)

Ingredients

- Half cup golden raisins
- 1/4 cup sweet white wine, like Asti Spumante
- 7/8 cup fat-free milk
- One large egg
- Four tablespoons unsalted butter, cut into pieces
- Three cups of unbleached all-purpose flour
- 1/4 cup sugar
- One and 1/4teaspoons salt
- Two and a half teaspoons bread machine yeast
- 1/4 cup coarsely chopped pine nuts
- 1/4 cup finely chopped orange confit
- One egg beat with one tablespoon of the drained wine from the raisins for glaze

Instructions

1. In a small bowl, cover the raisins with the wine. Macerate for at least an hour at room temperature.

2. Place the ingredients, except the raisins, pine nuts, and orange confit, in the pan according to the order in the manufacturer's instructions. Program for the Dough cycle; press Start. The dough ball will be soft.

3. Line a baking sheet with parchment paper. Drain the raisins, reserving one tablespoon of the liquid for the glaze. When the machine beeps at the end of the cycle, press Stop and unplug the machine. Turn the dough out onto a lightly floured work surface. Pat the dough into a large free form rectangle and sprinkle

with the raisins, pine nuts, and orange confit. Press in.

4. Fold the dough into thirds and knead a few times to distribute the fruit and nuts evenly. Divide the dough in half, then divide each half into four equal portions.
5. Afterward, shape each portion into a tight round and place it on the baking sheet, at least 3 inches apart. Cover with a clean tea towel and let rise until doubled in bulk, about 45 minutes.
6. Twenty minutes before baking, preheat the oven to 400oF.
7. Brush the tops of the rolls with the glaze. Bake for 20 to 25 minutes, or until golden brown. Cool on a rack.

Semolina Pizza Dough

(Ready in about one hour and 35 minutes I Servings-6 individual crusts I Difficulty- Moderate)

Ingredients

- One and a half cups water
- Three tablespoons olive oil
- Three and 1/3 cups of unbleached all-purpose flour
- 2/3 cup semolina pasta flour (durum flour)
- One tablespoon sugar
- Two teaspoons salt
- Two and a half teaspoons bread machine yeast

Instructions

1. Place all the ingredients in the pan according to the order in the manufacturer's instructions. Program for the Dough or Pizza Dough cycle and press Start.
2. When the machine beeps at the end of the cycle, press Stop and unplug the machine. Immediately remove the pan from the machine, and turn the dough out onto a lightly floured work surface. Divide into the desired number of portions. Flatten each portion into a disc by kneading a few times and folding the edges into the center.
3. Cover with a damp towel on the work surface to rest for 30 minutes until the dough has increased about 20 percent in size.
4. Roll out and shape the dough as directed in your pizza recipe. Or place the dough in plastic food storage bags and refrigerate for up to 24 hours. To use, let rest for 20 minutes at room temperature before rolling out. The dough balls may also be stored in the freezer for up to 3 months; let the dough defrost in the refrigerator overnight before using.

Cornmeal Pizza Dough

(Ready in about one hour and 35 minutes I Servings-16 I Difficulty- Moderate)

Ingredients

- One and a half cups water
- 1/4 cup olive oil
- Three and 2/3 cups of unbleached all-purpose flour
- 1/3 cup medium-grind yellow cornmeal
- One teaspoon salt
- or Two and a half teaspoons bread machine yeast

Instructions

1. Place all the ingredients in the pan according to the order in the manufacturer's instructions. Program for the Dough or Pizza Dough cycle and press Start.
2. When the machine beeps at the end of the cycle, press Stop and unplug the machine. Immediately remove the pan from the machine, and turn the dough out onto a lightly floured work surface. Divide into the desired number of portions. Flatten the dough into a disc by kneading a few times then folding the edges into the center. Cover with a damp towel on the work surface to rest for 30 minutes until the dough has increased about 20 percent in size.
3. Roll out and shape the dough as directed in your pizza recipe. Or place the dough in plastic food storage bags and refrigerate for up to 24 hours. To use, let rest for 20 minutes at room temperature before rolling out. The dough balls may also be stored in the freezer for up to 3 months; let the dough defrost in the refrigerator overnight before using.

Suzanne's Chicago-style Deep-Dish Pizza

(Ready in about one hour and 35 minutes I Servings-8 I Difficulty- Moderate)

Ingredients

- One large onion, coarsely chopped
- Two cups of ground sirloin
- Two cups of ground pork
- One teaspoon whole fennel seed
- Three fresh plum tomatoes
- One recipe Cornmeal Pizza Dough
- Four cups of mozzarella cheese, shredded
- 3/4 cup grated Romano cheese
- One and a half teaspoons dried oregano
- One and a half teaspoons dried basil
- Two cups of Hunt's Spaghetti Sauce or Two cups of Essential Tomato-Herb Pizza Sauce
- 1/3 cup olive oil

Instructions

1. Place the onion and meats in a medium sauté pan. Cook over medium heat until the meat is no longer pink and onion is cooked; blot up excess fat with a paper towel. Add the fennel seed. Set aside to cool.
2. Skin and chop the tomatoes. Place in a sieve and drain for 10 minutes.
3. Twenty to thirty minutes before baking, place a pizza stone on the lower third rack of the oven, and preheat it to 400°F. Brush a 14-inch deep-dish pizza pan with oil and press in the pizza dough, making sure it is even on the bottom and up the sides to the rim; do not stretch. Let rest for 15 minutes.
4. Toss the mozzarella, Romano, and herbs together in a bowl. Sprinkle the dough with two-thirds of the cheese mixture.
5. Then spread with the entire can of sauce and drizzle with some olive oil. Distribute the meat mixture over the top for the next layer. Top with the tomatoes and the remaining cheese mixture. Drizzle with the remaining olive oil.

6. Bake for 15 minutes, lower the oven temperature to 350°F and bake for an additional 40 to 45 minutes. Cover with foil for the last 10 minutes if the cheese is too brown. When done, the crust will be golden brown; lift with a metal spatula to check the bottom. Remove the pizza from the oven and let it rest on a rack for 10 minutes before cutting. Serve while still hot.

Cheese Pizza Torta

(Ready in about one hour and 35 minutes | Servings-16 | Difficulty- Moderate)

Ingredients

- Three tablespoons yellow cornmeal or coarse semolina, for dusting
- Half cup mozzarella cheese, shredded
- Half cup Italian fontina cheese, shredded
- Half cup smoked provolone, shredded
- ¾ cup of soft goat cheese (such as Montrachet or domestic chibis) or a half cup of crumbled feta
- Half cup grated Parmesan
- One recipe Basic Pizza Dough
- 1/3 cup Essential Tomato-Herb Pizza Sauce or commercial marinara sauce
- Fresh-ground black pepper
- One egg beat with one tablespoon milk for glaze

Instructions

1. Place a baking stone on the lower third oven rack and preheat the oven to 375°F. Oil an 8-inch springform pan and dust with cornmeal or semolina.
2. Combine all the cheeses, except 1/4 cup of the Parmesan, in a small bowl and toss together.
3. Place the dough on a lightly floured work surface. Divide the dough into three equal portions. With a rolling pin, roll the dough out to very thin 9-inch rounds. Carefully place 1 round in the prepared pan and press the excess dough up the pan's sides. Spread with half of the tomato sauce and sprinkle half of the cheese mixture and a few grinds of pepper, leaving a 1-inch border all around.
4. Brush the edge of the dough with the egg glaze. Position the second dough round on top, again pressing the excess dough up the sides of the pan, spread with the tomato sauce, and sprinkle evenly with the remaining cheese mixture and a little more pepper. Brush the edge of the dough with the egg glaze.
5. Place the last dough round on top. Bring the edges of the two bottom layers of dough up to the top, and roll the edges together in sections to seal in the cheeses; the edges will naturally form a rope pattern. Brush the top all over with the egg glaze and sprinkle with the reserved 1/4 cup Parmesan.
6. Immediately place the pan in the oven and bake until thoroughly browned about 30 to 35 minutes. Remove from the oven to a wire rack and remove the springform sides. Let rest for 10 minutes. Slide the torta onto a cutting board, cut it while hot with a serrated knife, and serve.

Roman Bread

(Ready in about one hour and 35 minutes | Servings-one flatbread | Difficulty- Moderate)

Ingredients

For the dough:
- One cup of water
- Three cups of bread flour
- One tablespoon sugar
- 1/3 cup chopped yellow onion
- One and a half teaspoons salt
- Two and a half teaspoons bread machine yeast

For the topping:
- Three tablespoons olive oil
- One and a half tablespoons dried rosemary, crushed
- Coarse sea salt, for sprinkling

Instructions

1. To make the dough, place the ingredients in the pan according to the order in the manufacturer's instructions. Program for the Dough cycle; press Start.
2. Brush a large rectangular baking sheet with olive oil. When the machine beeps at the end of the cycle, press Stop and unplug the machine. Immediately remove the pan and turn the dough out onto the baking sheet. With oiled fingers or a rolling pin, press and flatten the dough into a 1-inch-thick oval. Cover with plastic wrap and let rise at room temperature until doubled in bulk, about 40 minutes.
3. Twenty minutes before baking, place a baking stone on the lowest rack of a cold oven, and preheat it to 425°F. If you are not using a baking stone, preheat the oven to 400°F.
4. Using a small, sharp knife, slash the dough's top with a big tic-tac-toe grid, no more than 1/2-inch deep. Drizzle with olive oil and sprinkle with the rosemary. Bake for 20 to 25 minutes, until browned. When the bread comes out of the oven, sprinkle it with the coarse salt. Serve cut into squares the day it is made, warm, or at room temperature.

Millet and Potato Long Rolls

(Ready in about one hour and 35 minutes | Servings-10 | Difficulty- Moderate)

Ingredients

- One cup of whole wheat flour
- Half cup raw whole millet
- 1/4 cup sesame seeds
- Half cup instant potato flakes
- One cup of boiling water
- One and a half cups warm water
- One large egg plus one egg white (reserve yolk for glaze) or equivalent of a liquid egg substitute
- Two tablespoons unsalted butter or margarine, cut into pieces
- Three and a half cups of bread flour
- 1/3 cup light brown sugar
- One and a half teaspoons salt

- One tablespoon bread machine yeast
- Three tablespoons sesame seeds, for sprinkling before baking

Instructions

1. Combine the Half cup of the whole wheat flour, the millet, and sesame seeds in the work bowl of a food processor. Grind to a coarse flour and set aside. Stir the potato flakes and the boiling water together in a small bowl until thick; cool for 5 minutes.
2. Place all the ingredients in the pan according to the order in the manufacturer's instructions. Add the mashed potatoes on top of the wet ingredients and the sesame-millet flour, and the remaining Half cup whole wheat flour with the dry ingredients. Program for the Dough cycle; press Start.
3. Line a large baking sheet with parchment paper. When the machine beeps at the end of the cycle, press Stop and unplug the machine. Turn the dough out onto the work surface and divide into ten equal portions. Form the rolls by patting each portion into an 8-inch oval and rolling up from a long edge, like a mini-loaf of bread. Place rolls seam side down and at least 2 inches apart on the baking sheet. Flatten each with your palm to 3 inches wide. Cover loosely with plastic wrap and let rise at room temperature until puffy, about 45 minutes.
4. Twenty minutes before baking, preheat the oven to 375°F.
5. Beat the reserved egg yolk with a teaspoon of water in a small bowl. Brush the tops of the rolls with the glaze and sprinkle with the sesame seeds. Bake in the oven center until lightly brown and firm to the touch, about 18 to 23 minutes. Immediately remove the rolls from the baking sheet to a rack to cool. Slice the rolls with a serrated knife.

Virginia Light Rolls

(Ready in about one hour and 35 minutes I Servings-16 I Difficulty- Moderate)

Ingredients

- One cup of plus one tablespoon milk
- Three tablespoons honey
- Two large eggs
- Six tablespoons butter or margarine, cut into pieces
- Four and 1/4 cups unbleached all-purpose flour
- One and a half teaspoons salt
- Two and a half teaspoons bread machine yeast
- Four tablespoons melted butter or margarine, for brushing

Instructions

1. Place all the ingredients in the pan according to the order in the manufacturer's instructions. Program for the Dough cycle; press Start. The dough ball will be soft, but add no more than 2 to 3 extra tablespoons of flour, as needed, if you think it necessary.
2. Line a large baking sheet with parchment paper. When the machine beeps at the end of the cycle, press Stop and unplug the machine. Turn the

dough out onto a lightly floured surface. Divide the dough in half, then roll each half into a 2-3-inch cylinder. With a metal dough scraper or a chef's knife, cut the cylinder into eight equal portions.

3. Repeat with the second cylinder, making a total of 16 equal portions. Shape each portion like a miniature loaf by patting it into an oval, then rolling up from a short side to make a small compact cylinder about 4 inches long. Place the rolls in two rows of 8 with their long sides touching. Brush some melted butter on the tops of the rolls. Cover loosely with plastic wrap and rise at room temperature until doubled in bulk, about 45 minutes.
4. Twenty minutes before baking, preheat the oven to 375°F.
5. Place the baking sheet in the oven center and bake for 25 to 28 minutes, until golden brown. Remove the rolls from the pan and cool on a rack. Serve warm or cool to room temperature and reheat.

English Muffins

(Ready in about one hour and 35 minutes I Servings-12 I Difficulty- Moderate)

Ingredients

- One and a half cups fat-free milk
- Two tablespoons unsalted butter, melted
- One large egg
- Four and a half cups of unbleached all-purpose flour
- Two teaspoons salt
- Two and 3/4 teaspoons bread machine yeast
- 1/3 cup yellow cornmeal or coarse semolina, for sprinkling

Instructions

1. Place all the ingredients in the pan according to the order in the manufacturer's instructions. Program for the Dough cycle; press Start. The dough ball will be soft and very slightly moist. The softer you leave the dough, the lighter the muffins. You can always add a bit more flour when you remove the dough from the machine.
2. Lightly sprinkle the work surface with cornmeal or semolina. When the machine beeps at the end of the cycle, press Stop and unplug the machine. Turn the dough out onto the work surface and, with a rolling pin, roll into a rectangle about Half inch thick. Sprinkle the top surface with cornmeal or semolina to prevent sticking while rolling. Cut out the muffins with a 3-inch biscuit cutter or with the rim of a drinking glass. Roll out the trimmings and cut out the remaining muffins. Cover with a clean tea towel, or place them in the refrigerator if they are rising too fast while the others are baking.
3. Preheat an electric griddle to 350° to 375°F, or heat a cast-iron stovetop griddle over medium heat until a drop of water sprinkled on the griddle dances across the surface. Lightly oil the surface.
4. Immediately place several muffins on the hot griddle. Cook for about 10 minutes on each side, turning them when they are quite brown. English muffins take time to bake all the way through, and

they will swell and be very puffy while baking. Remove the muffins from the griddle with a spatula and let cool on a rack.

Hamburger Buns and Hotdog

(Ready in about one hour and 35 minutes | Servings-8| Difficulty- Moderate)

Ingredients

- One cup of water
- One large egg
- Four tablespoons unsalted butter, cut into pieces
- Two tablespoons sugar
- Three cups of bread flour
- 1/4 cup nonfat dry milk
- Two tablespoons instant potato flakes
- One tablespoon gluten
- One and a half teaspoons salt
- Two and 1/4teaspoons bread machine yeast
- One egg yolk beat with one tablespoon water for glaze
- One and a half tablespoons sesame seeds, for sprinkling

Instructions

1. Place all the ingredients in the pan according to the order in the manufacturer's instructions. Program for the Dough cycle; press Start.
2. Line a large baking sheet with parchment paper. When the machine beeps at the end of the cycle, press Stop and unplug the machine. Immediately turn the dough out onto a lightly floured work surface. With a dough knife, divide the and a half-pound dough into eight equal portions or the 2-pound dough into 12 equal portions. For hamburger buns form
3. each portion into tight rounds. For long rolls, flatten each portion into an oval about 6 inches long and rolling up tightly from a long end to form a cylinder. Place the rolls on the lined baking sheet at least 1-inch apart. Press with your palm to flatten each roll. Cover loosely with plastic wrap and let rest for 30 minutes.
4. Preheat the oven to 375°F.
5. Brush the rolls with the egg glaze and sprinkle with sesame seeds. Bake for 15 to 22 minutes, depending on the size of the roll until lightly browned. Remove the rolls from the sheet with a spatula and let cool completely on a rack. Slice in half horizontally to serve.

Little Italian Bread Rolls

(Ready in about one hour and 35 minutes | Servings-3 | Difficulty- Moderate)

Ingredients

For the biga starter:
- One cup of water
- One and 1/4cups unbleached all-purpose flour
- 1/ 4 teaspoon of bread machine yeast

For the dough:
- One tablespoon olive oil
- One tablespoon lard, cut into pieces
- One cup of unbleached all-purpose flour
- Half cup white pastry flour (not cake flour)
- Two teaspoons salt
- Two teaspoons bread machine yeast
- 1/4 cup white cornmeal, for sprinkling

Instructions

1. To make the biga starter, place the starter ingredients in the pan according to the manufacturer's instructions. Program for the Dough cycle and set a kitchen timer for 10 minutes. When the timer rings, press Stop and unplug the machine. Let the starter rest in the machine for 3 hours.
2. To make the dough, add all the dough ingredients to the starter in the pan. Program for the Dough cycle; press Start. After Knead 2, press Reset, and program for the Dough cycle again, allowing the dough to be kneaded a second time. When the machine beeps at the end of the cycle, press Stop and unplug the machine. Let the finished dough sit in the machine for 2 hours.
3. Turn the dough out onto a clean work surface; divide it into three equal portions. Flatten each portion into a 7-inch round with your palms. Roll up each round into a tight log. Cover with oiled plastic wrap, and let rest for 10 minutes.
4. With a rolling pin, roll each log into a 10-by-3-inch rectangle. Cover again with the plastic wrap and let them rest for 5 minutes.
5. Preheat the oven to 450°F. Line a large baking sheet with parchment paper and sprinkle with cornmeal.
6. To make carciofo, rolls that resemble artichokes, cut 2-inch slits that go about three-quarters of the way across, spaced Half inch apart, down one long side of the dough. Starting at a short end, roll up the dough. Place, with the fringed edge standing up, on the baking sheet.
7. With your fingers, pull down the strips of dough to make a petal effect. Repeat with the other two rectangles.
8. To make montasu, or scrolls, roll up the two short ends of the rectangle toward the center with your thumbs pressing and pushing until the two rolls almost meet in the middle, with a 1-inch space between the two. Twist one roll 90° and lay it on top of the other roll. Press firmly in the center to adhere the two rolls together and hold the shape. Place on the baking sheet. Repeat with the other two rectangles.
9. To make the crocetta, little cross rolls, roll up the two short ends of the rectangle towards the center until they almost meet, but leave a 1-inch space in between. Twist one roll two complete turns to form a double twist in the center section. Pull one roll up and over the second roll, centering the double twist on the second roll. Twist and turn the top roll under the bottom, forming a cross. Place on the baking sheet. Repeat with the other two rectangles.
10. Let stand, uncovered, for 10 minutes. Brush gently with water and bake for 10 minutes. Reduce the oven temperature to 400°F and bake for an additional 10 to 15 minutes, until crusty and golden brown. Place the baking sheet on a rack to cool. Serve the rolls within a few hours.

David Soohoo's Bao

(Ready in about one hour and 35 minutes | Servings-6 | Difficulty- Moderate)

Ingredients

For the bao dough:
- 2/3 cup water
- Four tablespoons unsalted butter, melted
- One large egg
- Three and a half cups bread flour
- Five tablespoons sugar
- One tablespoon nonfat dry milk
- One tablespoon bread machine yeast

For the filling:
- 1/4 cup water
- One tablespoon rice wine or dry sherry
- Two tablespoons oyster sauce
- One tablespoon hoisin sauce
- Two tablespoons soy sauce
- One teaspoon sesame oil
- One tablespoon sugar
- Three tablespoons all-purpose flour
- 1/4-pound prepared char Siu (Chinese barbecued pork)
- Three tablespoons diced yellow onion or scallions, green part only for the egg glaze
- One large egg beat with one tablespoon sugar
- One and a half tablespoons white sesame seeds

Instructions

1. To make the dough, place all the dough ingredients in the pan according to the order in the manufacturer's instructions, but add only Two cups of the bread flour. Program for the Dough cycle; press Start. About 5 minutes into Knead 2, slowly add the remaining One and a half cups flour. The dough will be stiff at first, but it will be pliable and smooth by the end of the kneading phase. It is important not to add more water; if the batter is too moist, the bao will flatten as they bake.
2. While the dough is rising, prepare the filling: Make the gravy by combing the water, rice wine or sherry, oyster sauce, hoisin, soy sauce, sesame oil, and sugar in the top of a double boiler. Mix in the flour. Place over simmering water and, constantly stirring, cook until thick and smooth. The gravy should be the consistency of mayonnaise.
3. Remove from the water bath and cool in the refrigerator.
4. Chop the pork into a large dice and place it in a large bowl with the onions. Add the gravy and mix. Cover and refrigerate until needed.
5. Line a large baking sheet with parchment paper. When the machine beeps at the end of the cycle, press Stop and unplug the machine. Turn the dough out onto a clean wooden work surface. Roll into a fat 3-inch-wide log. Cut the log into six equal portions. Place a dough disc on a wooden work surface (don't shape on cool marble or ceramic

6. because it will stiffen the dough). With the palm of your hand, press down on the center and rotate your palm, spiraling out from the center. The dough will shape into a 3-inch-diameter circle (not lopsided, please) with a pretty spiral pattern radiating from the center like a flower. Don't use any flour. Repeat with the remaining portions of dough.
7. Using a one and a half-ounce ice cream scoop (size 40) or another utensil, place a scoop of about two tablespoons of the filling in the center of the round of dough. Bring the dough up over the filling and, holding the two sides between your thumb and third finger and pinching with your pointer finger, pleat the edges to encase the filling. Place the bao on their sides, and at least 4 inches apart, on the prepared baking sheet. Cover loosely with plastic wrap and rise at room temperature until doubled in bulk, 45 minutes to 1 hour. If the filling is cold, the bao will take One and a half hours to rise.
8. Twenty minutes before baking, preheat the oven to 350°F.
9. Brush each bao with the egg glaze and sprinkle with sesame seeds. Bake in the oven center for 30 to 40 minutes, until big, puffy, and golden brown. If you have a convection oven, this will take about 20 minutes. Eat the bao the day they are baked, or freeze in plastic freezer bags for up to 2 months. Reheat in a microwave (no need to defrost) for 2 to 3 minutes for a quick dinner.

White Rolls

(Ready in about one hour and 35 minutes | Servings-12 | Difficulty- Moderate)

Ingredients
- One teaspoon Easy bake yeast
- Two and ¼ cups strong white bread flour
- One teaspoon fine sea salt
- One and ¼ cup of water

Instructions
1. Add all the ingredients into the pan in the correct order for your machine.
2. Fit the pan into the bread machine and close the lid.
3. Select the white dough setting and the size. Press Start.
4. When the program has finished, turn the dough on to a lightly floured surface and knead lightly, knocking out the air, until smooth and elastic.
5. Divide the dough into 12 equal pieces and, with floured hands, shape into rolls. Arrange, smooth side up, on an oiled baking sheet.
6. Cover with oiled film and leave to rise until doubled in size.
7. Meanwhile, preheat the oven to 220°C (Fan 200°C), 425°F, Gas 7.
8. Remove the film, put it into the hot oven, and cook for about 15 minutes until golden brown and cooked through.
9. Transfer to a wire rack and leave to cool.

White Rolls with Granary

(Ready in about one hour and 35 minutes | Servings-12 | Difficulty- Moderate)

Ingredients

- One teaspoon Easy bake yeast
- One and ¾ cup strong white bread flour
- ¾ cup granary-style or malted flour, plus extra for dusting
- One teaspoon fine sea salt
- Two teaspoon malt extract
- One tablespoon milk powder (optional)
- One tablespoon butter, cut into small pieces
- One and ¼ cup of water

Instructions

1. Add all the ingredients into the pan in the correct order for your machine.
2. Fit the pan into the bread machine and close the lid.
3. Select the white dough setting and the size. Press Start.
4. When the program has finished, turn the dough on to a lightly floured surface and knead lightly, knocking out the air, until smooth and elastic.
5. Cut the dough into 12 pieces and shape it into rolls. Arrange, smooth side up, and spaced about 2.5cm/1 in apart on an oiled baking tray.
6. Cover with oiled film and leave to rise until doubled in size.
7. Meanwhile, preheat the oven to 220°C (Fan 200°C), 425°F, Gas 7.
8. Remove the film and dust the tops with a little extra flour.
9. Put into the hot oven and cook for about 15 minutes until golden brown and cooked through. Transfer to a wire rack and leave to cool.

Whole meal Rolls

(Ready in about one hour and 35 minutes | Servings-10 | Difficulty- Moderate)

Ingredients

- One teaspoon Easy bake yeast
- Two and ¾ cups strong whole meal flour, plus extra for dusting
- One and ¼ teaspoon fine sea salt
- Two teaspoon malt extract
- One tablespoon olive oil
- One and ¾ cups of water (or half water and half milk)

Instructions

1. Add all the ingredients into the pan in the correct order for your machine.
2. Fit the pan into the bread machine and close the lid.
3. Select the whole wheat dough setting and the size. Press Start.
4. When the program has finished, turn the dough onto a floured surface and knead lightly, knocking out the air until smooth.
5. Cut the dough into ten pieces and, keeping the surface floured, shape into rolls, flattening them slightly to look like baps. Arrange, smooth side up, and spaced about 2.5cm/1 in apart on an oiled baking sheet.
6. Cover with oiled film and leave to rise until doubled in size.

7. Meanwhile, preheat the oven to 200°C (Fan 180°C), 400°F, Gas 6.
8. Remove the film and dust the rolls with a little extra flour.
9. Put into the hot oven and cook for 15-20 minutes until golden brown and cooked through.
10. Transfer to a wire rack and leave to cool.

Bridge Rolls

(Ready in about one hour and 35 minutes | Servings-24 | Difficulty- Moderate)

Ingredients

- One small egg with milk
- One teaspoon Easy bake yeast
- Two and 1/6 cups of strong white bread flour
- One teaspoon fine sea salt
- One tablespoon golden caster sugar
- Two and ¾ tablespoons of butter, cut into small pieces
- Beaten egg to glaze
- Lightly beat the egg
- One and ¼ cups of milk.

Instructions

1. Add all the ingredients, including the egg mixture, into the pan in the correct order for your machine.
2. Fit the pan into the bread machine and close the lid.
3. Select the white dough setting and the size. Press Start.
4. When the program has finished, turn the dough on to a lightly floured surface and knead lightly, knocking out the air, until smooth and elastic.
5. Cut the dough into 24 pieces and shape it into fingers. Arrange, smooth side up and quite close together, on an oiled baking tray.
6. Cover with oiled film and leave to rise until doubled in size (this should take only 15-20 minutes).
7. Meanwhile, preheat the oven to 220°C (Fan 200°C), 425°F, Gas 7.
8. Remove the film and brush the tops gently with the beaten egg glaze.
9. Put into the hot oven and cook for about 15 minutes until golden brown and cooked through. Transfer to a wire rack and leave to cool.

Granary Baps

(Ready in about one hour and 35 minutes | Servings-8-10 | Difficulty- Moderate)

Ingredients

- One teaspoon Easy bake yeast
- Two and 1/6 cups of granary-style or malted flour
- One teaspoon fine sea salt
- One tablespoon malt extract
- One and ¼ cup of water
- One and ¼ cup of milk
- Rolled oats for topping

Instructions

1. Put all the ingredients, except the oats, into the pan in the correct order for your machine.

2. Fit the pan into the bread machine and close the lid.
3. Select the white dough setting and the size. Press Start.
4. When the program has finished, turn the dough on to a lightly floured surface and knead lightly, knocking out the air, until smooth and elastic.
5. Cut the dough into 8-10 pieces and shape it into balls. Flatten the balls to about 10cm/4 in diameter. Arrange, smooth side up, and spaced about 2.5cm/1 in apart on an oiled baking tray.
6. Cover with oiled film and leave to rise until doubled in size.
7. Meanwhile, preheat the oven to 220°C (Fan 200°C), 425°F, Gas 7.
8. Remove the film, lightly brush the tops with water and sprinkle with rolled oats.
9. Put into the hot oven and cook for about 20 minutes until golden brown and cooked through.
10. Transfer to a wire rack and leave to cool.

Squash or Pumpkin Cloverleaf Rolls

(Ready in about one hour and 35 minutes I Servings-16 I Difficulty- Moderate)

Ingredients

- One winter squash (about 11/3 pounds) or One cup of canned pumpkin puree
- Half cup of water
- Half cup milks
- 1/3 cup butter, melted
- Four and a half cups of unbleached all-purpose flour
- Three tablespoons light or dark brown sugar
- Grated zest of one orange
- Two teaspoons salt
- Two and 3/4 teaspoons bread machine yeast

Instructions

1. Preheat the oven to 350°F.
2. If you are using winter squash, wash the squash and cut off the top with a sharp chef's knife. Take care when cutting, because some varieties are very hard. Cut in half and scrape out the seeds and spongy fibers. Leave butternut squash or pumpkin in halves, or cut larger squash into large cubes leaving the skin intact.
3. Place in a baking dish, flesh down, and add a half-inch of water. Cover and bake for 1 to One and a half hours, depending on the pieces' size, or until the flesh is tender when pierced with a knife. Drain, cool, then scoop out the squash flesh and discard the skin. Puree the pulp until smooth in a food mill or food processor. You should have about one cup of. Cool, cover, then refrigerate or freeze until needed. Warm slightly in the microwave before placing it in the bread machine.
4. Place all the ingredients in the pan according to the order in the manufacturer's instructions. Program for the Dough cycle; press Start.
5. Oil 16 standard muffin cups (one full pan plus 4 cups in a second pan) When the machine beeps at the end of the cycle, immediately remove the dough and place it on a lightly floured work surface; divide into four equal portions.
6. Divide each of those pieces into four equal portions. Divide each of the 16 portions into three portions and form them into small balls about a walnut's size. You want them all about the same size; this is important, or else the rolls will look funny after baking. Arrange three balls of dough touching each other in each of the muffin cups. Cover loosely with plastic wrap and let rise until doubled in bulk, about 30 minutes.
7. Meanwhile, preheat the oven to 375°F.
8. Bake for 15 to 18 minutes, or until golden brown. Immediately remove the rolls from the pan. Let cool on racks or serve warm.

Morning Sticky Buns

(Ready in about one hour and 35 minutes I Servings-12 I Difficulty- Moderate)

Ingredients

For the dough:
- One and 1/4cups fat-free milk
- One teaspoon vanilla extract
- Three tablespoons unsalted butter, cut into pieces
- Three cups of unbleached all-purpose flour
- Three tablespoons sugar
- One and 1/4teaspoons salt
- Two and a half teaspoons bread machine yeast

For the cinnamon filling:
- 3/4 cup light or dark brown sugar
- One tablespoon ground cinnamon
- Six tablespoons unsalted butter softened

For the caramel:
- 1/3 cup unsalted butter
- One cup of light or dark brown sugar
- 1/4 cup light corn syrup
- One cup of chopped pecans

Instructions

1. To make the dough, place all the dough ingredients in the pan according to the manufacturer's instructions. Program for the Dough cycle; press Start. The dough ball will be soft, yet at the same time smooth and springy. Combine
2. the sugar and cinnamon for the filling in a small bowl. Set aside.
3. To make the caramel, 10 minutes before the end of the Dough cycle, oil the sides and bottom of a 13-by-9- inch glass or metal baking pan.
4. Combine the butter, brown sugar, and corn syrup in a small skillet or heavy saucepan over low heat, stirring constantly. When the butter is melted and the sugar is dissolved, remove it from the heat. Immediately pour into the baking pan. Spread evenly over the bottom with a rubber spatula. Sprinkle with the nuts. Set aside. When the machine beeps at the end of the cycle, press Stop and unplug the machine. Turn the dough out onto a lightly floured work surface. Roll it into a 12-by-15- inch rectangle. Add the filling: Leaving a 1-inch border around all the edges,

spread the surface evenly with the six tablespoons soft butter, then sprinkle evenly with the sugar and cinnamon, which will be quite a light filling. Roll up jelly-roll fashion starting from a long edge, and pinch the seam to seal. With a serrated knife using a gentle sawing motion, cut the roll into 12 equal portions, each slice about One and a half inches thick. Place the slices close together on top of the caramel, spiral cut side down. Cover loosely with plastic wrap and let the rolls rise at room temperature for 45 minutes, or until puffy and even with the rim of the pan.

5. Preheat the oven to 350°F.
6. Bake the buns until the tops are brown, 30 to 35 minutes. Remove from the oven and let stand no more than 5 minutes on a wire rack. Place the cooling rack on top of the pan and, securely holding the hot pan with oven mitts, invert the pan on top of the rack, taking care not to touch the hot caramel. Let cool for at least 20 minutes, then transfer to a serving plate. Pull the buns apart and serve warm.

Hot Cross Buns

(Ready in about one hour and 35 minutes I Servings-12 I Difficulty- Moderate)

Ingredients

For the dough:

- 3/4 cup fat-free milk
- Half teaspoon vanilla extract
- Two large eggs
- Four tablespoons unsalted butter, cut into pieces
- Two and 3/4 cups unbleached all-purpose flour
- 1/3 cup white whole wheat flour or an additional 1/3 cup unbleached all-purpose flour
- 1/4 cup light brown sugar
- One and a half teaspoons salt
- One teaspoon ground mace
- One tablespoon bread machine yeast
- 2/3 cup dried currants
- 1/3 cup finely chopped dried apricots or dried plums

For the icing:

- 3/4 cup sifted confectioners' sugar
- 1/4 teaspoon vanilla extract, almond extract, lemon oil, or Fiori di Sicilia
- One and 1/4tablespoons fat-free milk

Instructions

1. To make the dough, place the dough ingredients, except the dried fruit, in the pan according to the order in the manufacturer's instructions. Program for the Dough cycle; press Start. The dough ball will be soft.
2. Line a baking sheet with parchment paper. When the machine beeps at the end of the cycle, press Stop and unplug the machine. Immediately turn the dough out onto a lightly floured work surface. Pat the dough into a large freeform rectangle and sprinkle with the dried fruit. Press in. Fold the dough into thirds and knead a few times to distribute the fruit evenly.
3. Divide the dough in half. Roll each portion into a 10-inch-long log and, with a bench knife, cut into six equal portions. Form each portion into a round bun and place the buns 2 inches apart on the baking sheet. Let rise, uncovered, at room temperature until doubled in bulk, about 40 minutes.
4. Twenty minutes before baking, preheat the oven to 375oF.
5. With a sharp knife, gently cut across, no deeper than Half-inch, over the surface of each bun. Bake for 15 to 20 minutes, or until browned.
6. While the buns are baking, prepare the icing: Mix the icing ingredients together in a small bowl. Beat hard until the icing is smooth and a bit firm for piping. Remove the rolls from the oven and place the baking sheet on a rack. Place the icing in a pastry bag fitted with a small plain tip, and pipe a cross over the top of each hot bun into the indentation where you cut the cross before baking. Let stand for at least 20 minutes to set before devouring.

Chapter 17-Sweet, Grainy, Seedy, and Nutty Bread Recipes

This chapter provides you with the recipes of sweet, seedy, nutty, and grainy bread that you can easily make with the help of your respective bread machine.

Whole-Wheat Seed Bread

(Ready in about 3 hours 10 minutes I Servings- One loaf I Difficulty- Moderate)

Ingredients

- One and 1/Three cups of whole wheat bread flour
- One and 1/Three cups of water
- Three tablespoons of honey
- One teaspoon of salt
- Two tablespoons of softened Butter
- Half cup of flaxseed
- One and a half cups of bread flour
- Half cup of sunflower seeds
- One teaspoon of active dry yeast

Instructions

1. Put all the required ingredients in the container of the bread machine in the manufacturer's suggested order, except for sunflower seeds.
2. Select the basic cycle and press the start button.
3. Add sunflower seeds on the beeping of the kneading cycle.
4. Serve fresh.

Multigrain Bread

(Ready in about 2 hours 40 minutes I Servings- One loaf I Difficulty- Moderate)

Ingredients

- 3/4 Cup of multigrain cereal

- Three tablespoons of Softened Unsalted Butter
- Two and a 1/4 Cups of Bread Flour
- One Cup of warm milk
- One teaspoon of Bread Machine Yeast
- 1/4 Cup of Brown Sugar packed:
- One teaspoon of salt

Instructions

1. Put all the required ingredients in the container of the bread machine in the suggested order by the manufacturer.
2. Select a basic cycle, light crust, and press the start button.
3. Serve fresh

Toasted Pecan Bread

(Ready in about 3 hours 5 minutes I Servings- One loaf I Difficulty- Moderate)

Ingredients

- Two and a half tablespoons of butter
- One and 1/4 cups of water
- Half cup of old-fashioned oatmeal
- Three cups of bread flour
- Half cup chopped pecans
- Two teaspoons of bread machine yeast
- Two tablespoons of dry milk
- Three tablespoons of sugar
- One and a 1/4 teaspoons of salt

Instructions

1. Put all the required ingredients in the container of the bread machine in the suggested order by the manufacturer.
2. Select Grain and light crust. Press the start button.
3. Serve fresh.

Market Seed Bread

(Ready in about 3 hours 10 minutes I Servings- One loaf I Difficulty- Moderate)

Ingredients

- Two tablespoons of olive oil
- One cup of tepid water
- One cup of whole wheat bread flour
- 1/3 cup of mixed seeds (pumpkin, sunflower, sesame, linseed, & poppy)
- One teaspoon of salt
- One and a half teaspoons of dried yeast
- One tablespoon of sugar
- Two cups of White bread flour

Instructions

1. Put all the required ingredients in the container of the bread machine in the suggested order by the manufacturer. Add seeds in the end.
2. Select white bread cycle—Press the start button. Check the dough's consistency if it needs more water or flour. Add one tablespoon at a time.
3. Serve fresh.

Cracked Wheat Bread

(Ready in about 1 hour 10 minutes I Servings- One loaf I Difficulty- Moderate)

Ingredients

- One and a half teaspoons of salt
- Two and 1/4 cups of bread flour
- One and a half tablespoons of butter
- One and a 1/3 cup of water
- Two tablespoons of honey
- Two and a 1/4 teaspoons of active dry yeast
- 1 and 1/4 cups of whole wheat flour
- Half cup of cracked wheat

Instructions

1. Put all ingredients in the pan of the bread machine, as per the suggested order.
2. Select a basic setting, the crust of your liking. Press the start buttons.
3. Serve fresh and enjoy.

Double Coconut Bread

(Ready in about 4 hours 10 minutes I Servings- One loaf I Difficulty- Moderate)

Ingredients

- One egg yolk only
- One cup of unsweetened coconut milk
- One and a half teaspoons of coconut extract
- Three cups of white flour
- 3/4 teaspoon of salt
- One and a half tablespoons of vegetable oil
- 1/3 cup of coconut
- One and a half teaspoons of bread machine yeast
- Two and a half tablespoons of sugar

Instructions

1. Put all the required ingredients in the container of the bread machine in the suggested order by the manufacturer.
2. Select sweet cycle—Press the start button.
3. Serve fresh and enjoy

Honeyed Bulgur Bread

(Ready in about 2 hours 10 minutes I Servings- One loaf I Difficulty- Moderate)

Ingredients

- Two tablespoons of honey
- 1/4 cup of extra coarse bulgur wheat
- 1/4 cup of boiling water
- One package of active dry yeast
- One teaspoon of salt
- Half cup of bread flour
- One tablespoon of vegetable oil
- 1 and 1/4 cups of all-purpose flour
- 3/4 cup of water
- One tablespoon of skim milk

Instructions

1. Put all the required ingredients in the container of the bread machine in the suggested order by the manufacturer.
2. Select the basic cycle and Press the start button.
3. Enjoy fresh.

Flaxseed Honey Bread

(Ready in about 3 hours 40 minutes I Servings- One loaf I Difficulty- Moderate)

Ingredients

- 1/4 cup of vegetable oil
- One and a half cup of bread flour
- Three tablespoons of honey
- One and a half teaspoon of salt
- One teaspoon of ground ginger
- One and a half cup of whole wheat flour
- One and a 1/3 cup of lukewarm water
- One and a half teaspoon of instant yeast
- Half cup of ground flax seed

Instructions

1. Put all the ingredients in the pan of the bread machine as per the suggested order.
2. Select the basic cycle and medium crust—Press the start button.
3. Check dough. It should not be too sticky or too dry. Add water or flour one tablespoon at a time.
4. Enjoy fresh with butter.

Chia Sesame Bread

(Ready in about 3 hours 10 minutes I Servings- One loaf I Difficulty- Moderate)

Ingredients

- One tablespoon of organic apple cider vinegar
- 1/4 cup of olive oil
- Two teaspoons of salt
- 2/3 cup of almond meal flour
- Three whole eggs mixed
- One cup of ground sesame seeds
- Half cup of gluten-free tapioca flour
- One cup of ground chia seeds
- One cup of warm water
- 1/3 cup of Gluten-free coconut flour
- Three tablespoons of psyllium husks ground

Instructions

1. In a bowl, add all dry ingredients and sift them together. Take out any large bits.
2. Put all the required ingredients in the container of the bread machine in the suggested order by the manufacturer.
3. Select gluten-free, Press the start button and check dough's consistency. It should not be too wet or too dry. Add one tablespoon of water or flour if it's too dry or too wet.
4. Serve fresh.

Quinoa Whole Wheat Bread

(Ready in about 3 hours 10 minutes I Servings- One loaf I Difficulty- Moderate)
Ingredients

- Two tablespoons of honey
- One and ¼ cups of water
- One tablespoon of olive oil
- Half teaspoon of salt
- One and ¾ cups of whole wheat flour
- One and 3/4 cups of bread flour
- One dash of toasted sesame oil
- 1/3 cup of uncooked quinoa
- One and 3/4 teaspoons of active dry yeast

Instructions

1. Put all the required ingredients in the container of the bread machine in the suggested order by the manufacturer.
2. Select basic, light crust—Press the start button.
3. Serve fresh.

Peanut Butter Bread

(Ready in about 3 hours 10 minutes I Servings- One loaf I Difficulty- Moderate)

Ingredients

- One and a half cups of bread flour
- Half cup of peanut butter
- Half teaspoon of salt
- One and a half cups of whole wheat flour
- Two and a ¼ teaspoons of active dry yeast
- Three tablespoons of gluten flour
- One and ¼ cups of warm water
- ¼ cup of brown sugar

Instructions

1. Put all the required ingredients in the container of the bread machine in the suggested order by the manufacturer.
2. Select whole wheat, light crust. Press the start button.
3. Serve fresh.

Toasted Hazelnut Bread

(Ready in about 2 hours 45 minutes I Servings- One loaf I Difficulty- Moderate)

Ingredients

- Two tablespoons of hazelnut liqueur
- Three cups of flour
- ¾ cups of chopped hazelnuts
- One whole egg
- Three tablespoons of sugar
- ¾ teaspoon of salt
- One teaspoon of active dry yeast
- Three tablespoons of butter
- One cup of milk

For Glaze

- Two teaspoons of milk
- One tablespoon of hazelnut liqueur
- Half cup of powdered sugar

Instructions

1. Put all the required ingredients in the container of the bread machine in the suggested order by the manufacturer except for nuts.
2. Select basic and light crust. Press the start button.
3. Add nuts on the signal.
4. Meanwhile, mix all the ingredients of glaze. Drizzle over warm bread and serve.

Oatmeal Seed Bread

(Ready in about 3 hours 10 minutes I Servings- One loaf I Difficulty- Moderate)

Ingredients

- Two tablespoons of softened Butter
- One and ¾ cups of water
- One tablespoon of olive oil
- Two cups of bread flour
- ¼ cup of honey
- 2/3 cup of Quick-cooking oats
- Two cups of whole wheat flour
- Half cup of sunflower seeds
- Two tablespoons of dry milk
- Two and a half teaspoons of bread machine yeast
- One and a ¼ teaspoons of salt

Instructions

1. Put all the required ingredients in the container of the bread machine in the suggested order by the manufacturer, except for seeds.
2. Select basic, light crust. Do not try the delay cycle.
3. Press the start button.
4. Serve fresh.

Nutty Wheat Bread

(Ready in about 3 hours 10 minutes I Servings- One loaf I Difficulty- Moderate)

Ingredients

- One and a half tablespoons of unsalted butter, cut into half-inch pieces
- One and a ⅓ cups of buttermilk
- One and a half tablespoons of maple syrup
- One teaspoon of salt
- One and a ¼ cups of bread flour
- Two and a ¼ teaspoons bread machine yeast
- ¾ cups of mixed seeds and nuts (pecans, sunflower seeds, pumpkin seeds, and walnuts)
- Two and a ¼ cups of whole wheat flour

Instructions

1. All ingredients should be at room temperature
2. Put all the required ingredients in the container of the bread machine in the suggested order by the manufacturer. Do not add seeds and nuts yet.
3. Select whole wheat, light crust. Press the start button.
4. Add in the seeds, nuts on the ingredients signal.
5. Serve warm.

Sunflower Bread

(Ready in about 2 hours 10 minutes I Servings- One loaf I Difficulty- Moderate)

Ingredients

- Two and a half cups of white bread flour
- One and 1/4 cups of water
- Two tablespoons of dry milk
- Half cup of sunflower seeds
- Half teaspoon of salt
- ¾ cup of wheat bread flour
- Two tablespoons of butter
- Two teaspoons of fast rise yeast
- Three tablespoons of honey

Instructions

1. Put all the required ingredients in the container of the bread machine in the suggested order by the manufacturer.
2. Select the cycle you like the best. Even use the delay cycle.
3. Press the start button and enjoy fresh bread.

Raisin Seed Bread

(Ready in about 3 hours 10 minutes I Servings- One loaf I Difficulty- Moderate)

Ingredients

- Two teaspoons of cinnamon
- Half teaspoon of salt
- Three cups of whole-wheat flour
- One cup of warm water
- One cup of raisins
- Four tablespoons of honey
- One teaspoon of seeds

- Half cup of coconut oil
- Two teaspoons of active dry yeast

Instructions

1. Put all the required ingredients in the container of the bread machine in the suggested order by the manufacturer.
2. Select whole-wheat crust to your liking—press the start button.

Quinoa Oatmeal Bread

(Ready in about 3 hours 50 minutes I Servings- One loaf I Difficulty- Moderate)

Ingredients

- Half cup of whole wheat flour
- One cup of buttermilk
- One and a half of bread flour
- Half cup of quick-cooking oats
- One and a half teaspoons of bread machine yeast
- 2/3 cup of water
- One tablespoon of honey
- 1/3 cup of uncooked quinoa
- Four tablespoons of melted unsalted butter
- One teaspoon of salt
- One tablespoon of sugar

Instructions

1. Cook quinoa in 2/3 cup of water. Cool it.
2. Add all ingredients with cooked quinoa to the bread machine in the suggested order by the manufacturer.
3. Select whole grain and Press the start button.
4. Enjoy fresh.

Chocolate Chip Peanut Butter Banana Bread

(Ready in about 3 hours 10 minutes I Servings- One loaf I Difficulty- Moderate)

Ingredients

- Three whole Eggs
- Half cup of softened butter
- One and a half cups of mashed bananas (very ripe)
- 1 and 1/4 cups of sugar
- Half cup of vegetable oil
- One and a half cups of all-purpose flour
- One teaspoon of salt
- Half cup of plain Greek yogurt
- One teaspoon of vanilla
- One cup of peanut butter and chocolate chips
- One teaspoon of baking soda

Instructions

1. Add all ingredients, except chocolate chips and nuts, to the bread machine in the manufacturer's suggested order.
2. Select a batter bread cycle. Press the start button.

3. Add chocolate chips and nuts at the ingredient signal and take out the paddle.
4. Enjoy fresh bread.

Chocolate Sour Cream Bread

(Ready in about 3 hours 40 minutes I Servings- One loaf I Difficulty- Moderate)

Ingredients

- 3 and 3/4 cups of flour
- Three tablespoons of butter
- 3/4 cup of sour cream
- Two and a 1/4 teaspoons of yeast
- One tablespoon of sugar
- 3/4 cup of water
- Chocolate chips
- One teaspoon of salt

Instructions

1. Place all ingredients in the container of the bread machine in the suggested order by the manufacturer.
2. Select a basic cycle. Light crust. Press the start button.
3. Serve fresh bread.

Nectarine Cobbler Bread

(Ready in about 3 hours 40 minutes I Servings- One loaf I Difficulty- Moderate)

Ingredients

- One package of active dry yeast
- Two and a half cups of bread flour
- One teaspoon of salt
- 1/4 teaspoon of nutmeg
- One cup of nectarine
- One tablespoon of gluten flour
- 1/4 cup of packed brown sugar
- 1/4 teaspoon of cinnamon
- 1/3 cup of peach juice
- Half cup of whole wheat flour
- One teaspoon of vanilla extract
- 1/3 cup chopped dried peaches
- 1/3 cup of sour cream
- One tablespoon of butter
- 1/8 teaspoon of baking soda

Instructions

1. All ingredients should be at room temperature.
2. Put all the required ingredients in the container of the bread machine in the suggested order by the manufacturer.
3. Select the sweet bread cycle—Press the start button.
4. Enjoy fresh bread.

Sour Cream Maple Bread

(Ready in about 3 hours 10 minutes I Servings- One loaf I Difficulty- Moderate)

Ingredients

- Half cup of melted butter
- Two and a half cups of all-purpose flour

- Half teaspoon of baking soda
- Half cup of sugar
- One teaspoon of baking powder
- Half teaspoon of salt
- Two cups of mashed ripe bananas
- Four teaspoons of maple syrup
- Two teaspoons of nutmeg
- 1/4 cup of sour cream
- 1/3 cup of walnuts and pecans
- One teaspoon of vanilla
- 1/3 cup of raisins
- Two whole eggs mixed

Instructions

1. Add all ingredients, except for raisins and walnuts, to the bread machine in the manufacturer's suggested order.
2. Select cake cycle. Press the start button. Add nuts at the ingredient signal.
3. Serve fresh bread.

Barmbrack Bread

(Ready in about 3 hours 10 minutes I Servings- One loaf I Difficulty- Moderate)

Ingredients

- Two cups of bread flour
- One coin enclosed in foil
- Half teaspoon of salt
- Half cup of golden raisins
- Half teaspoon of ground allspice
- One and a half teaspoons of active dry yeast
- 1/4 cup of sugar
- Two tablespoons of orange zest
- Half cup of currants
- Two tablespoons of non-fat powdered milk
- Two tablespoons of softened butter
- 3/4 cup and two tablespoons of water

Instructions

1. Place all ingredients into the bread machine, except coin, currants, and raisins, in the manufacturer's suggested order.
2. Select the basic cycle. Medium crust. Press the start button.
3. Add raisins and currants at the ingredients signal. Spray the foil coin with spray oil generously.
4. Ten minutes before the baking cycle begins, place the coin under the surface. Let the bread bake.
5. Enjoy.

Apple Butter Bread

(Ready in about 4 hours 10 minutes I Servings- One loaf I Difficulty- Moderate)

Ingredients

- Half cup of apple butter
- One cup of water
- One tablespoon of sugar
- Two tablespoons of vegetable oil

- One cup of whole wheat flour
- Two cups of bread flour
- One and a half teaspoons of yeast
- One teaspoon of salt

Instructions

1. Put all the required ingredients in the container of the bread machine in the suggested order by the manufacturer.
2. Select sweet cycle—Press the start button.
3. Adjust dough consistency by adding one tablespoon of flour if too sticky and one tablespoon of water if too dry.
4. Enjoy fresh bread.

Crusty Honey Bread

(Ready in about 3 hours 10 minutes I Servings- One loaf I Difficulty- Moderate)

Ingredients

- One teaspoon of sugar
- One tablespoon of honey
- One and 1/8 cup of warm water
- One tablespoon of olive oil
- One package of bread machine yeast
- One teaspoon of salt
- Three cups of bread flour

Instructions

1. Put all the required ingredients in the container of the bread machine in the suggested order by the manufacturer.
2. Select white bread cycle. Medium crust. Press the start button.
3. Enjoy fresh bread.

Honey Granola Bread

(Ready in about 3 hours 10 minutes I Servings- One loaf I Difficulty- Moderate)

Ingredients

- Two tablespoons of butter
- One and 1/4 cups of water
- Three cups of bread flour
- 3/4 cup of granola cereal
- Four tablespoons of honey
- One and a half teaspoons of bread machine yeast
- Two tablespoons of dry milk
- One teaspoon of salt

Instructions

1. Put all the required ingredients in the container of the bread machine in the suggested order by the manufacturer.
2. Select the basic cycle. Light or medium crust. Press the start button.
3. Enjoy.

Black Bread

(Ready in about 4 hours 15 minutes I Servings- One loaf I Difficulty- Moderate)

Ingredients

- Two and 2/Three tablespoons of applesauce

- One and 1/Three cups of water
- One teaspoon of salt
- One teaspoon of coffee granules, instant
- One and a half tablespoons of cider vinegar
- One teaspoon of dried onion flakes
- Two cups of all-purpose flour
- Two and a half teaspoons of active dry yeast
- 1/4 teaspoon of fennel seed
- One and 1/Three tablespoons of dark molasses
- One and 1/Three cups of rye flour
- Two and a half teaspoons of caraway seeds
- 2/3 cup of oat bran
- One teaspoon of sugar
- Two tablespoons of cocoa powder, unsweetened

Instructions

1. Put all the required ingredients in the container of the bread machine in the suggested order by the manufacturer.
2. Select the basic cycle. Press the start button.
3. Serve fresh bread.

Apple Cider Bread

(Ready in about 3 hours 40 minutes I Servings- One loaf I Difficulty- Moderate)

Ingredients

- One and 1/4 cup of apple cider
- Two tablespoons of softened butter
- Two and 1/4 teaspoons of active dry yeast
- Three cups of white bread flour
- One teaspoon of ground cinnamon
- One teaspoon of salt
- Two tablespoons of packed brown sugar

Instructions

1. Place all ingredients in the container of the bread machine in the suggested order by the manufacturer.
2. Select the basic cycle. Light crust. Press the start button.
3. Enjoy fresh bread.

Pumpkin Coconut Bread

(Ready in about 4 hours 10 minutes I Servings- One loaf I Difficulty- Moderate)

Ingredients

- One and a half teaspoons of coconut extract
- Half cup of pumpkin puree
- One egg yolk only
- Half cup of coconut milk, unsweetened
- One and a half tablespoons of olive oil
- 1/3 cup of coconut
- One and a half teaspoons of bread machine yeast
- Two and a half tablespoons of sugar
- Three cups of regular flour
- 3/4 teaspoon of salt

Instructions

1. Place all ingredients in the container of the bread machine in the suggested order by the manufacturer.
2. Select the sweet bread cycle. Crust to your liking. Press the start button.
3. Enjoy fresh bread.

Vanilla Almond Milk Bread

(Ready in about 3 hours 40 minutes I Servings- One loaf I Difficulty- Moderate)

Ingredients

- Two tablespoons of olive oil
- Two tablespoons of honey
- Two cups of whole wheat flour
- Two and a ¼ teaspoons of active dry yeast
- One and ¼ cups of bread flour
- One and ¼ cups of vanilla almond milk
- One tablespoon of vital gluten
- One and a half teaspoon of salt

Instructions

1. Put all the required ingredients in the container of the bread machine in the suggested order by the manufacturer.
2. Select the wheat bread cycle. Light crust. Press the start button.
3. Enjoy.

Triple Chocolate Bread

(Ready in about 3 hours 40 minutes I Servings- One loaf I Difficulty- Moderate)

Ingredients

- One teaspoon of vanilla extract
- Two cups of bread flour
- Two tablespoons of brown sugar
- One tablespoon of margarine or butter
- 2/3 cup of milk
- One teaspoon of active dry yeast
- One tablespoon unsweetened cocoa
- Half teaspoon of salt
- One whole egg
- Half cup of semisweet chocolate chips

Instructions

1. Put all the required ingredients in the container of the bread machine in the suggested order by the manufacturer.
2. Select the basic cycle. Press the start button.
3. Enjoy fresh bread.

Chocolate Oatmeal Banana Bread

(Ready in about 3 hours 40 minutes I Servings- One loaf I Difficulty- Moderate)

Ingredients

- Two tablespoons of milk
- Two bananas, mashed
- 1/3 cup of melted butter
- Two cups of bread flour
- Two whole eggs
- Half teaspoon of salt

- 2/3 cups of sugar
- One and 1/4 teaspoon of baking powder
- Half cup of chocolate chips
- Half teaspoon of baking soda
- Half cup of chopped walnuts

Instructions

1. Put all the required ingredients in the container of the bread machine in the suggested order by the manufacturer.
2. Select the quick bread cycle—Press the start button.
3. Enjoy fresh bread.

Old-Fashioned Sesame-Wheat Bread

(Ready in about 3 hours 40 minutes I Servings- One loaf I Difficulty- Moderate)

Ingredients

- 3/4 cup water
- 3/8 cup milk
- Two tablespoons butter, cut into pieces
- Two and 1/4 cups bread flour
- 3/4 cup whole wheat flour
- Two tablespoons light or dark brown sugar
- One tablespoon sesame seed
- One tablespoon plus one teaspoon gluten
- One and a half teaspoons salt
- Two and a half teaspoons bread machine yeast

Instructions

1. Place all the ingredients in the pan according to the order in the manufacturer's instructions. Set crust on medium and program for the Basic cycle; press Start.
2. When the baking cycle ends, immediately remove the pan's bread and place it on a rack. Let cool to room temperature before slicing

Three-Seed Whole Wheat Bread

(Ready in about 3 hours 40 minutes I Servings- One loaf I Difficulty- Moderate)

Ingredients

- One and 1/4 cups water
- Two tablespoons sunflower seed oil
- One and a half cups bread flour
- One and a half cups whole wheat flour
- Three tablespoons nonfat dry milk
- Two tablespoons brown sugar
- One tablespoon gluten
- One teaspoon salt
- Two and a half teaspoons bread machine yeast
- 1/3 cup raw sunflower seeds
- Two tablespoons sesame seeds
- Two teaspoons poppy seeds

Instructions

1. Place the ingredients, except the seeds, in the pan according to the

order in the manufacturer's instructions. Set crust on medium and program for the Basic or Whole Wheat cycle; press Start.

2. When the machine beeps, or between Knead 1 and Knead 2, add all the seeds.

3. When the baking cycle ends, immediately remove the pan's bread and place it on a rack. Let cool to room temperature before slicing.

Chocolate Challah

(Ready in about 3 hours 40 minutes I Servings- One loaf I Difficulty- Moderate)

Ingredients

- One cup of water
- One large egg plus one egg yolk
- Two tablespoons vegetable oil
- Two teaspoons vanilla extract
- Three cups of bread flour
- Half cup sugars
- 1/4 cup unsweetened Dutch-process cocoa powder
- One tablespoon gluten
- One and a half teaspoons salt
- Two and 1/4teaspoons bread machine yeast
- Half cup semisweet chocolate chips

Instructions

1. Place the ingredients, except the chocolate chips, in the pan according to the order in the manufacturer's instructions.

2. Set crust on medium and program for the Basic or Sweet Bread cycle; press Start. At the beep, add the chocolate chips.

3. When the baking cycle ends, immediately remove the pan's bread and place it on a rack. Let cool to room temperature before slicing.

Chocolate Bread with Dates and Pistachios

(Ready in about 3 hours 40 minutes I Servings- One loaf I Difficulty- Moderate)

Ingredients

- 7/8 cup water
- One large egg
- Three tablespoons vegetable oil
- Three cups of bread flour
- Half cup sugars
- 1/4 cup unsweetened Dutch-process cocoa powder
- One tablespoon gluten
- One and 1/4teaspoons salt
- Two and a half teaspoons bread machine yeast
- 2/3 cup snipped pitted dates
- 1/4 cup chopped pistachios

Instructions

1. Place the ingredients, except the dates and pistachios, in the pan according to the order in the manufacturer's instructions. Set crust on medium and program for the Basic or Sweet Bread cycle; press Start.

2. When the machine beeps, or between machine beeps, or between Knead 1 and Knead 2, add the dates and pistachios.

3. When the baking cycle ends, immediately remove the pan's bread and place it on a rack. Let cool to room temperature before slicing.

Chocolate Cherry Bread

(Ready in about 3 hours 40 minutes I Servings- One loaf I Difficulty- Moderate)

Ingredients

- One cup of milk
- One large egg
- Half teaspoon vanilla extract
- Half teaspoon almond extract
- Three tablespoons unsalted butter, cut into pieces
- Two and 7/8 cups bread flour
- 1/3 cup unsweetened Dutch-process cocoa powder
- 1/4 cup light brown sugar
- One tablespoon gluten
- One and ¼ teaspoons salt
- Two and a half teaspoons bread machine yeast
- 3/4 cup snipped glazed tart dried cherries

Instructions

1. Place the ingredients, except the cherries, in the pan according to the order in the manufacturer's instructions. Set crust on medium and program for the Basic or Sweet Bread cycle; press Start

2. When the machine beeps, or between Knead 1 and Knead 2, add the cherries.

3. When the baking cycle ends, immediately remove the pan's bread and place it on a rack. Let cool to room temperature before slicing.

Pain Aux Troi S Parfums

(Ready in about 3 hours 40 minutes I Servings- One loaf I Difficulty- Moderate)

Ingredients

- Half cup milk
- Half cup of water
- One large egg plus one egg yolk
- Three tablespoons pistachio oil or melted unsalted butter
- One teaspoon mint extract
- Two and 2/3 cups of bread flour
- 1/4 cup sugar
- Three tablespoons unsweetened Dutch-process cocoa powder
- One tablespoon plus one teaspoon gluten
- One teaspoon salt
- Two and a half teaspoons bread machine yeast
- Half cup bittersweet chocolate chips
- 1/3 cup chopped pistachios

Instructions

1. Place the ingredients, except the chocolate chips and pistachios, in the pan according to the manufacturers' order. Set crust on light and program for the Sweet Bread cycle; press Start.
2. When the machine beeps, or between Knead 1 and Knead 2, add the chocolate chips and pistachios.
3. When the baking cycle ends, immediately remove the pan's bread and place it on a rack. Let cool to room temperature before slicing.

Poppy Seed Egg Bread

(Ready in about 3 hours 40 minutes I Servings- One loaf I Difficulty- Moderate)

Ingredients

- Half cup of milk
- Three large eggs
- Two tablespoons unsalted butter, cut into pieces
- Three cups of bread flour
- One tablespoon sugar
- One tablespoon gluten
- Two teaspoons poppy seeds
- One and a half teaspoons salt
- Two teaspoons bread machine yeast

Instructions

1. Place all the ingredients in the pan according to the order in the manufacturer's instructions. Set crust on medium and program for the Basic or Tender cycle; press Start.
2. When the baking cycle ends, immediately remove the pan's bread and place it on a rack. Let cool to room temperature before slicing.

Sprouted Wheat Berry Bread

(Ready in about 3 hours 40 minutes I Servings- One loaf I Difficulty- Moderate)

Ingredients

- One and 1/8 cups buttermilk
- Two tablespoons canola oil
- Two tablespoons honey
- Two cups of bread flour
- One and 1/4cups graham or whole wheat flour
- One and a half tablespoons gluten
- One and a half teaspoons salt
- One tablespoon plus Half teaspoons bread machine yeast
- One cup of chopped sprouted wheat berries

Instructions

1. Place the ingredients, except the wheat berries, in the pan according to the order in the manufacturer's instructions. Set crust on dark and program for the Basic or Whole Wheat cycle; press Start.
2. Set a kitchen timer for 12 minutes. When the timer rings, open the lid and sprinkle in the wheat berries around the sides of the dough ball while the machine is running, being careful to avoid the

rotating blade. Close the lid. The wheat berries will be slowly incorporated.
3. When the baking cycle ends, immediately remove the pan's bread and place it on a rack. Let cool to room temperature before slicing.

Sennebec Hill Bread

(Ready in about 3 hours 40 minutes I Servings- One loaf I Difficulty- Moderate)

Ingredients

- One and 1/4cups water
- Three tablespoons canola oil
- Two tablespoons molasses
- Two large egg yolks
- One and a half cups bread flour
- 3/4 cup whole wheat flour
- Half cup medium or dark rye flour
- Three tablespoons rolled oats
- Three tablespoons yellow cornmeal
- Three tablespoons toasted wheat germ
- Half cup nonfat dry milk
- One and a half tablespoons gluten
- One and a half teaspoons salt
- One tablespoon bread machine yeast

Instructions

1. Place all the ingredients in the pan according to the order in the manufacturer's instructions. Set crust on dark and program for the Whole Wheat cycle's dark and program; press Start.
2. When the baking cycle ends, immediately remove the pan's bread and place it on a rack. Let cool to room temperature before slicing.

Stonehenge Bread

(Ready in about 3 hours 40 minutes I Servings- One loaf I Difficulty- Moderate)

Ingredients

- Three tablespoons whole millet
- 1/4 cup bulgur wheat
- Three tablespoons polenta
- One and 1/4cups boiling water
- Three tablespoons honey
- Three tablespoons unsalted butter, cut into pieces
- Two cups of bread flour
- Half cup whole wheat flour
- 1/4 cup medium rye flour
- 1/4 cup rolled oats
- Two tablespoons bran
- One and a half tablespoons gluten
- One and a half teaspoons salt
- One tablespoon plus Half teaspoon bread machine yeast

Instructions

1. Place the millet, bulgur wheat, polenta, boiling water, honey, and butter in a bowl. Let soak for 15 minutes to soften the grains, melt the butter, and cool until warm.

2. Place the ingredients in the pan according to the order in the manufacturer's instructions, adding the grains and their soaking liquid as the liquid ingredients. Set crust on dark and program for the Basic or Whole Wheat cycle; press Start.

3. When the baking cycle ends, immediately remove the pan's bread and place it on a rack. Let cool to room temperature before slicing.

Nine-Grain Honey Bread

(Ready in about 3 hours 40 minutes I Servings- One loaf I Difficulty- Moderate)

Ingredients

- One and 1/4 cups boiling water
- Half cup 9-grain cereal
- Three tablespoons honey
- Three tablespoons unsalted butter, cut into pieces
- One and 2/3 cups of bread flour
- One cup of whole wheat flour
- 1/3 cup dry buttermilk powder
- One and a half tablespoons gluten
- One and ¼ teaspoons salt
- One tablespoon bread machine yeast

Instructions

1. Pour the boiling water over the cracked grain cereal in a bowl. Add the honey and butter. Let stand for 1 hour to soften the grains.

2. Place the ingredients in the pan according to the order in the manufacturer's instructions, adding the cereal and its soaking liquid as the liquid ingredients. Set crust on dark and program for the Basic or Whole Wheat cycle; press Start.

3. When the baking cycle ends, immediately remove the pan's bread and place it on a rack. Let cool to room temperature before slicing.

Super-Grain Bread

(Ready in about 3 hours 40 minutes I Servings- One loaf I Difficulty- Moderate)

Ingredients

- One heaping tablespoon of raw amaranth seeds
- Half cup of water
- 2/3 cup buttermilk
- One large egg
- Two tablespoons butter, cut into pieces
- Two tablespoons honey
- One and 3/4 cups bread flour
- Half cup whole wheat or spelled flour
- Two tablespoons quinoa flour
- Two tablespoons barley flour
- Two tablespoons brown rice flour
- Two tablespoons instant potato flakes
- Two tablespoons cornmeal
- Two tablespoons rolled oats
- One and a half tablespoons gluten
- One and a half teaspoons salt

- One and a half teaspoon bread machine yeast

Instructions

1. Heat a deep, heavy saucepan over medium heat. Place the amaranth in the pan. Stir immediately with a natural bristle pastry brush. Stir constantly. The amaranth will pop like popcorn. Immediately remove to a bowl to cool.

2. Place all the ingredients, including the popped amaranth, in the pan according to the order in the manufacturer's instructions, adding the popped amaranth with the dry ingredients. Set crust on dark and program for the Whole Wheat cycle; press Start. The dough ball should be moist and springy.

3. When the baking cycle ends, immediately remove the pan's bread and place it on a rack. Let cool to room temperature before slicing.

Toasted Walnut Bread

(Ready in about 3 hours 40 minutes I Servings- One loaf I Difficulty- Moderate)

Ingredients

- 3/4 cup walnut pieces
- One cup of water
- Two large egg whites, lightly beaten
- One and a half tablespoons butter, cut into pieces
- Three cups of bread flour
- Two tablespoons sugar
- Two tablespoons nonfat dry milk
- One tablespoon gluten
- 3/4 teaspoon salt
- Two teaspoons bread machine yeast

Instructions

1. Preheat the oven to 350°F.

2. Spread the walnuts on a baking sheet and place in the center of the oven for 4 minutes to toast lightly. Set aside to cool.

3. Place the ingredients, except the walnuts, in the pan according to the order in the manufacturer's instructions.

4. Set crust on medium and program for the Basic or Fruit and Nut cycle; press Start. When the machine beeps, or between Knead 1 and Knead 2, add the walnuts.

5. When the baking cycle ends, immediately remove the pan's bread and place it on a rack. Let cool to room temperature before slicing.

Sunflower Oatmeal Bread

(Ready in about 3 hours 40 minutes I Servings- One loaf I Difficulty- Moderate)

Ingredients

- Half cup of water
- 5/8 cup buttermilk
- One large egg
- One and a half tablespoon butter, cut into pieces
- Two tablespoons honey
- One tablespoon molasses

- Two and a half cups bread flour
- Half cup rolled oats
- Half cup whole wheat flour
- Half cup raw sunflower seeds
- One tablespoon gluten
- One and a half teaspoons salt
- Two and a half teaspoons bread machine yeast

Instructions

1. Place all the ingredients in the pan according to the order in the manufacturer's instructions. Set crust on medium and program for the Basic cycle; press Start.
2. When the baking cycle ends, immediately remove the pan's bread and place it on a rack. Let cool to room temperature before slicing.

Zuni Indian Bread

(Ready in about 3 hours 40 minutes I Servings- One loaf I Difficulty- Moderate)

Ingredients

- One cup of buttermilk
- One large egg
- Two tablespoons sunflower seed oil
- Two cups of bread flour
- 2/3 cup whole wheat flour
- 1/3 cup cornmeal
- Half cup raw sunflower seeds
- Two tablespoons dark brown sugar
- One and a half tablespoons gluten
- One and a half teaspoons salt
- Two and 3/4 teaspoons bread machine yeast

Instructions

1. Place all the ingredients in the pan according to the order in the manufacturer's instructions. Set crust on dark and program for the Whole Wheat cycle; press Start.
2. When the baking cycle ends, immediately remove the pan's bread and place it on a rack. Let cool to room temperature before slicing.

Orange-Cumin Bread

(Ready in about 3 hours 40 minutes I Servings- One loaf I Difficulty- Moderate)

Ingredients

- Half cup orange juice
- 2/3 cup fat-free milk
- Three tablespoons butter, cut into pieces
- Two and 2/3 cups of bread flour
- 1/3 cup whole wheat flour
- 1/4 cup light brown sugar
- One tablespoon gluten
- One and a half teaspoons cumin seed, crushed in a mortar and pestle
- One and a half teaspoons salt
- Two and a half teaspoons bread machine yeast

Instructions

1. Place all the ingredients in the pan according to the order in the manufacturer's instructions. Set crust on dark and program for the Basic cycle; press Start. The dough ball will be firm and smooth, yet springy.
2. When the baking cycle ends, immediately remove the pan's bread and place it on a rack. Let cool to room temperature before slicing.

Moroccan Bread with Sesame and Aniseed

(Ready in about 3 hours 40 minutes I Servings- Two loaf I Difficulty- Moderate)

Ingredients

- One and 1/4cups water
- Two and 3/4 cups bread flour
- Half cup whole wheat flour
- Two teaspoons sesame seeds
- Two teaspoons aniseeds
- Two teaspoons salt
- Two and a half teaspoons bread machine yeast
- Two tablespoons yellow cornmeal, for sprinkling

Instructions

1. Place all the dough ingredients in the pan according to the order in the manufacturer's instructions. Program for the Dough cycle; press Start.
2. Turn the dough out onto a work surface and divide it into two equal portions. Knead each portion into a ball and let rest for 10 minutes covered with a clean tea towel. With your fingers, moisten the surface of each dough ball with some olive oil; press with your palm to flatten each into a disc 1-inch thick and 6 inches in diameter. Dust the work surface with a bit of flour to keep the dough from sticking to it and cover the discs with the towel. Let rest for One and a half to 2 hours, until puffy. Prick the surface of each loaf with the tines of a fork to gently release the gas.
3. Preheat the oven to 400°F. Sprinkle a baking sheet with cornmeal and place the loaves on the baking sheet.
4. Place the loaves in the oven (it won't be up to temperature or hot yet) and bake for exactly 12 minutes. Reduce the oven temperature to 300°F and bake for an additional 35 to 40 minutes, or until the bread is brown and sounds hollow when tapped on the bottom with your finger. Remove to a rack to cool before cutting into wedges to serve.

Potato Bread with Caraway Seeds

(Ready in about 3 hours 40 minutes I Servings- One loaf I Difficulty- Moderate)

Ingredients

- One and 1/3 cups of warm water
- Two tablespoons instant potato flakes
- One and a half tablespoons butter or lard

- Two and 2/3 cups of bread flour
- 1/3 cup potato starch flour
- One and a half tablespoons sugar
- Two teaspoons gluten
- Two teaspoons caraway seeds
- One and a half teaspoons salt
- Two and 1/4 teaspoons bread machine yeast

Instructions

1. Place the instant potato flakes in the water in a bowl. Let stand for 5 minutes. The flakes will expand and soften, and the water becomes cloudy.
2. Place the ingredients in the pan according to the manufacturer's instructions, adding the potato water with the butter or lard as the liquid ingredients. Set crust on dark and program for the Quick Yeast Bread or Rapid cycle; press Start. The dough ball will be smooth and soft. If the dough rises more than two-thirds of the way up the pan, gently deflate the dough a bit. This will keep the dough from hitting the window during baking.
3. When the baking cycle ends, immediately remove the pan's bread and place it on a rack. Let cool to room temperature before slicing.

Fig and Walnut Bread

(Ready in about 3 hours 40 minutes | Servings- One loaf | Difficulty- Moderate)

Ingredients

- One cup plus two tablespoons water
- One-pound box white bread machine mix
- Two teaspoons gluten
- One yeast packet (included in the mix)
- 3/4 cup chopped dried figs
- 1/4 cup chopped walnuts

Instructions

1. Place the ingredients, except the figs and walnuts, in the pan according to the order in the manufacturer's instructions. Set the crust for dark and program for the Basic or Fruit and Nut cycle; press Start. When the machine beeps, or between Knead 1 and Knead 2, add the figs and walnuts.
2. When the baking cycle ends, immediately remove the pan's bread and place it on a rack. Let cool to room temperature before slicing

Polish Poppy Seed Bread

(Ready in about 3 hours 40 minutes | Servings- One loaf | Difficulty- Moderate)

Ingredients

- One cup plus two tablespoons fat-free milk

- One egg yolk
- One teaspoon almond extract
- One-pound box white bread machine mix
- Half cup chopped slivered blanched almonds
- 1/3 cup currants
- One tablespoon poppy seed
- One tablespoon light brown sugar
- Two teaspoons gluten
- One yeast packet (included in the mix)

Instructions

1. Place all the ingredients in the pan according to the order in the manufacturer's instructions. Set the crust for medium and program for the Basic cycle; press Start.
2. When the baking cycle ends, immediately remove the pan's bread and place it on a rack. Let cool to room temperature before slicing

Hazelnut and Cinnamon Bread

(Ready in about 3 hours 40 minutes | Servings- One loaf | Difficulty- Moderate)

Ingredients

- One and 1/4 teaspoon Easy bake yeast
- One cup of extra strong or Canadian white bread flour
- One cup of strong whole meal flour
- One teaspoon fine sea salt
- 3/4 teaspoon ground cinnamon
- One and 1/4 cup of water
- One tablespoon walnut oil
- One tablespoon clear honey
- Half cup of hazelnuts, toasted and finely chopped

Instructions

1. Put all the ingredients, except for the hazelnuts, into the pan in the correct order for your machine. Fit the pan into the bread machine and close the lid.
2. Select the basic whole wheat raisin setting, medium crust, and the appropriate size. Press Start.
3. When the machine indicates (with a beeping sound), add the hazelnuts and close the lid again.
4. When the program has finished, lift the pan out of the machine, turn the bread out on to a wire rack and leave to cool completely

Chapter 19-Ketogenic Bread Recipes

People nowadays tend to go on various diets, and keto is one among them. While following a keto diet, you can savor the delicious taste of the ketogenic bread. The recipes of ketogenic bread you can have while on a diet are provided in this chapter.

Basic Low-Carb Bread

(Ready in about 3 hours 40 minutes I Servings- One loaf I Difficulty- Moderate)

Ingredients

- One and a half teaspoon of Bread Machine Yeast
- One and a half tablespoon of sugar
- ¼ cup of Vegetable Oil
- One cup of Water Warm
- Three cups of low carb flour
- Three teaspoons of Wheat Gluten

Instructions

1. Spray the bread machine pan with cooking spray.
2. Activate yeast in warm water with sugar. After 8-10 minutes, add to the pan.
3. Add rest of the ingredients as well, as per the suggested order by the manufacturer.
4. Select the low-carb cycle or basic. Press the start button
5. Enjoy.

Almond Flour Yeast Bread

(Ready in about 3 hours 40 minutes I Servings- One loaf I Difficulty- Moderate)

Ingredients

- Two and 1/4 cups of Almond Flour
- One and 1/4 cups of water
- 1/3 cup of Psyllium Husk Powder
- 3/4 cup of Ground Flax Seed
- Half cup of Wheat Gluten
- Two teaspoons of Coconut Palm Sugar
- 1/3 cup of seed mix
- Six whole Eggs, lightly mixed
- Two tablespoons of yeast
- 1/3 cup of Extra Virgin Olive Oil
- One teaspoon of Sea Salt

Instructions

1. Put all the required ingredients in the container of the bread machine in the suggested order by the manufacturer.

2. Select a gluten-free or basic cycle. Medium crust. Press the start button.
3. Scrap the sides of the pan with a rubber spatula after the kneading cycle.
4. Enjoy fresh bread.

Almond Milk Bread

(Ready in about 3 hours 20 minutes I Servings- One loaf I Difficulty- Moderate)

Ingredients

- One and a half teaspoons of salt
- One tablespoon sliced unsalted butter
- Two teaspoons of fast-rising yeast
- Three cups of almond flour
- One and 1/8 cups of almond milk
- One tablespoon of sugar
- One teaspoon of xanthan gum

Instructions

1. Put all the required ingredients in the container of the bread machine in the suggested order by the manufacturer.
2. Select the basic cycle. Medium crust and Press the start button.
3. Enjoy fresh bread.

Flaxseed Bread

(Ready in about 3 hours 40 minutes I Servings- One loaf I Difficulty- Moderate)

Ingredients

- Half cup of ground flax seed
- Two teaspoons of bread machine yeast
- Three tablespoons of honey
- One and 1/3 Cup of warm water
- One and a half teaspoon of salt
- Two tablespoons of vegetable oil
- One and a half cup of gluten-free flour
- One and 1/3 Cup of almond flour

Instructions

1. Put all the required ingredients in the container of the bread machine in the suggested order by the manufacturer.
2. Select the basic cycle. Crust to your liking. Press the start button.
3. Serve fresh bread.

Almond Flour Bread

(Ready in about 3 hours 40 minutes I Servings- One loaf I Difficulty- Moderate)

Ingredients

- 1/4 cup of ground flaxseed meal
- Four whole eggs and one egg white
- One teaspoon of baking soda
- One teaspoon of cinnamon
- One tablespoon of apple cider vinegar
- Two tablespoons of honey
- Two tablespoons of coconut oil
- Half teaspoon of kosher salt

- Two and a half cups of blanched almond flour

Instructions

1. Put all the required ingredients in the container of the bread machine in the suggested order by the manufacturer.
2. Select the basic cycle. Crust to your liking. Press the start button.
3. Enjoy fresh bread.

Sandwich Bread

(Ready in about 3 hours 30 minutes I Servings- One loaf I Difficulty- Moderate)

Ingredients

- Three tablespoons of sugar
- 1/3 cup of half and half
- Three tablespoons of softened butter
- One and a half teaspoons of salt
- One cup of milk
- One and a half teaspoons of instant yeast
- Three and 3/4 cups of almond flour
- One teaspoon of xanthan gum

Instructions

1. Put all the required ingredients in the container of the bread machine in the suggested order by the manufacturer.
2. Select white bread cycle—Press the start button.
3. Enjoy fresh bread.

Macadamia Bread

(Ready in about 3 hours 40 minutes I Servings- One loaf I Difficulty- Moderate)

Ingredients

- ¾ cup of ripe bananas
- 2/3 cup of warm water
- Two tablespoons of softened butter
- Half cup of ground macadamia nuts
- One whole egg
- Three tablespoons of white sugar
- Two and ¾ teaspoons of bread machine
- One and ¼ teaspoons of salt
- Three and ¼ cups of almond flour
- One and a 1/4 teaspoon of xanthan gum

For Glaze,

- ¼ cup of sliced almonds
- One egg yolk mixed with one teaspoon of water

Instructions

1. Put all the required ingredients in the container of the bread machine in the suggested order by the manufacturer.
2. Select white bread cycle—Press the start button.
3. After the rising cycle, brush with yolk glaze and sprinkle the almonds on top.
4. Serve fresh bread.

Toasting Bread

(Ready in about 2 hours 50 minutes I Servings- One loaf I Difficulty- Moderate)

Ingredients

- A ¼-1/3 cup of water
- One teaspoon of vinegar
- One cup of lukewarm milk
- Half teaspoon of baking powder
- One and a half teaspoon of salt
- Two and 1/4 teaspoon of instant yeast
- Three and a half cups of all-purpose flour
- Two tablespoons of vegetable oil
- One and a half teaspoon of sugar

Instructions

1. Put all the required ingredients in the container of the bread machine in the suggested order by the manufacturer.
2. Add less water in a warm climate and more in colder weather.
3. Select basic white bread cycle. Press the start button.
4. Before the baking cycle, take the dough out and roll it in cornmeal, although this step is optional. Place back into the machine and let it bake.
5. Enjoy fresh bread.

Mediterranean Bread

(Ready in about 3 hours 40 minutes I Servings- One loaf I Difficulty- Moderate)

Ingredients

- ⅓ cup of crumbled feta cheese
- One cup of water
- Three and ¼ cups of almond flour
- One and ¼ teaspoons of salt
- One tablespoon of honey
- Extra virgin olive oil: 1 tablespoon
- Two teaspoons of dried oregano
- ¾ teaspoon of bread machine yeast
- Three cloves of minced garlic
- Half cup of sliced Kalamata olive
- One and 1/4 teaspoon of xanthan gum

Instructions

1. Put all the required ingredients in the container of the bread machine in the suggested order by the manufacturer.
2. Select the basic cycle. Press the start button.
3. Enjoy with soups

Italian Bread

(Ready in about 3 hours 40 minutes I Servings- One loaf I Difficulty- Moderate)

Ingredients

- One and a half teaspoon of salt
- Four and 1/4 cup of gluten-free whole wheat flour
- Two tablespoons of sugar
- One and a half cup of water
- Two teaspoons of bread machine yeast

- Two tablespoons of olive oil
- Two teaspoons of xanthan gum

Instructions

1. Place all ingredients in the container of the bread machine in the suggested order by the manufacturer.
2. Select the whole wheat cycle. Press the start button.
3. Serve fresh bread.

Keto Baguette

(Ready in about 2 hours 40 minutes I Servings- One loaf I Difficulty- Moderate)

Ingredients

- One and ¼ cups of warm water
- One teaspoon of salt
- Three and a half cups of gluten-free flour
- One and a half teaspoon of xanthan gum
- One package of active dry yeast

Instructions

1. Put all the required ingredients in the container of the bread machine in the suggested order by the manufacturer.
2. Select the dough cycle. Press the start button.
3. Take the dough out on a clean, floured surface.
4. Cut into half pieces. Make a 12" long shape from each piece.
5. Put on an oiled baking pan. Cover with a warm towel.
6. Let it rise for one hour. Let the oven preheat to 450 F.
7. Bake for 15-20 minutes, until golden brown.
8. Serve fresh.

Keto Brioche Bread

(Ready in about 2 hours 40 minutes I Servings- One loaf I Difficulty- Moderate)

Ingredients

- One and ¾ cups of keto-flour
- Two whole eggs and one yolk
- One and ¾ teaspoons of active dry yeast
- Three tablespoons of sugar
- ¾ teaspoon of salt
- Eight tablespoons of unsalted butter
- Two tablespoons of almond flour
- ¼ cup of water
- Two tablespoons of water

Instructions

1. Add all ingredients, except butter, to the bread machine in the manufacturer's suggested order.
2. Select basic bread cycle. Light crust and Press the start button. Cut butter into small pieces.
3. After the first kneading cycle, add one tablespoon of butter at a time.
4. Enjoy fresh bread.

Keto Focaccia

(Ready in about 3 hours 10 minutes I Servings- One loaf I Difficulty- Moderate)

Ingredients

- Three cups of whole wheat flour
- One cup of lukewarm water
- Two teaspoons of chopped garlic
- One and a half teaspoons of active dry yeast
- Two tablespoons of olive oil
- One tablespoon of chopped fresh rosemary
- half teaspoon of salt
- One and a half teaspoons of chopped fresh rosemary
- One teaspoon of xanthan gum

Instructions

1. Put all the required ingredients in the container of the bread machine in the suggested order by the manufacturer.
2. Select the dough cycle. Press the start button.
3. Take the dough out from the bread machine and put it in a 12" pizza pan. With clean fingers, dimple the bread.
4. Brush with olive oil and sprinkle fresh rosemary. Cover with wrap.
5. Let the oven preheat to 400 F.
6. Bake for 20-25 minutes, until golden brown.
7. Serve fresh bread.

Oregano Onion Focaccia

(Ready in about 3 hours 40 minutes I Servings- One loaf I Difficulty- Moderate)

Ingredients

Dough

- 3/4 cup of water
- One tablespoon of sugar
- Two tablespoons of olive oil
- One and a half teaspoons of yeast
- One teaspoon of salt
- Two tablespoons of shredded parmesan cheese
- 3/4 cup of shredded mozzarella cheese
- Two cups of almond flour
- 3/4 teaspoon of xanthan gum

Toppings

- Two minced garlic cloves
- Three tablespoons of butter
- Two medium sliced onions

Instructions

1. Add all ingredients of dough to the bread machine in the suggested order by the manufacturer.
2. Select the dough cycle. Press the start button.
3. Meanwhile, melt butter on medium flame and sauté garlic and onion until caramelized.
4. Take the dough out on an oiled baking sheet. Make the dough into 12" circles. Let it rise for half an hour until it doubles.
5. Let the oven preheat to 400 F. with a wooden spoon, make a depression into the dough.
6. Place topping on the dough. Bake for 15-20 minutes until golden brown.
7. Enjoy fresh bread.

Zucchini Ciabatta

(Ready in about 3 hours 40 minutes I Servings- One loaf I Difficulty- Moderate)

Ingredients

- One and a half teaspoons of Salt
- One and a half cups of Water
- One and a half teaspoons of Yeast
- One tablespoon of olive oil
- Three and 1/4 cups of flour
- One teaspoon of sugar
- Half cup of grated zucchini

Instructions

1. Make sure to dry well the grated zucchini.
2. Place all the required ingredients in the container of the bread machine in the suggested order by the manufacturer.
3. Select the dough cycle. Press the start button.
4. Once the dough cycle is completed, take the dough out. Try not to add any more flour to the dough.
5. Place in a floured bowl for 15 minutes, cover with plastic wrap.
6. Take out on the floured surface and half them. Make 13 by 14 oval shape. Let it rise for 45 minutes covered with a towel.
7. Let the oven preheat to 425 F. dimple the dough and put it in the middle rack's oven.
8. Bake for almost half an hour. During the baking process, spray with water after every 5-10 minutes.
9. Enjoy fresh bread.

Chapter 20-Gluten-Free Bread Recipes

The present youth is health-conscious and sometimes prefer to eat bread that is gluten-free or low in gluten. You can also make gluten-free bread in your bread machine. Some of the recipes for gluten-free bread are compiled in this chapter.

Gluten-Free White Bread

(Ready in about 3 hours 40 minutes I Servings- One loaf I Difficulty- Moderate)

Ingredients

- One and 1/3 cup of milk
- Two eggs mixed
- One teaspoon of vinegar
- Six tablespoons of oil
- One and a half cup of Whole-wheat flour
- Two teaspoons of quick yeast
- One teaspoon of salt
- Two tablespoons of sugar

Instructions

1. Mix the milk with vinegar and oil.
2. Put all the required ingredients in the container of the bread machine in the suggested order by the manufacturer.
3. Select basic rapid or gluten-free cycle. Press the start button.
4. Enjoy fresh bread.

Brown Rice Bread

(Ready in about 3 hours 40 minutes I Servings- One loaf I Difficulty- Moderate)

Ingredients

- Four cups of bread flour
- Half cup of cooked brown rice
- One and a half teaspoons of salt
- One and 1/4 cups of warm water
- Two and ¼ teaspoons of bread machine yeast
- One teaspoon of sugar

Instructions

1. Place all ingredients in the container of the bread machine in the suggested order by the manufacturer.
2. Select the basic cycle. Medium crust. Press the start button.
3. Enjoy fresh bread.

Brown Rice & Cranberry Bread

(Ready in about 3 hours 40 minutes I Servings- One loaf I Difficulty- Moderate)

Ingredients

- 1/4 cup of non-fat milk powder
- Two tablespoons of liquid honey
- 1/8 teaspoon of black pepper
- One and 1/4 cup of water
- One tablespoon of olive oil
- Three cups of bread flour
- 3/4 cup of cooked brown rice
- One and 1/4 teaspoon of salt
- 2/3 cup of dried cranberries
- 1/4 cup of pine nuts
- 3/4 teaspoon of celery seeds
- One teaspoon of bread machine

Instructions

1. Add all ingredients, except cranberries, to the bread machine in the suggested order by the manufacturer.
2. Select the basic cycle. Crust to your liking. Press the start button. Add cranberries to the signal ingredient.

3. Enjoy.

Gluten-Free Peasant Bread

(Ready in about 3 hours 40 minutes | Servings- One loaf | Difficulty- Moderate)

Ingredients

- One and a half tablespoons of vegetable oil
- Two teaspoons of xanthan gum
- One and a half cups of warm water
- One teaspoon of cider vinegar
- Two and a half cups of gluten-free baking flour
- One tablespoon of active dry yeast
- One teaspoon of salt
- Two whole eggs
- One tablespoon of white sugar

Instructions

1. Place all ingredients in the container of the bread machine in the suggested order by the manufacturer.
2. Select the basic cycle. Light crust. Press the start button.
3. Enjoy fresh bread.

Gluten-Free Hawaiian Loaf

(Ready in about 3 hours 40 minutes | Servings- One loaf | Difficulty- Moderate)

Ingredients

- Three tablespoons of oil
- Three and a half tablespoons of honey
- Two whole eggs
- One cup of pineapple juice
- Four cups of gluten-free flour
- Three tablespoons of skim dry milk
- One tablespoon of fast-rising yeast

Instructions

1. Put all the required ingredients in the container of the bread machine in the suggested order by the manufacturer.
2. Select the gluten-free cycle. Dark crust. Press the start button.
3. Enjoy fresh bread.

Vegan Gluten-Free Bread

(Ready in about 1 hour 45 minutes | Servings- One loaf | Difficulty- Moderate)

Ingredients

- One and a half teaspoon of xanthan gum
- Two tablespoons of olive oil
- Two and ¼ cups of gluten-free flour blend
- One tablespoon of ground flax seeds
- One and 2/5 cups of warm water
- Two and 1/4 teaspoon of Easy Bake yeast
- One teaspoon of sea salt

Instructions

1. Put all the required ingredients in the container of the bread machine in the suggested order by the manufacturer.
2. Select a gluten-free cycle—Press the start button.
3. Before the baking cycle begins, brush olive oil on the loaf and sprinkle seeds.
4. Enjoy fresh bread.

Gluten-Free Almond and Dried Fruit Holiday Bread

(Ready in about 3 hours 40 minutes | Servings- One loaf | Difficulty- Moderate)

Ingredients

For the dough:

- One and a half cups water
- Two teaspoons almond extract
- One teaspoon apple cider vinegar or rice vinegar
- Three large eggs, broken into a measuring cup to equal 3/4 cup (add water if needed)
- Two cups of white rice flour
- Half cup of potato starch flour
- Half cup tapioca flour or arrowroot
- Half cup dry buttermilk powder or nonfat dry milk
- 1/3 cup sugar or three tablespoons powdered fructose
- One tablespoon xanthan gum
- One and a half teaspoons ground cardamom
- Half teaspoon ground mace or nutmeg
- Grated zest of one lemon or one teaspoon dried lemon peel
- One and a half teaspoons salt
- One tablespoon bread machine yeast
- Half cup mixed dried fruit bits
- Two tablespoons currants
- 1/3 cup toasted slivered almonds

Instructions

1. To make the dough, place the ingredients, except the raisins, in the pan according to the order in the manufacturer's instructions. Set crust on medium and program for the Non-Gluten or Quick Yeast Bread cycle; press Start.
2. Set a kitchen timer for 5 minutes. When the timer rings, open the lid and add the dried fruit and almonds. Close the lid.
3. When the baking cycle ends, immediately remove the pan from the machine and place it on a rack. Let cool for 10 minutes before removing the loaf from the pan.
4. Place it on a rack with a plate underneath.
5. To make the lemon glaze, combine the confectioners' sugar, butter, and lemon juice in a small bowl. Immediately pour over the top of the loaf, letting it dribble down the sides. Let cool to room temperature before slicing.

Gluten-Free Cinnamon Raisin Bread

(Ready in about 3 hours 40 minutes | Servings- One loaf | Difficulty- Moderate)

Ingredients

- One and 1/4cups water
- One teaspoon apple cider vinegar or rice vinegar
- Three tablespoons vegetable or nut oil
- Three large eggs, broken into a measuring cup to equal 3/4 cup (add water if needed)
- One and 3/4 cups white rice flour
- One and 1/8 cups brown rice flour
- Half cup dry buttermilk powder or nonfat dry milk
- Three tablespoons sugar or powdered fructose
- Two teaspoons xanthan gum
- One and a half teaspoons ground cinnamon
- One and a half teaspoons salt
- Two and 3/4 teaspoons bread machine yeast
- 3/4 cup golden raisins or dried cranberries

Instructions

1. Place the ingredients, except the raisins, in the pan according to the order in the manufacturer's instructions. Set crust on medium and program for the Non-Gluten or Quick Yeast Bread cycle; press Start.
2. Set a kitchen timer for 5 minutes. When the timer rings, open the lid and add the raisins. Close the lid.
3. When the baking cycle ends, immediately remove the pan from the machine and place it on a rack. Let cool for 10 minutes before removing the loaf from the pan. Let the loaf cool to room temperature before slicing.

Gluten-Free Mock Light Rye

(Ready in about 3 hours 40 minutes I Servings- One loaf I Difficulty- Moderate)

Ingredients

- One and 1/4cups water
- Three tablespoons dark molasses
- One teaspoon apple cider or rice vinegar
- 1/4 cup vegetable or canola oil
- Three large eggs, broken into a measuring cup to equal 3/4 cup (add water if needed)
- Two and 1/4cups white rice flour
- 7/8 cup brown rice flour
- Half cup nonfat dry milk
- 1/4 cup dark brown sugar
- One tablespoon xanthan gum
- One tablespoon plus one teaspoon caraway seeds
- Grated zest of one large orange or two teaspoons dried orange peel
- One and a half teaspoons salt
- Two and 3/4 teaspoons bread machine yeast

Instructions

1. Place all the ingredients in the pan according to the order in the manufacturer's instructions. Set crust on dark and
2. program for the Non-Gluten or Quick Yeast Bread cycle; press Start.
3. When the baking cycle ends, immediately remove the pan from the machine and place it on a rack. Let cool for 10 minutes before removing the loaf from the pan. Let the loaf cool to room temperature before slicing.

Gluten-Free Ricotta Potato Bread

(Ready in about 3 hours 40 minutes I Servings- One loaf I Difficulty- Moderate)

Ingredients

- One and 1/3 cups of water
- 3/4 cup ricotta cheese
- One teaspoon apple cider vinegar or rice vinegar
- Three tablespoons vegetable or canola oil
- Three large eggs, broken into a measuring cup to equal 3/4 cup (add water if needed)
- Two and 1/4cups white rice flour
- Half cup instant potato flakes
- 1/3 cup potato starch flour
- 1/3 cup tapioca flour
- Half cup dry buttermilk powder or nonfat dry milk
- Three tablespoons sugar or powdered fructose
- Two teaspoons xanthan gum
- One and a half teaspoons salt
- 3/4 teaspoon baking soda
- Two and 3/4 teaspoons bread machine yeast

Instructions

1. Place all the ingredients in the pan according to the order in the manufacturer's instructions. Set crust on medium and program for the Non-Gluten or Quick Yeast Bread cycle; press Start
2. When the baking cycle ends, immediately remove the pan from the machine and place it on a rack. Let cool for 10 minutes before removing the loaf from the pan. Let the loaf cool to room temperature before slicing.

Gluten-Free Buttermilk White Bread

(Ready in about 3 hours 40 minutes I Servings- One loaf I Difficulty- Moderate)

Ingredients

- One cup of buttermilk
- Half cup of water
- One teaspoon apple cider vinegar or rice vinegar
- Four tablespoons butter or margarine, cut into pieces
- Four large egg whites, beaten until foamy
- One cup of white rice flour
- One cup of brown rice flour
- 3/1 cup potato starch flour
- 1/4 cup tapioca flour

- Three tablespoons light or dark brown sugar
- One tablespoon plus Half teaspoon xanthan gum
- One and a half teaspoons salt
- One tablespoon plus Half teaspoon machine yeast

Instructions

1. Place all the ingredients in the pan according to the order in the manufacturer's instructions. Set crust on medium and program for the Non-Gluten or Quick Yeast Bread cycle; press Start.
2. When the baking cycle ends, immediately remove the pan from the machine and place it on a rack. Let cool for 10 minutes before removing the loaf from the pan. Let the loaf cool to room temperature before slicing.

Gluten-Free Chickpea, Rice, and Tapioca Flour Bread

(Ready in about 3 hours 40 minutes I Servings- One loaf I Difficulty- Moderate)

Ingredients

- One and 1/4cups water
- One teaspoon apple cider vinegar or rice vinegar
- Three tablespoons maple syrup
- Three tablespoons olive oil
- Three large eggs, broken into a measuring cup to equal 3/4 cup (add water if needed)
- One cup of chickpea flour
- One cup of brown rice flour
- Half cup cornstarch
- Half cup tapioca flour
- Half cup nonfat dry milk
- Two tablespoons light brown sugar
- One tablespoon plus one teaspoon xanthan gum
- One and a half teaspoons salt
- Two 3/4 teaspoons bread machine yeast

Instructions

1. Place all the ingredients in the pan according to the order in the manufacturer's instructions. Set crust on dark and program for the Non-Gluten or Quick Yeast Bread cycle; press Start.
2. When the baking cycle ends, immediately remove the pan from the machine and place it on a rack. Let cool for 10 minutes before removing the loaf from the pan. Let the loaf cool to room temperature before slicing.

Low-Gluten White Spelt Bread

(Ready in about 3 hours 40 minutes I Servings- One loaf I Difficulty- Moderate)

Ingredients

- One cup of water
- 1/4 cup apple juice concentrate, thawed
- One and a half tablespoons canola oil or soft butter
- Three cups of white spelt flour
- 1/4 cup oat bran or cornmeal
- One tablespoon full-fat soy flour

- One and 1/4teaspoons salt
- One tablespoon bread machine yeast

Instructions

1. Place all the ingredients in the pan according to the order in the manufacturer's instructions. Set crust on medium and program for the Basic cycle; press Start. Test the dough ball, add 1 to 2 teaspoons spelt flour or water as needed, but leave the dough moist and slightly tacky.
2. When the baking cycle ends, immediately remove the pan from the machine and place it on a rack. Let cool for 10 minutes before removing the loaf from the pan. Let the loaf cool to room temperature before slicing.

Traditional Egg Bread

(Ready in about 3 hours 40 minutes I Servings- One loaf I Difficulty- Moderate)

Ingredients

Dry ingredients

- Two tablespoons active dry yeast
- Two and 1 /4 cups of Light Flour Blend
- One and 1 /4 cups of millet flour
- 1 /4 cup milk powder or Dari Free
- Two tablespoons granulated cane sugar
- Two and a half teaspoons baking powder
- One teaspoon xanthan gum
- Half teaspoon kosher or fine sea salt
- 1 /8 teaspoon ascorbic acid, optional

Wet ingredients

- One tablespoon honey or agave nectar
- 3 /4 cup water, warmed to 80°F (27°C)
- Three large eggs, at room temperature, beaten
- Six tablespoons of salted butter, melted and slightly cooled
- Two teaspoons apple cider vinegar

Instructions

1. Set the pan on the counter and insert the beater paddle(s). Unless otherwise directed by your machine's manufacturer, add the liquids first, then the dry ingredients, and finally the yeast.
2. Measure the yeast into a small bowl and set aside. Combine the remaining dry ingredients in a large mixing bowl, mixing until thoroughly combined. Set the bowl beside the yeast and pan.3. Mix the honey and water together in a 4-cup (1 liter) glass measuring cup. Add the remaining wet ingredients and mix again. Pour into the pan. Add the dry ingredients over the liquids' top, spreading them out with a spatula to completely cover the liquids. Make a shallow well in the center and pour in the yeast.
3. Place the pan in the machine, settle it in the center, and lock it in place. Close the lid and select: Gluten-free cycle, Loaf size, Medium crust, then press Start
4. About 3 minutes into the mixing process, open the lid and use the spatula to scrape down the pan's sides, avoiding the paddle. Push any flour that has accumulated around the edges and under the dough into the center. Check again once or twice during kneading, scraping the edges, corners, and under the dough. If the dough looks too wet or too dry, add a little flour blend or tiny amounts of warm water. Once

the mixing/kneading is done, leave the lid closed during the rise and bake cycles.

5. At the end of the bake cycle, lift the lid and check the temperature. When the bread reaches 206°F to 210°F (97°C to 99°C) on an instant-read thermometer inserted in the center, it is done. Remove the pan from the machine and set it on its side on a wire cooling rack. Leave the bread in the pan for a couple of minutes, then turn the pan upside down and slide the loaf onto the wire rack. Carefully remove the paddle if it is embedded in the bottom of the loaf. Let the bread cool, upside down, for at least 2 hours before slicing.

6. Store the bread in a resealable plastic bag or airtight container on the counter for up to 3 days. For longer storage, cut into even slices, double-wrap tightly in plastic, place in a resealable plastic bag, and freeze for up to 3 months.

Potato Bread

(Ready in about 3 hours 40 minutes | Servings- One loaf | Difficulty- Moderate)

Ingredients

Dry ingredients

- One tablespoon instant yeast
- Two and a half cups of Light Flour Blend or Whole-Grain Flour Blend
- Half cup of potato starch (not potato flour)
- Half cup Dari Free or milk powder
- Two tablespoons sugar
- Two teaspoons tapioca flour/starch
- Two teaspoons psyllium husk flakes or powder
- Two teaspoons kosher or fine sea salt
- 1 /8 teaspoon ascorbic acid, optional

Wet ingredients

- One and ¼ cups of water warmed to about 80°F (27°C)
- Two large eggs, at room temperature, beaten
- Two teaspoons apple cider vinegar
- Two tablespoons of non-dairy butter substitute, melted and slightly cooled
- One and a half cups of rice or mashed cooked and peeled potatoes

Instructions

1. Set the pan on the counter and insert the beater paddle(s). Unless otherwise directed by your machine's manufacturer, add the liquids first, then the dry ingredients, and finally the yeast.

2. Measure the yeast into a small bowl and set aside. In a large mixing bowl, mix the remaining dry ingredients together.

3. Mix the water, eggs, vinegar, and butter in a 4-cup (1 liter) glass measuring cup until smooth. Pour into the pan. Add the potatoes. Use a spatula to spread the dry ingredients over the wet ingredients. Make a shallow well in the center and pour in the yeast.

4. Place the pan in the machine, settle it in the center, and lock it in place. Close the lid and select the

Gluten-free cycle, Loaf size, Medium crust, and then press Start.

5. After the first kneading cycle, scrape the sides and bottom of the pan with a spatula to make sure all the dry ingredients are incorporated.

6. At the end of the bake cycle, lift the lid and check the temperature. The bread is done when it registers 206°F to 210°F (97°C to 99°C) on an instant-read thermometer inserted in the center of the loaf. Remove the pan from the machine and place it on its side on a wire rack. Leave the bread in the pan for a couple of minutes, then turn the pan upside down and slide the loaf onto the wire rack. Carefully remove the paddle if it is embedded in the bottom of the loaf. Let the bread cool while upside down for at least 2 hours before slicing.

7. Store the bread in a resealable plastic bag or airtight container on the counter for up to 3 days. For longer storage, cut into even slices, double-wrap tightly in plastic, place in a resealable plastic bag, and freeze for up to 3 months.

Herbed Sandwich Bread

(Ready in about 3 hours 40 minutes | Servings- One loaf | Difficulty- Moderate)

Ingredients

Dey ingredients

- Two tablespoons active dry yeast
- Three cups of Light Flour Blend
- 1 /4 cup granulated cane sugar
- One tablespoon baking powder
- Two teaspoons xanthan gum
- Two teaspoons kosher salt
- One teaspoon dried dill weed
- One teaspoon dried oregano
- One teaspoon dried basil
- One teaspoon dried thyme
- One teaspoon onion powder
- 1 /8 teaspoon ascorbic acid, optional

Wet ingredients

- Three large eggs, at room temperature, beaten
- One cup of plus two tablespoons 1% milk or water, warmed to about 80°F (27°C)
- 1 /4 cup olive oil
- Two teaspoons apple cider vinegar

Instructions

1. Set the pan on the counter and insert the beater paddle(s). Unless otherwise directed by your machine's manufacturer, add the liquids first, then the dry ingredients, and finally the yeast.

2. Measure the yeast into a small bowl and set aside. In a large mixing bowl, mix the remaining dry ingredients together.

3. In a 4-cup (1 liter) glass measuring cup, mix the wet ingredients together and pour into the pan. Use a spatula to spread the dry ingredients over the wet ingredients, covering completely. Make a shallow well in the center and pour in the yeast.

4. Place the pan in the machine, settle it in the center, and lock it in place. Close the lid and select: Gluten-

free cycle, Loaf size, Medium crust, and then press start

5. About 3 minutes after the machine has started mixing/kneading, open the lid and use a spatula to scrape the sides of the pan, avoiding the paddle, and push any loose flour into the center of the pan. Check again once or twice during the knead cycle, scraping any loose flour into the dough. If the dough/batter looks too wet or too dry, add a little flour blend or tiny amounts of warm water. Once the mix/knead-cycle is done, leave the lid closed during the rise and bake cycles.

6. At the end of the bake cycle, lift the lid and check the temperature. When the bread reaches 206°F to 210°F (97°C to 99°C) on an instant-read thermometer inserted in the center, it is done. Remove the pan from the machine and set it on its side on a wire cooling rack. Leave the bread in the pan for a couple of minutes, then turn the pan upside down and slide the loaf onto the wire rack. Carefully remove the paddle if it is embedded in the bottom of the loaf. Cool the loaf upside down for at least 2 hours before slicing.

7. Store the bread in a resealable plastic bag or airtight container on the counter for up to 3 days. For longer storage, cut into even slices, double-wrap tightly in plastic, place in a resealable plastic bag, and freeze for up to 3 months.

Easy Sorghum Sandwich Bread

(Ready in about 3 hours 40 minutes I Servings- One loaf I Difficulty- Moderate)

Ingredients

Dry ingredients

- Two tablespoons active dry yeast
- Two cups of Light Flour Blend
- One cup of sorghum flour
- 1 /4 cup granulated cane sugar
- 1 /4 cup milk powder or Dari Free
- Two teaspoons xanthan gum2 teaspoons baking powder
- One teaspoon kosher salt
- 1 /8 teaspoon ascorbic acid, optional

Wet ingredients

- Three large eggs, at room temperature, beaten
- One cup of water, heated to about 80°F (27°C)
- 1 /4 cup olive oil
- Two teaspoons apple cider vinegar

Instructions

1. Set the pan on the counter and insert the beater paddle(s). Unless otherwise directed by your machine's manufacturer, add the liquids first, then the dry ingredients, and finally the yeast.

2. Measure the yeast into a small bowl and set aside. In a large mixing bowl, mix the remaining dry ingredients together.

3. In a 4-cup (1 liter) glass measuring cup, mix the wet ingredients together and pour into the pan. Use a spatula to spread the dry ingredients over the wet ingredients, covering completely. Make a shallow well in the center and pour in the yeast.

4. Place the pan in the machine, settle it in the center, and lock it in place. Close the lid and select the Gluten-free cycle, Loaf size, Medium crust, and then press Start.

5. About 3 minutes into the mixing process, open the lid and use a spatula to scrape down the pan's sides, avoiding the paddle. Push any flour that has accumulated around the edges and under the dough into the center. Check again once or twice during kneading, scraping the edges, corners, and under the dough. If the dough looks too wet or too dry, add a little flour blend or tiny amounts of warm water. Once the mix/knead-cycle is done, leave the lid closed during the rise and bake cycles.

6. At the end of the bake cycle, lift the lid and check the temperature. When the bread reaches 206°F to 210°F (97°C to 99°C) on an instant-read thermometer inserted in the center, it is done. Remove the pan from the machine and set it on its side on a wire cooling rack. Leave the bread in the pan for a couple of minutes, then turn the pan upside down and slide the loaf onto the wire rack. Carefully remove the paddle if it is embedded in the bottom of the loaf. Let the bread cool for at least 2 hours before slicing.

7. Store the bread in a resealable plastic bag or airtight container on the counter for up to 3 days. For longer storage, cut into even slices, double-wrap tightly in plastic, place in a resealable plastic bag, and freeze for up to 3 months.

Sorghum-Oat Buttermilk Bread

(Ready in about 3 hours 40 minutes I Servings- One loaf I Difficulty- Moderate)

Ingredients

Dry ingredients

- Four teaspoons active dry yeast
- One and a half cups of sorghum flour
- One cup of Light Flour Blend
- Half cup gluten-free oat flour
- Half cup of buttermilk powder
- Three tablespoons of granulated cane sugar
- Two teaspoons xanthan gum
- Two teaspoons kosher or fine sea salt
- One and a half teaspoons baking powder
- Half teaspoon baking soda
- 1 /8 teaspoon ascorbic acid, optional

Wet Ingredients

- Two teaspoons honey
- One cup of plus two tablespoons water warmed to 80°F (27°C)
- Three large eggs, at room temperature, beaten
- 1 /4 cup olive oil
- One teaspoon apple cider vinegar

Instructions

1. Set the pan on the counter and insert the beater paddle(s). Unless otherwise directed by your machine's manufacturer, add the liquids first, then the dry ingredients, and finally the yeast.

2. Measure the yeast into a small bowl and set aside. In a large mixing bowl, mix the remaining dry ingredients together.

3. Mix the honey and water together in a 4-cup (1 liter) glass measuring cup to dissolve the honey. Add the remaining wet ingredients and mix again. Pour into the pan. Use a spatula to spread the dry ingredients over the wet ingredients, covering completely. Make a shallow well in the center and pour in the yeast.

4. Place the pan in the machine, settle it in the center, and lock it in place. Close the lid and select the Gluten-free cycle, Loaf size, Medium crust, and then press Start.

5. About 3 minutes after the machine has started mixing/kneading, open the lid and use a spatula to scrape the sides of the pan, avoiding the paddle, and push any loose flour into the center of the pan. Check again once or twice during kneading, scraping the edges, corners, and under the dough. If the dough looks too wet or too dry, add a little flour blend or tiny amounts of warm water. Once the mix/knead-cycle is done, leave the lid closed during the rise and bake cycles.

6. At the end of the bake cycle, lift the lid and check the temperature. When the bread reaches 206°F to 210°F (97°C to 99°C) on an instant-read thermometer inserted in the center, it is done. Remove the pan from the machine and set it on its side on a wire cooling rack. Leave the bread in the pan for a couple of minutes, then turn the pan upside down and slide the loaf onto the wire rack. Carefully remove the paddle if it is embedded in the bottom of the loaf. Let the bread cool upside down for at least 2 hours before slicing.

7. Store the bread in a resealable plastic bag or airtight container on the counter for up to 3 days. For longer storage, cut into even slices, double-wrap tightly in plastic, place in a resealable bag, and freeze for up to 3 months.

Oat Bread

(Ready in about 3 hours 40 minutes I Servings- One loaf I Difficulty- Moderate)

Ingredients

Dry ingredients
- Two tablespoons active dry yeast
- Two cups of Light Flour Blend
- One cup of gluten-free oat flour
- 1 /4 cup gluten-free oats or oatmeal
- 1 /4 cup granulated cane sugar
- Four teaspoons baking powder
- Two teaspoons xanthan gum
- One and 1 /4 teaspoons kosher or fine sea salt
- 1 /8 teaspoon ascorbic acid, optional

Wet ingredients
- Three large eggs, at room temperature, beaten
- One cup of plus two tablespoons of water warmed to about 80°F (27°C)
- 1 /4 cup of olive oil
- Two teaspoons apple cider vinegar

Topping
- Water for brushing
- Gluten-free oats, for sprinkling

Instructions

1. Set the pan on the counter and insert the beater paddle(s). Unless otherwise directed by your machine's manufacturer, add the liquids first, then the dry ingredients, and finally the yeast.

2. Measure the yeast into a small bowl and set aside. In a large mixing bowl, mix the remaining dry ingredients together.

3. In a 4-cup (1 liter) glass measuring cup, mix the wet ingredients together and pour into the pan. Use a spatula to spread the dry ingredients over the wet ingredients, covering completely. Make a shallow well in the center and pour in the yeast.

4. Place the pan in the machine, settle it in the center, and lock it in place. Close the lid and select: Gluten-free cycle, Loaf size, Medium crust, then press Start

5. About 3 minutes into the mixing process, open the lid and use a spatula to scrape down the pan's sides, avoiding the paddle. Push any flour that has accumulated around the edges into the center. Check again once or twice during kneading, scraping the edges, corners, and under the dough. If the dough looks too wet or too dry, add a little flour blend or tiny amounts of warm water. When the mix/knead-cycle is done, brush the top of the loaf with a little water and sprinkle with oats, then close the lid and leave it closed during the rise and bake cycles.

6. At the end of the bake cycle, lift the lid and check the temperature. When the bread reaches 206°F to 210°F (97°C to 99°C) on an instant-read thermometer inserted in the center, it is done. Remove the pan from the machine and set it on its side on a wire cooling rack. Leave the bread in the pan for a couple of minutes, then turn the pan upside down and slide the loaf onto the wire rack. Carefully remove the paddle if it is embedded in the bottom of the loaf. Let the bread cool for at least 2 hours before slicing.

7. Store the bread in a resealable plastic bag or airtight container on the counter for up to 3 days. For longer storage, cut into even slices, double-wrap tightly in plastic, place in a resealable plastic bag, and freeze for up to 3 months.

Honey Oat Bread

(Ready in about 3 hours 40 minutes I Servings- One loaf I Difficulty- Moderate)

Ingredients

Dry ingredients
- Two tablespoons active dry yeast
- One tablespoon active dry yeast
- Two cups of Light Flour Blend
- One cup of gluten-free oat flour
- 1 /4 cup milk powder or Dari Free
- Two tablespoons granulated cane sugar
- Two teaspoons xanthan gum
- Two teaspoons baking powder
- Two teaspoons kosher or fine sea salt
- 1 /8 teaspoon ascorbic acid, optional

Wet ingredients
- 1 /4 cup honey
- One cup of water warmed to 80°F (27°C)
- Three large eggs, at room temperature, beaten
- 1 /4 cup olive oil

- Two teaspoons apple cider vinegar

Topping
- Milk or water for brushing
- Gluten-free oats, for sprinkling

Instructions

1. Set the pan on the counter and insert the beater paddle(s). Unless otherwise directed by your machine's manufacturer, add the liquids first, then the dry ingredients, and finally the yeast.
2. Measure the yeast into a small bowl and set aside. In a large mixing bowl, mix the remaining dry ingredients together.
3. Mix the honey and water together in a 4-cup (1 liter) glass measuring cup to dissolve the honey. Add the remaining wet ingredients and mix again. Pour into the pan. Use a spatula to spread the dry ingredients over the wet ingredients, covering completely. Make a shallow well in the center and pour in the yeast.
4. Place the pan in the machine, settle it in the center, and lock it in place. Close the lid and select Gluten-free cycle, Loaf size, Medium crust, then press Start.
5. About 3 minutes into the mixing process, open the lid and use a spatula to scrape down the pan's sides and under the dough, avoiding the paddle. Push any flour that has accumulated into the center. Check again once or twice during kneading, scraping the edges, corners, and under the dough. If the dough looks too wet or too dry, add a little flour blend or tiny amounts of warm water.
6. When the mixing and kneading are done, gently brush the top of the bread with a little milk or water and sprinkle oats. Close the lid and do not open it during the rise and bake cycles.
7. At the end of the bake cycle, lift the lid and check the temperature. When the bread reaches 206°F to 210°F (97°C to99°C) on an instant-read thermometer inserted in the center, it is done. Remove the pan from the machine and set it on its side on a wire cooling rack. Leave the bread in the pan for a couple of minutes, then turn the pan upside down and slide the loaf onto the wire rack. Carefully remove the paddle if it is embedded in the bottom of the loaf. Let the loaf cool upside down for at least 2 hours before slicing.
8. Store the bread in a resealable plastic bag or airtight container on the counter for up to 3 days. For longer storage, cut into even slices, double-wrap tightly in plastic, place in a resealable plastic bag, and freeze for up to 3 months.

Walnut Oat Bread

(Ready in about 3 hours 40 minutes I Servings- One loaf I Difficulty- Moderate)

Ingredients

Dry Ingredients
- Two tablespoons active dry yeast
- Two cups of Light Flour Blend
- One cup of gluten-free oat flour
- Half cup of chopped walnuts
- 1 /4 cup of granulated cane sugar
- Four teaspoons of baking powder
- Two teaspoons xanthan gum
- One and 1 /4 teaspoons kosher or fine sea salt

- 1 /8 teaspoon ascorbic acid, optional

Wet ingredients
- Three large eggs, at room temperature, beaten
- One cup of plus one tablespoon water warmed to about 80°F (27°C)
- 1 /4 cup of olive oil
- Two teaspoons apple cider vinegar

Topping
- Water for brushing
- Gluten-free oats, for sprinkling

Instructions

1. Set the pan on the counter and insert the beater paddle(s). Unless otherwise directed by your machine's manufacturer, add the liquids first, then the dry ingredients, and finally the yeast.
2. Measure the yeast into a small bowl and set aside. In a large mixing bowl, mix the remaining dry ingredients together.
3. In a 4-cup (1 liter) glass measuring cup, mix the wet ingredients together and pour into the pan. Use a spatula to spread the dry ingredients over the wet ingredients, covering completely. Make a shallow well in the center and pour in the yeast.
4. Place the pan in the machine, settle it in the center, and lock it in place. Close the lid and select the Gluten-free cycle, Loaf size, Medium crust, and then press Start.
5. About 3 minutes into the mixing process, open the lid and use a spatula to scrape down the pan's sides, avoiding the paddle. Push any flour that has accumulated around the edges and under the dough into the center. Check again once or twice during kneading, scraping the edges, corners, and under the dough. If the dough looks too wet or too dry, add a little flour blend or tiny amounts of warm water.
6. Once the mix/knead cycle is done, gently brush the dough's top with a little water and sprinkle with oats. Gently press the oats into the dough to help them stick. Leave the lid closed and do not open it during the rise and bake cycles.
7. At the end of the bake cycle, lift the lid and check the temperature. When the bread reaches 206°F to 210°F (97°C to 99°C) on an instant-read thermometer inserted in the center, it is done. Remove the pan from the machine and set it on its side on a wire cooling rack. Turn the pan upside down and slide the loaf onto the wire rack. Carefully remove the paddle if it is embedded in the bottom of the loaf. Cool the bread on its side for at least 2 hours before slicing.
8. Store the bread in a resealable plastic bag or airtight container on the counter for up to 3 days. For longer storage, cut into even slices, double-wrap tightly in plastic, place in a resealable plastic bag, and freeze for up to 3 months.

Buckwheat Sandwich Bread

(Ready in about 3 hours 40 minutes I Servings- One loaf I Difficulty- Moderate)

Ingredients

Dry Ingredients
- Two tablespoons of active dry yeast
- Two cups of Light Flour Blend
- One cup of buckwheat flour

- Half cup milk powder or Dari Free
- 1 /4 cup flaxseed meal or ground flaxseed
- One tablespoon baking powder
- Two teaspoons xanthan gum
- One and a half teaspoons kosher or fine sea salt
- 1 /8 teaspoon ascorbic acid, optional

Wet Ingredients

- 1 /4 cup pure maple syrup, at room temperature
- One cup of plus two tablespoons water, heated to about 80°F (27°C)
- Three large eggs, at room temperature, beaten
- Three tablespoons olive oil
- Two teaspoons apple cider vinegar

Instructions

1. Set the pan on the counter and insert the beater paddle(s). Unless otherwise directed by your machine's manufacturer, add the liquids first, then the dry ingredients, and finally the yeast.
2. Measure the yeast into a small bowl and set aside. In a large mixing bowl, mix the remaining dry ingredients together.
3. Mix the maple syrup and water together in a 4-cup (1 liter) glass measuring cup to dissolve the syrup. Add the remaining wet ingredients and mix again. Pour into the pan. Use a spatula to spread the dry ingredients over the wet ingredients, covering completely. Make a shallow well in the center and pour in the yeast.
4. Place the pan in the machine, settle it in the center, and lock it in place. Close the lid and select: Gluten-free cycle, Loaf size, Medium crust, and then press Start
5. About 3 minutes into the mixing process, open the lid and use a spatula to scrape down the pan's sides, avoiding the paddle. Push any flour that has accumulated around the edges and under the dough into the center. Check again once or twice during kneading, scraping the edges, corners, and under the dough. If the dough looks too wet or too dry, add a little flour blend or tiny amounts of warm water. Once the mix/knead-cycle is done, leave the lid closed during the rise and bake cycles.
6. At the end of the bake cycle, lift the lid and check the temperature. When the bread reaches 206°F to 210°F (97°C to 99°C) on an instant-read thermometer inserted in the center, it is done. Remove the pan from the machine and set it on its side on a wire cooling rack. Leave the bread in the pan for a couple of minutes, then turn the pan upside down and slide the loaf onto the wire rack. Carefully remove the paddle if it is embedded in the bottom of the loaf. Cool the loaf upside down for at least 2 hours before slicing.
7. Store the bread in a resealable plastic bag or airtight container on the counter for up to 3 days. For longer storage, cut into even slices, double-wrap tightly in plastic, place in a resealable plastic bag and freeze for up to months.

Light Rye Bread

(Ready in about 3 hours 40 minutes I Servings- One loaf I Difficulty- Moderate)

Ingredients

Dry ingredients

- Two tablespoons active dry yeast
- Two cups of Light Flour Blend
- One cup of plus two tablespoons buckwheat flour
- 1 /4 cup milk powder or
- Two tablespoons firmly packed brown sugar
- Two tablespoons caraway seeds or one teaspoon caraway powder, optional
- Two tablespoons flaxseed meal or ground flaxseed (double this amount if not using caraway seeds)
- One tablespoon baking powder
- Two teaspoons xanthan gum
- Two teaspoons dried minced onions or shallots
- One and a half teaspoons gluten-free rye flavoring, optional
- One teaspoon kosher salt
- Half teaspoon dried dill weed
- 1 /8 teaspoon ascorbic acid, optional

Wet ingredients

- Three tablespoons honey
- One cup plus one tablespoon water, heated to about 80°F (27°C)
- Three large eggs, at room temperature, beaten
- Three tablespoons olive oil
- Two teaspoons apple cider vinegar
- One teaspoon finely grated orange zest, optional

Instructions

1. Set the pan on the counter and insert the beater paddle(s). Unless otherwise directed by your machine's manufacturer, add the liquids first, then the dry ingredients, and finally the yeast.
2. Measure the yeast into a small bowl and set aside. In a large mixing bowl, mix the remaining dry ingredients together. Mix the honey and water together in a 4-cup (1 liter) glass measuring cup to dissolve the honey. Add the remaining wet ingredients and mix again. Pour into the pan. Use a spatula to spread the dry ingredients over the wet ingredients, covering completely. Make a shallow well in the center and pour in the yeast.
3. Place the pan in the machine, settle it in the center, and lock it in place. Close the lid and select: Gluten-free cycle, Loaf size, Medium crust, and then press Start
4. About 3 minutes into the mixing process, open the lid and use a spatula to scrape down the pan's sides, avoiding the paddle. Push any flour that has accumulated around the edges and under the dough into the center. Check again once or twice during kneading, scraping the edges, corners, and under the dough. If the dough looks too wet or too dry, add a little flour blend or tiny amounts of warm water. Once

the mix/knead-cycle is done, leave the lid closed during the rise and bake cycles.

5. At the end of the bake cycle, lift the lid and check the temperature. When the bread reaches 206°F to 210°F (97°C to 99°C) on an instant-read thermometer inserted in the center, it is done. Remove the pan from the machine and set it on its side on a wire cooling rack. Leave the bread in the pan for a couple of minutes, then turn the pan upside down and slide the loaf onto the wire rack. Carefully remove the paddle if it is embedded in the bottom of the loaf. Let the bread cool upside down for at least 2 hours before slicing.

6. Store the bread in a resealable plastic bag or airtight container on the counter for up to 3 days. For longer storage, cut into even slices, double-wrap tightly in plastic, place in a resealable bag, and freeze for up to 3 months.

Dary Rye Bread

(Ready in about 3 hours 40 minutes I Servings- One loaf I Difficulty- Moderate)

Ingredients

Dry ingredients

- Two tablespoons active dry yeast
- Two cups of Light Flour Blend
- One cup of buckwheat flour
- Two tablespoons unsweetened cocoa powder
- Two tablespoons firmly packed brown sugar
- Two tablespoons caraway seeds or one teaspoon caraway powder, optional
- Two tablespoons flaxseed meal or ground flaxseed (double this amount if not using caraway seeds)
- One tablespoon baking powder
- Two teaspoons xanthan gum
- Two teaspoons instant espresso powder or instant coffee
- 1 /8 teaspoon ascorbic acid, optional
- Two teaspoons dried minced onions or shallots
- One and a half teaspoons gluten-free rye flavor, optional
- One teaspoon kosher salt
- Half teaspoon dried dill weed

Wet ingredients

- Three tablespoons molasses (not blackstrap)
- One cup of plus one tablespoon water, heated to about 80°F (27°C)
- Three large eggs, at room temperature, beaten
- Three tablespoons olive oil
- Two teaspoons apple cider vinegar
- One teaspoon finely grated orange zest, optional

Instructions

1. Set the pan on the counter and insert the beater paddle(s). Unless otherwise directed by your machine's manufacturer, add the liquids first, then the dry ingredients, and finally the yeast.

2. Measure the yeast into a small bowl and set aside. In a large mixing bowl, mix the remaining dry ingredients together. Mix the molasses and water together in a 4-cup (1 liter) glass measuring cup to dissolve the molasses. Add the remaining wet ingredients and mix again. Pour into the pan. Use a spatula to spread the dry ingredients over the wet ingredients, covering completely. Make a shallow well in the center and pour in the yeast.

3. Place the pan in the machine, settle it in the center, and lock it in place. Close the lid and select: Gluten-free cycle, Loaf size, Medium crust, and then press Start

4. About 3 minutes into the mixing process, open the lid and use a spatula to scrape down the pan's sides, avoiding the paddle. Push any flour that has accumulated around the edges or under the dough into the center. Check again once or twice during kneading, scraping the edges, corners, and under the dough. If the dough looks too wet or too dry, add a little flour blend or tiny amounts of warm water. Once the mix/knead-cycle is done, leave the lid closed during the rise and bake cycles.

5. At the end of the bake cycle, lift the lid and check the temperature. When the bread reaches 206°F to 210°F (97°C to 99°C) on an instant-read thermometer inserted into the center, it is done. Remove the pan from the machine and set it on its side on a wire cooling rack. Leave the bread in the pan for a couple of minutes, then turn the pan upside down and slide the loaf onto the wire rack. Carefully remove the paddle if it is embedded in the bottom of the loaf. Let the bread cool upside down for at least 2 hours before slicing.

6. Store the bread in a resealable plastic bag or airtight container on the counter for up to 3 days. For longer storage, cut into even slices, double-wrap tightly in plastic, place in a resealable plastic bag, and freeze for up to 3 months.

Delectable Brown Bread

(Ready in about 3 hours 40 minutes I Servings- One loaf I Difficulty- Moderate)

Ingredients

Dry ingredients

- Two tablespoons active dry yeast
- One and 1 /4 cups sorghum flour
- One cup of Light Flour Blend
- One cup of millet flour
- 1 /3 cup flaxseed meal or ground flaxseed
- Three tablespoons firmly packed brown sugar
- One tablespoon baking powder
- Two teaspoons xanthan gum1 teaspoon kosher salt
- 1 /8 teaspoon ascorbic acid, optional

Wet ingredients

- Two tablespoons molasses (not blackstrap)
- One and 1 /3 cups of buttermilk, warmed to about 80°F (27°C)
- Three large eggs, at room temperature, beaten

- 1 /4 cup of olive oil
- One teaspoon cider vinegar

Instructions

1. Set the pan on the counter and insert the beater paddle(s). Unless otherwise directed by your machine's manufacturer, add the liquids first, then the dry ingredients, and finally the yeast.
2. Measure the yeast into a small bowl and set aside. In a large mixing bowl, mix the remaining dry ingredients together.
3. Mix the molasses and buttermilk together in a 4-cup (1 liter) glass measuring cup to dissolve the molasses. Add the remaining wet ingredients and mix again. Pour into the pan. Use a spatula to spread the dry ingredients over the wet ingredients, covering completely. Make a shallow well in the center and pour in the yeast.
4. Place the pan in the machine, settle it in the center, and lock it in place. Close the lid and select: Gluten-free cycle, Loaf size, Medium crust, and press Start
5. About 3 minutes into the mixing process, open the lid and use a spatula to scrape down the pan's sides, avoiding the paddle. Push any flour that has accumulated around the edges and under the dough into the center. Check again once or twice during kneading, scraping the edges, corners, and under the dough. If the dough looks too wet or too dry, add a little flour blend or tiny amounts of warm water. Once the mix/knead-cycle is done, leave the lid closed during the rise and bake cycles.
6. At the end of the bake cycle, lift the lid and check the temperature. When the bread reaches 206°F to 210°F (97°C to 99°C) on an instant-read thermometer inserted in the center, it is done. Remove the pan from the machine and set it on its side on a wire cooling rack. Leave the bread in the pan for a couple of minutes, then turn the pan upside down and slide the loaf onto the wire rack. Carefully remove the paddle if it is embedded in the bottom of the loaf. Let the bread cool upside down for at least 2 hours before slicing.
7. Store the bread in a resealable plastic bag or airtight container on the counter for up to 3 days. For longer storage, cut into even slices, double-wrap tightly in plastic, place in a resealable plastic bag, and freeze for up to 3 months.

California Brown Bread

(Ready in about 3 hours 40 minutes | Servings- One loaf | Difficulty- Moderate)

Ingredients

Dry ingredients

- One tablespoon active dry yeast
- Two cups of Light Flour Blend
- 3 /4 cup sorghum flour
- 1 /4 cup milk powder or Dari Free
- 1 /4 cup corn flour or masa harina
- Two tablespoons granulated cane sugar
- One tablespoon baking powder
- Two teaspoons xanthan gum
- One and a half teaspoons kosher or fine sea salt
- Half cup dried currants or golden raisins, optional

- 1 /8 teaspoon ascorbic acid, optional

Wet ingredients

- Half cup molasses (not blackstrap)
- One cup of plus one tablespoon water, heated to about 80°F (27°C)
- Two large eggs, at room temperature, beaten
- 1 /4 cup olive oil
- Two teaspoons apple cider vinegar

Instructions

1. Set the pan on the counter and insert the beater paddle(s). Unless otherwise directed by your machine's manufacturer, add the liquids first, then the dry ingredients, and finally the yeast.
2. Measure the yeast into a small bowl and set aside. Mix the remaining dry ingredients—except the currants—together in a large mixing bowl. Stir in the currants, if using.
3. In a 4-cup (1 liter) glass measuring cup, mix the molasses and warm water to dissolve the molasses. Mix in the remaining wet ingredients and pour them into the pan. Use a spatula to spread the dry ingredients over the wet ingredients, covering completely. Make a shallow well in the center and pour in the yeast.
4. Place the pan in the machine, settle it in the center, and lock it in place. Close the lid and select the Gluten-free cycle, Loaf size, Medium crust, and press Start
5. About 3 minutes after the machine has started mixing/kneading, open the lid, and use a spatula to scrape the sides of the pan, avoiding the paddle. Push any loose flour into the center of the pan. Check again once or twice during the knead cycle, scraping the sides, corners, and under the dough. If the dough looks too wet or too dry, add a little flour blend or tiny amounts of warm water. Once the mix/knead-cycle is done, leave the lid closed during the rise and bake cycles.
6. At the end of the bake cycle, lift the lid and check the temperature. When the bread reaches 206°F to 210°F (97°C to 99°C) on an instant-read thermometer inserted in the center, it is done. Remove the pan from the machine and set it on its side on a wire cooling rack. Leave the bread in the pan for a couple of minutes, then turn the pan upside down and slide the loaf onto the wire rack. Carefully remove the paddle if it is embedded in the bottom of the loaf. Let the bread cool upside down for at least 2 hours before slicing.
7. Store the bread in a resealable plastic bag or airtight container on the counter for up to 3 days. For longer storage, cut into even slices, double-wrap tightly in plastic, place in a resealable plastic bag, and freeze for up to 3 months.

Paleo Bread

(Ready in about 3 hours 40 minutes | Servings- One loaf | Difficulty- Moderate)

Ingredients

Dry ingredients

- One tablespoon active dry yeast

- One cup of arrowroot
- One cup of tapioca flour
- 2 /3 cup coconut sugar
- 1 /3 cup coconut flour
- One teaspoon kosher or fine sea salt
- One and a half teaspoons baking soda
- 1 /4 teaspoon cream of tartar
- 3 /4 cup flaxseed meal or ground flaxseed
- One cup of sunflower seeds, ground to the consistency of sand in a food processor

Wet ingredients

- One cup of water warmed to about 80°F (27°C)
- Two large eggs, at room temperature, beaten
- 1 /3 cup coconut oil, melted and slightly cooled
- Two teaspoons apple cider vinegar

Instructions

1. Set the pan on the counter and insert the beater paddle(s). Unless otherwise directed by your machine's manufacturer, add the liquids first, then the dry ingredients, and finally the yeast.
2. Measure the yeast into a small bowl and set aside. In a large mixing bowl, mix the remaining dry ingredients together.
3. In a 4-cup (1 liter) glass measuring cup, mix the wet ingredients together. Scrape the mixture into the pan. Use a spatula to spread the dry ingredients over the wet ingredients. Make a shallow well in the center and pour in the yeast.
4. Place the pan in the machine, settle it in the center, and lock it in place. Close the lid and select: Gluten-free cycle, Loaf size, Medium crust, then press Start
5. After the first kneading cycle, scrape the sides and bottom of the pan with the spatula to make sure all the dry ingredients are incorporated. Once the mix/knead-cycle is done, leave the lid closed during the rise and bake cycles.
6. At the end of the bake cycle, lift the lid and check the temperature. When the bread registers 206°F to 210°F (97°C to 99°C) on an instant-read thermometer inserted in the center, it is done. Remove the pan from the machine and set it on its side on a wire rack. Leave the bread in the pan for a couple of minutes, then turn the pan upside down and slide the loaf onto the wire rack. Carefully remove the paddle if it is embedded in the bottom of the loaf. Let the bread cool on its side for at least 2 hours before slicing.
7. Store the bread in a resealable plastic bag or airtight container on the counter for up to 3 days. For longer storage, cut into even slices, double-wrap tightly in plastic, place in a resealable plastic bag, and freeze for up to 3 months.

Monkey Bread

(Ready in about 3 hours 40 minutes I Servings- One loaf I Difficulty- Moderate)

Ingredients

Dry ingredients

- Two tablespoons instant yeast
- Two and a half cups of Light Flour Blend or Whole-Grain Flour Blend
- Half cup of millet flour
- 1 /4 cup granulated cane sugar
- One tablespoon baking powder
- One tablespoon psyllium husk flake or powder1 teaspoon dough enhancer
- Half teaspoon kosher or fine sea salt

Wet ingredients

- Half cup unsweetened coconut milk
- Three large eggs, at room temperature, beaten
- Four tablespoons non-dairy butter substitute, melted and slightly cooled
- Two teaspoons apple cider vinegar

Topping

- Six tablespoons non-dairy butter substitute, melted
- One cup of firmly packed brown sugar
- Two tablespoons ground cinnamon

Instructions

1. Set the pan on the counter and insert the beater paddle(s). Unless otherwise directed by your machine's manufacturer, add the liquids first, then the dry ingredients, and finally the yeast.
2. Measure the yeast into a small bowl and set aside. In a large mixing bowl, mix the remaining dry ingredients together.
3. In a 4-cup (0.5 liters) glass measuring cup, mix the wet ingredients together and pour them into the pan. Use a spatula to spread the dry ingredients over the wet ingredients. Make a shallow well in the center and pour in the yeast.
4. Place the pan in the machine, settle it in the center, and lock it in place. Close the lid and select Dough cycle, loaf size, and Start.
5. While the machine is mixing and kneading, open the lid and use a spatula to scrape down the pan's sides, pushing any flour that has accumulated around the edges and under the dough into the center. Let the machine mix the dough until it is smooth and has no lumps, about 5 minutes. Press the stop button to cancel the cycle, turn off the machine, and remove the pan.
6. Put the melted butter for the topping in a shallow bowl. In a separate shallow bowl, mix the brown sugar and cinnamon. Oil a 10-cup (2.4 liters) Bundt pan and set it next to the butter and cinnamon sugar.
7. Turn out the dough onto a lightly oiled work surface. With lightly oiled hands, pat or roll the dough into an 8 × 12-inch (20 × 30 cm) rectangle. Cut into one and a half-inch (4 cm) pieces and roll each piece into a ball. Dip the dough balls into butter, then roll them in cinnamon-sugar. Arrange the dough balls evenly in the Bundt pan, building the layers by placing them slightly offset from the row below. Cover with plastic wrap and let rest for 30 to 40 minutes.
8. Preheat the oven to 350°F (180°C).
9. Bake until an instant-read thermometer inserted into the loaf center reads at least 190°F (88°C), 30 to 35 minutes. Transfer the pan to a wire rack. Leave the bread in the pan for 3 minutes, then set a plate on top and, holding the two together with pot holders to protect your hands, quickly flip them so that the bread falls out of the pan and onto the plate. Let the bread

cool slightly before serving. This bread is best on the day it is baked.

Mexican Salsa Bread

(Ready in about 3 hours 40 minutes I Servings- One loaf I Difficulty- Moderate)

Ingredients

Dry ingredients

- Two tablespoons active dry yeast
- Three cups of Light Flour Blend
- 1 /4 cup corn flour or masa harina
- 1 /4 cup granulated cane sugar
- One tablespoon baking powder
- One tablespoon chopped fresh cilantro
- Two and a Half teaspoons tomato powder
- Two teaspoons xanthan gum
- One teaspoon red pepper flake, or to taste
- One teaspoon onion powder
- One teaspoon smoked sea salt or kosher salt
- 1 /8 teaspoon ascorbic acid, optional

Wet ingredients

- Three large eggs, at room temperature, beaten
- One cup of plus Three tablespoons water warmed to about 80°F (27°C)
- 1 /4 cup olive oil
- Two teaspoons apple cider vinegar

Instructions

1. Set the pan on the counter and insert the beater paddle(s). Unless otherwise directed by your machine's manufacturer, add the liquids first, then the dry ingredients, and finally the yeast.
2. Measure the yeast into a small bowl and set aside. In a large mixing bowl, mix the remaining dry ingredients together.3. In a 4-cup (1 liter) glass measuring cup, mix the wet ingredients together and pour into the pan. Use a spatula to spread the dry ingredients over the wet ingredients, covering completely. Make a shallow well in the center and pour in the yeast.
3. Place the pan in the machine, settle it in the center, and lock it in place. Close the lid and select: Gluten-free cycle, Loaf size, Medium crust, and then press Start
4. About 3 minutes into the mixing process, open the lid and use a spatula to scrape down the pan's sides, avoiding the paddle. Push any flour that has accumulated around the edges and under the dough into the center. Check again once or twice during kneading, scraping the edges, corners, and under the dough. If the dough looks too wet or too dry, add a little flour blend or tiny amounts of warm water. Once the mix/knead-cycle is done, leave the lid closed during the rise and bake cycles.
5. At the end of the bake cycle, lift the lid and check the temperature. When the bread reaches 206°F to 210°F (97°C to 99°C) on an instant-read thermometer inserted in the center, it is done. Remove the pan from the machine and set it on its side on a wire cooling rack. Leave the bread in the pan for a couple of minutes, then turn the pan upside down and slide the loaf onto the wire rack. Carefully remove the paddle if it is embedded in the bottom of the loaf. Let

the bread cool upside down for at least 2 hours before slicing.

6. Store the bread in a resealable plastic bag or airtight container on the counter for up to 3 days. For longer storage, cut into even slices, double-wrap tightly in plastic, place in a resealable plastic bag, and freeze for up to 3 months.

Pizza Pie Bread

(Ready in about 3 hours 40 minutes I Servings- One loaf I Difficulty- Moderate)

Ingredients

Dry ingredients

- Two tablespoons active dry yeast
- Three cups of Light Flour Blend
- Half cup milk powder
- Three tablespoons granulated cane sugar
- Two tablespoons very finely grated Parmesan cheese or powdered cheddar cheese
- One tablespoon baking powder
- One tablespoon dried oregano
- Two teaspoons xanthan gum
- Two teaspoons kosher salt
- Two teaspoons dried basil
- One and a Half teaspoons onion powder
- One and a Half teaspoons tomato powder (see Resources)
- 1 /4 teaspoon garlic powder
- 1 /8 teaspoon ascorbic acid, optional

Wet ingredients

- Three large eggs, at room temperature, beaten
- One cup of plus Two tablespoons water, heated to about 80°F (27°C)
- 1 /4 cup olive oil
- Two teaspoons apple cider vinegar

Instructions

1. Set the pan on the counter and insert the beater paddle(s). Unless otherwise directed by your machine's manufacturer, add the liquids first, then the dry ingredients, and finally the yeast.
2. Measure the yeast into a small bowl and set aside. In a large mixing bowl, mix the remaining dry ingredients together.
3. In a 4-cup (1 liter) glass measuring cup, mix the wet ingredients together and pour into the pan. Use a spatula to spread the dry ingredients over the wet ingredients, covering completely. Make a shallow well in the center and pour in the yeast.
4. Place the pan in the machine, settle it in the center, and lock it in place. Close the lid and select: Gluten-free cycle, Loaf size, Medium crust, and then Start
5. About 3 minutes into the mixing process, open the lid and use a spatula to scrape down the pan's sides, avoiding the paddle. Push any flour that has accumulated around the edges and under the dough into the center. Check again once or twice during kneading, scraping the edges, corners, and under the dough. If the dough looks too wet or too dry, add a little flour blend or tiny amounts of warm water. Close

the lid and do not open it during the rise and bake cycles.

6. At the end of the bake cycle, lift the lid and check the temperature. When the bread reaches 206°F to 210°F (97°C to 99°C) on an instant-read thermometer inserted in the center, it is done. Remove the pan from the machine and set it on its side on a wire cooling rack. Leave the bread in the pan for a couple of minutes, then turn the pan upside down and slide the loaf onto the wire rack. Carefully remove the paddle if it is embedded in the bottom of the loaf. Let the loaf cool upside down for at least 2 hours before slicing.

7. Store the bread in a resealable plastic bag or airtight container on the counter for up to 3 days. For longer storage, cut into even slices, double-wrap tightly in plastic, place in a resealable plastic bag, and freeze for up to 3 months.

Gluten-Free Ricotta Potato Bread

(Ready in about 3 hours 40 minutes I Servings- One loaf I Difficulty- Moderate)

Ingredients

- One and 1/3 cups of water
- 3/4 cup ricotta cheese
- One teaspoon apple cider vinegar or rice vinegar
- Three tablespoons vegetable or canola oil
- Three large eggs, broken into a measuring cup to equal 3/4 cup (add
- water if needed)
- Two and 1/4cups white rice flour
- Half cup instant potato flakes
- 1/3 cup potato starch flour
- 1/3 cup tapioca flour
- Half cup dry buttermilk powder or nonfat dry milk
- Three tablespoons sugar or powdered fructose
- Two teaspoons xanthan gum
- One and a half teaspoons salt
- 3/4 teaspoon baking soda
- Two and 3/4 teaspoons bread machine yeast

Instructions

1. Place all the ingredients in the pan according to the order in the manufacturer's instructions. Set crust on medium and program for the Non-Gluten or Quick Yeast Bread cycle; press Start

2. When the baking cycle ends, immediately remove the pan from the machine and place it on a rack. Let cool for 10 minutes before removing the loaf from the pan. Let the loaf cool to room temperature before slicing.

Chapter 21-Sourdough Bread Recipes

Sourdough is a divine bread, and the bread machine can also help you make them. Some of the sourdough bread that you can make with the help of your bread machine is provided below with detailed recipes

Basic Sourdough Bread

(Ready in about 3 hours 22 minutes | Servings- One loaf | Difficulty- Moderate)

Ingredients

- One and a half teaspoons of salt
- Two teaspoons of active dry yeast
- One and a half teaspoons of sugar
- Six tablespoons of lukewarm water
- Two cups of ripe sourdough starter
- Two and a half cups of All-Purpose Flour
- Two tablespoons of vegetable oil

Instructions

1. Put all the required ingredients in the container of the bread machine in the suggested order by the
2. manufacturer.
3. Select French bread or long-rise cycle. Press the start button.
4. After ten minutes of kneading, check the dough and more flour or water, if necessary, to make the dough smooth and soft.
5. Serve fresh bread.

Whole-Wheat Sourdough Bread

(Ready in about 3 hours 10 minutes | Servings- One loaf | Difficulty- Moderate)

Ingredients

- One tablespoon and one teaspoon of oil
- Two teaspoons of sugar
- Half cup and three tablespoons of water

- ¾ cup of whole wheat sourdough starter
- One and a half teaspoon of Active Dry Yeast
- Two and a ¼ cups of whole wheat flour
- One teaspoon of salt

Instructions

1. All the ingredients should be at room temperature, oil, and water at 80 F.
2. Put all the required ingredients in the container of the bread machine in the suggested order by the manufacturer.
3. Select whole wheat and medium crust, not the delay feature. Check dough and add water and flour, if needed.
4. Serve fresh bread.

Multigrain Sourdough Bread

(Ready in about 3 hours 10 minutes | Servings- One loaf | Difficulty- Moderate)

Ingredients

- 3/4 cup of Sourdough Starter
- 2/3 cup of 7 Grain Cereal (Hot)
- One and a half tablespoon of butter
- 3/4 teaspoon of sea salt
- One tablespoon of Wheat Gluten
- Two tablespoons of Water or Flour to make the dough smooth
- Two and a half Tablespoon of packed Brown Sugar
- Three cups of All-Purpose Flour

- One and a half teaspoon of Active Dry Yeast
- 2/3 cup of water

Instructions

1. Put all the required ingredients in the container of the bread machine in the suggested order by the manufacturer.
2. Select basic bread. Light crust. Press the start button.
3. Serve fresh bread.

Faux Sourdough Bread

(Ready in about 3 hours 10 minutes I Servings- One loaf I Difficulty- Moderate)

Ingredients

- One and a half teaspoon of salt
- Half cup of plain yogurt
- One tablespoon of lemon juice
- Two teaspoons of Active dry yeast
- One tablespoon of canola oil
- Three cups of bread flour
- 3/4 cup of water

Instructions

1. Put all the required ingredients in the container of the bread machine in the suggested order by the manufacturer.
2. Select French or white bread cycle, light crust. Press the start button.
3. Serve fresh bread.

Sourdough Milk Bread

(Ready in about 3 hours 10 minutes I Servings- One loaf I Difficulty- Moderate)

Ingredients

- Four tablespoons of sugar
- Four cups of bread flour
- One and a ¼ teaspoon of salt
- One and a half cups of sour milk or regular milk
- One and a ¾ teaspoons of active dry yeast
- One and a half Tablespoons of oil

Instructions

1. If using sour milk, you can make it by adding one tablespoon of vinegar to one cup of room temperature milk. Let it rest for five minutes.
2. Put all the required ingredients in the container of the bread machine in the suggested order by the manufacturer.
3. Select a basic setting, medium crust. Press the start button.
4. Check dough after 5-10 minutes of kneading, add one tablespoon of water or flour if the dough is too dry or too wet, respectively.

Lemon Sourdough Bread

(Ready in about 3 hours 10 minutes I Servings- One loaf I Difficulty- Moderate)

Ingredients

- Two teaspoons of lemon juice
- 1/3 cup of plain yogurt
- Half cup of water

- One teaspoon of salt
- Two tablespoons of softened butter
- One and a 3/4 teaspoon of regular active dry yeast
- Two cups of bread flour
- Two teaspoons of sugar

Instructions

1. Put all the required ingredients in the container of the bread machine in the suggested order by the manufacturer.
2. Do not use a delay cycle: select white bread or French bread—Press the start button.
3. Enjoy fresh bread.

San Francisco Sourdough Bread

(Ready in about 3 hours 10 minutes I Servings- One loaf I Difficulty- Moderate)

Ingredients

- 3/4 cup of lukewarm water
- Two teaspoons of salt
- 1/4 teaspoon of baking soda
- One cup of room temperature sourdough starter
- Three cups of bread flour

Glaze

- One teaspoon of cornstarch
- Half cup of cold water

Instructions

1. Place all ingredients in the pan of the bread machine.
2. Select basic bread, light crust. Press the start button.
3. Enjoy warm bread.

Sourdough Beer Bread

(Ready in about 3 hours 10 minutes I Servings- One loaf I Difficulty- Moderate)

Ingredients

- Two tablespoons of vegetable oil
- One and 1/Three cups of sourdough starter
- Half cup of flat beer
- Three cups of bread flour
- One and a half teaspoons of salt
- 1/4 cup of water
- One and a half teaspoons of yeast
- One tablespoon of sugar

Instructions

1. Put all the required ingredients in the container of the bread machine in the suggested order by the manufacturer.
2. Select white bread, dark crust if you like—Press the start button.
3. Enjoy fresh bread.

Crusty Sourdough Bread

(Ready in about 3 hours 40 minutes I Servings- One loaf I Difficulty- Moderate)

Ingredients

- Three cups of bread flour

- Half cup of water
- One cup of Sourdough Starter
- Two tablespoons of sugar
- One teaspoon of bread machine yeast
- One and a half teaspoons of salt

Instructions

1. Put all the required ingredients in the container of the bread machine in the suggested order by the manufacturer.
2. Select the white cycle, light crust. Press the start button.
3. Enjoy fresh bread.

Sourdough Cheddar Bread

(Ready in about 3 hours 10 minutes | Servings- One loaf | Difficulty- Moderate)

Ingredients

- One cup of sourdough starter
- One and a half teaspoons of salt
- One and a half teaspoons of yeast
- Half cup of warm water
- One and a half tablespoons of sugar
- Three cups of bread flour
- 3⁄4 cup of grated sharp cheddar cheese

Instructions

1. Put all the required ingredients in the container of the bread machine in the suggested order by the manufacturer.
2. Select French bread, light crust. Press the start button.
3. Enjoy fresh bread.

Herb Sourdough

(Ready in about 3 hours 10 minutes | Servings- One loaf | Difficulty- Moderate)

Ingredients

- Three tablespoons of sugar
- 3⁄4 cup of water
- One and a half teaspoons of salt
- Three or three and a half cups of bread flour
- One teaspoon of dried parsley
- One and 1⁄4 cups of sourdough starter
- One and a half teaspoons of dried Rosemary
- Two tablespoons of Soy margarine

Instructions

1. Put all the required ingredients in the container of the bread machine in the suggested order by the manufacturer.
2. Start with three cups of flour. Select basic cycle, light crust. Press the start button.
3. Check dough after 5-10 minutes; if it needs more flour, add one tablespoon of flour.
4. Serve fresh bread.

Cranberry Pecan Sourdough

(Ready in about 3 hours 10 minutes | Servings- One loaf | Difficulty- Moderate)

Ingredients

- One dried package of sweetened cranberries

- Two tablespoons and one and a 1⁄4 cup of water
- Two teaspoons of salt
- 3⁄4 cup toasted chopped pecans
- Four cups of bread flour
- Two tablespoons of butter
- Two teaspoons of yeast
- Two tablespoons of non-fat powdered milk
- 1⁄4 cup of sugar

Instructions

1. Place all ingredients in the bread machine as per the suggested order by the manufacturer.
2. Select white bread setting, medium crust. Press the start button.
3. Enjoy fresh bread.

Dark Chocolate Sourdough

(Ready in about 3 hours 10 minutes | Servings- One loaf | Difficulty- Moderate)

Ingredients

- 3⁄4 cup of lukewarm water
- Half cup of cocoa powder
- One cup of sourdough starter
- One tablespoon of sugar
- Half cup of finely diced dark chocolate
- Three tablespoons of oil
- Two teaspoons of salt
- One tablespoon of active dry yeast
- Three cups of bread flour

Instructions

1. Put all the required ingredients in the container of the bread machine in the suggested order by the manufacturer.
2. Select the basic cycle. Light crust. Press the start button.
3. Check dough's consistency if it's too wet and sticky and requires more flour. Add one tablespoon of flour at a time.
4. Serve fresh bread.

German Beer Starter

(Ready in about 3 hours 40 minutes | Servings- One and a half cup starter | Difficulty- Moderate)

Ingredients

- 3/4 cup unbleached all-purpose or bread flour
- Two tablespoons rye flour Large pinch of active dry, bread machine, or SAF yeast
- One cup of flat beer

Instructions

1. Mix together the flour, yeast, and beer in a medium bowl. The mixture will be smooth and thick. Transfer to a plastic container or crock. Cover with a few cheesecloth layers and secure with a rubber band; then cover loosely with plastic wrap.
2. Let stand at warm room temperature for 24 hours to 48 hours (80°F is optimum), stirring a few times. It will be bubbly and smell strongly fermented. Use immediately or store in the

refrigerator, covered loosely, until you are ready to use it.

French Buttermilk Starter

(Ready in about 3 hours 40 minutes I Servings- One and a half cup starter I Difficulty- Moderate)

Ingredients

- 3/4 cup unbleached all-purpose or bread flour
- Large pinch of active dry, bread machine, or SAF yeast
- One to One and 1/4cups low-fat buttermilk

For the first feeding:

- Two tablespoons unbleached all-purpose or bread flour
- Three tablespoons water

Instructions

1. Mix together the 3/4 cup flour, yeast, and buttermilk in a medium bowl; the mixture should be thick like a pancake batter. Add a bit more flour to adjust the consistency, if necessary. Transfer to a plastic container or crock. Cover with a few cheesecloth layers and secure with a rubber band; then cover loosely with plastic wrap. Let stand at warm room temperature 24 hours (80°F is optimum). It will be bubbly, begin to ferment and smell delightful. There will be tiny yellow dots of butter from the buttermilk on the top.
2. After 36 hours, when the starter begins to smell sour, feed it with the Two tablespoons of flour and the water; mix to combine. Let stand for 1 to 2 more days until the desired degree of sourness is achieved. This starter can be used 3 or 4
3. days after it is initially mixed. The longer you let it sit, the sourer it will be; you can judge how sour the starter has become by the way it smells. If you are not ready to use it after 3 or 4 days, let it stand a few more days to continue to sour, or store it in the refrigerator, covered loosely, until you are ready to use it.

Next-Day White Sourdough Starter

(Ready in about 3 hours 40 minutes I Servings- Two and a half cup starter I Difficulty- Moderate)

Ingredients

- One 1/2-ounce package commercial dry sourdough starter
- Two cups of bread flour Pinch of active dry, bread machine, or SAF yeast
- Two cups of warm water (85°F)
- Half medium apple, peeled, cored, and cut into chunks

For the first feeding:

- 1/4 cup bread flour
- 1 /4 cup warm water

Instructions

1. Combine the packaged starter with the flour and yeast in a medium bowl. Mix in the warm water until the mixture is smooth. Stir in the apple chunks. Transfer to a plastic container or crock. Cover with a few cheesecloth layers and secure with a rubber band; then cover loosely with

plastic wrap. Let stand at warm room temperature for 24 hours (80°F is optimum), stirring the mixture 2 to 3 times. It will be bubbly and begin to ferment, giving off a tangy, sour aroma. It will be the consistency of a pancake batter.

2. Remove the apple chunks. Add the first feeding flour and water and mix to combine. Let stand for 8 hours longer. The starter will be ready to use. If you desire a sourer starter or do not wish to use it right away, cover the starter loosely and store it in the refrigerator for about 24 hours.

Next-Day Rye Sourdough Starter

(Ready in about 3 hours 40 minutes I Servings- Two and a half cup starter I Difficulty- Moderate)

Ingredients

- One 1/2-ounce package commercial dry sourdough starter
- One and a half cups dark rye flour
- Half cup bread flour Pinch of active dry, bread machine, or SAF
- yeast
- Two cups of warm water (85°F)
- One thin slice of onion
- 1/4 large clove garlic
- Four caraway seeds

For the first feeding:

- 1/4 cup rye flour
- 1/4 cup warm water

Instructions

1. Combine the starter package with the flour and yeast in a medium bowl. Mix in the warm water until smooth.
2. Stir in the onion, garlic, and caraway. Transfer to a plastic container or crock. Cover with a few cheesecloth layers and secure with a rubber band; then cover loosely with plastic wrap. Let stand at warm room temperature for 24 hours (80°F is optimum), stirring the mixture 2 to 3 times. It will be bubbly and begin to ferment, giving off a tangy, sour aroma. It will be the consistency of a pancake batter.
3. Remove the onion and garlic pieces. Add the first feeding flour and water, and mix to combine. Let stand for 8 hours longer. The starter will be ready to use. If you desire a sourer starter or do not wish to use it right away, cover the starter loosely and store it in the refrigerator for 24 hours.

Suzanne's Sourdough Starter

(Ready in about 3 hours 40 minutes I Servings- Two and a half cup starter I Difficulty- Moderate)

Ingredients

- One 8-ounce container sour cream (not imitation, low-fat, or nonfat)
- Half cup warm water
- Three tablespoons apple cider vinegar
- 1/8 teaspoon active dry, bread machine, or SAF yeast
- 3/4 to One cup of unbleached all-purpose or bread flour

Instructions

1. Mix the sour cream until smooth in a medium bowl. Add the water and vinegar, and sprinkle with the yeast. Add the flour. Add a bit more flour to adjust the consistency to that of a pancake batter.
2. Transfer to a plastic container or crock. Cover with a few cheesecloth layers and secure with a rubber band; then cover loosely with plastic wrap. Let stand at warm room temperature for 24 hours (80°F is optimum). It will start to bubble immediately and have a fresh, creamy smell that will gently sour. You can begin using the starter after 2 to 5 more days. The longer it sits, the sourer it will become. If you have not used the starter six days after you made it, store it in the refrigerator, covered loosely, until you are ready to use it.

Grape yeast Natural Starter

(Ready in about 3 hours 40 minutes I Servings- Two and a half cup starter I Difficulty- Moderate)

Ingredients

- 2 pounds ripe unwashed fresh organic red or white varietal grapes on the vine
- Unbleached bread flour or whole wheat flour
- One cup of lukewarm bottled mineral water (90°F to 100°F)
- One and a half cups bread flour or whole wheat flour

Instructions

1. Place the grape bunches in a 4-quart deep plastic bucket (the yeast is outside the skins). Use the back of a large spoon to crush the grapes, pressing out the must (unfermented grape juice) and leaving the skins hanging on the stem. Remove the stem and skins, and leave the crushed grapes, whole seeds in the bucket.
2. Cover with a double layer of cheesecloth fastened with a rubber band and let stand at warm room temperature (80° to 90°F) to ferment for 5 to 7 days naturally. Do not add anything else to the bucket during this time.
3. Strain the contents of the bucket through a wire mesh over a bowl, reserving the juice. Discard the solids. You will end up with about half as much juice as solids. Pour the juice into a measuring cup, note the measure, and then pour it into a clean plastic bucket. Add flour equal to the amount of grape juice and mix to create a thick slurry. Cover with a double layer of cheesecloth and stand at room temperature to naturally ferment for three days.
4. The starter, known as a chef at this point, will bubble and foam.
5. On the third day, add the mineral water and One and a half cups of flour to the starter, adding a bit more flour if you desire a thicker starter. Mix until smooth. Re-cover the starter, now a classic levain, and let rest at room temperature for 24 hours to 3 days, depending on how sour you want it.
6. At this point, this starter can be stirred down and used immediately. Or cover the starter loosely and store it in the refrigerator for up to 1 week

White Sourdough Bread

(Ready in about 3 hours 10 minutes I Servings- One loaf I Difficulty- Moderate)

Ingredients

- 3/4 cup sourdough starter Next-Day White Sourdough Starter
- Half cup fat-free milk
- Two tablespoons unsalted butter, melted
- One and a half tablespoons honey
- Three cups of bread flour
- One and a half teaspoons salt
- One and a half teaspoons SAF yeast or two teaspoons bread machine yeast

Instructions

1. Place all the ingredients in the pan according to the order in the manufacturer's instructions. Set crust on dark
2. and program for the Basic cycle; press Start.
3. When the baking cycle ends, immediately remove the pan's bread and place it on a rack. Let cool to room temperature before slicing.

Classic Sourdough Bread

(Ready in about 3 hours 40 minutes I Servings- One loaf I Difficulty- Moderate)

Ingredients

For the sponge:
- 3/4 cup Next-Day Rye Sourdough Starter
- One and 1/8 cups water
- One and 1/8 cups light or medium rye flour
- Half teaspoon SAF or bread machine yeast

For the dough:
- One tablespoon unsalted butter, melted
- Two and 1/4 cups bread flour
- One tablespoon sugar
- One tablespoon caraway seed
- One and a half teaspoons salt
- One teaspoon SAF yeast or One and a half teaspoons bread machine yeast

Instructions

1. To make the sponge, place the sponge ingredients in the pan. Program for the Dough cycle; press Start. When the machine beeps at the end of the cycle, press Stop and unplug the machine. Let the sponge starter sit in the machine for 8 hours, or as long as overnight.
2. To make the dough, place all the dough ingredients in the pan with the sponge according to the manufacturer's instructions. Set crust on medium and program for the Basic or French Bread cycle; press Start. The dough ball will be moist, tacky, and smooth.
3. When the baking cycle ends, immediately remove the pan's bread and place it on a rack. Let cool to room temperature before slicing.

Sourdough Cornmeal Bread

(Ready in about 3 hours 40 minutes I Servings- One loaf I Difficulty- Moderate)

Ingredients

- One and 1/4 cups white flour sourdough starter Next-Day White Sourdough Starter
- Half cup plus Two tablespoons fat-free milk

- Two tablespoons olive oil or lard
- Three tablespoons honey or molasses
- Two and a half cups bread flour
- 2/3 cup yellow cornmeal
- One and a half teaspoons salt
- One and a half teaspoons SAF yeast or two teaspoons bread machine yeast

Instructions

1. Place all the ingredients in the pan according to the order in the manufacturer's instructions. Set crust on medium and program for the Basic cycle; press Start.
2. When the baking cycle ends, immediately remove the pan's bread and place it on a rack. Let cool to room temperature before slicing.

Sourdough French Bread

(Ready in about 3 hours 40 minutes I Servings- One loaf I Difficulty- Moderate)

Ingredients

- Two cups of white flour sourdough starter Next-Day White Sourdough Starter
- Half cup of water
- Three and 1/4 to three and a Half cups bread flour
- Two teaspoons salt
- Two and 1/4teaspoons bread machine yeast
- Yellow cornmeal, for sprinkling

Instructions

1. Place all the dough ingredients in the pan according to the order in the manufacturer's instructions. Use Three cups of flour at first, adding more as needed, depending on your starter's consistency. Program for the Dough cycle; press Start. The dough ball will be firm, then get shiny and soften. When the machine beeps at the end of the cycle, press Stop and unplug the machine. Gently deflate the dough with your finger. Let the dough rest for another 3 hours in the environment of the machine. If it is rising slowly, leave it in there for up to 8 hours. Check by poking with your finger; it will be springy.
2. Turn the dough out onto a lightly floured work surface. Using a dough card, fold the edges over into the center to make a round loaf, adding flour as needed to prevent sticking. Spread a thick layer of flour on the work surface and turn the loaf over so that the smooth side will be face down in the flour. Cover with a clean tea towel and let rest at room temperature for about 1 hour.
3. Knead the loaf into a tight round again to deflate it. Line an 8-inch round bowl or colander with a clean tea towel. Sprinkle heavily with flour. Place the round of dough in it, smooth side down. Wrap tightly with plastic wrap and refrigerate for 12 to 24 hours. It will rise slowly.
4. Twenty minutes before baking, place a baking stone on the lowest rack of the oven, if desired, and preheat to 450°F. Line a baking sheet with parchment paper and sprinkle with some cornmeal.
5. Remove the dough from the refrigerator and gently turn it out and over onto the baking sheet (the smooth side will be on top now). It will appear to deflate slightly and probably look very moist. This is okay. Gently slash a crosshatch or square into the top of

the loaf, no more than 1/4 inch deep, with a small sharp knife. Immediately place in the hot oven.
6. Bake for 12 minutes. Reduce the oven temperature to 375°F and bake for an additional 25 to 30 minutes, or until the crust is deep brown, very crisp, and the loaf sounds hollow when tapped with your finger.
7. Remove the bread from the oven and place it on a rack. Let cool completely before slicing.

Levain Loaf

(Ready in about 3 hours 40 minutes I Servings- two loaf I Difficulty- Moderate)

Ingredients

For the sponge:
- One cup of lukewarm bottled mineral water
- Half cup Grape yeast Natural Starter or other sourdough starters
- Half teaspoon bread machine yeast
- 3/4 cup bread flour
- 3/4 cup whole wheat flour

For the dough:
- Sponge, above
- One teaspoon SAF or One and a half teaspoons bread machine yeast
- One and 3/4 cups bread flour
- One and a half teaspoons fine sea salt
- Yellow cornmeal, for sprinkling

Instructions

1. To make the sponge, place the water, starter, and yeast in the pan. Add the flours on top. Program for the Dough cycle; press Start. Set a kitchen timer for 10 minutes. The sponge will be very wet and sticky. Don't be tempted to add more flour. When the timer rings, press Stop and unplug the machine. Let rest at room temperature in the machine for 24 hours.
2. The next day, stir down the sponge by running the Dough cycle for 3 minutes.
3. To make the dough, sprinkle the yeast over the sponge. Add the flour and the salt. Program for the Dough cycle and press Start. The dough will be shiny, very moist to the point of being slightly sticky, and soft. Don't be tempted to add more flour. When the machine beeps at the end of the cycle, press Stop and unplug the machine. Gently deflate the dough with your finger. Set a timer and let the dough rest for another One and a half hours in the machine's warm environment.
4. Line a baking sheet with parchment paper and sprinkle with cornmeal. Turn the dough out onto a lightly floured work surface. Divide the dough into two equal pieces. Using a dough card, gently knead each piece into a ball. Place the balls on the baking sheet a few inches apart. Cover with a clean tea towel and let it rise at room temperature until doubled in bulk, about 1 hour.
5. Twenty minutes before baking, place a baking stone on the middle rack of the oven, if desired, and preheat to 425°F.
6. Sprinkle the top of each loaf with flour and rub it to coat. Slash an X into the tops, no more than 14 inches deep, with a small sharp knife. Bake for 35 to 40 minutes, or until the crusts are deep brown, very crisp, and sound hollow when tapped with your finger. The loaves will be full and high. I insert an instant-

read thermometer into a soft crease on the side; it should read about 200°F. Remove the loaves from the oven and place them on a rack. Let cool completely before slicing.

Sourdough Buckwheat Bread

(Ready in about 3 hours 40 minutes I Servings- One loaf I Difficulty- Moderate)

Ingredients

- One cup of white flour sourdough starter Next-Day White Sourdough Starter
- 1/4 cup buttermilk
- One large egg
- Grated zest of 1 orange
- Two tablespoons unsalted butter, melted
- Two cups of bread flour
- Half cup whole wheat flour
- Half cup buckwheat flour
- Three tablespoons light brown sugar
- One and a half teaspoons salt
- One and a half teaspoons SAF yeast or two teaspoons bread machine yeast

Instructions

1. When the baking cycle ends, immediately remove the pan's bread and place it on a rack. Let cool to room temperature before slicing.
2. Place all the ingredients in the pan according to the order in the manufacturer's instructions. Set crust on dark and program for the Basic cycle; press Start.

Sourdough Sunflower-Seed Honey Bread

(Ready in about 3 hours 40 minutes I Servings- One loaf I Difficulty- Moderate)

Ingredients

- One cup of sourdough starter Next-Day White Sourdough Starter
- Half cup fat-free milk
- 1/4 cup margarine, cut into pieces
- One cup of bread flour
- Two cups of whole wheat flour
- 1/4 cup dark brown sugar
- 1/3 cup raw sunflower seeds
- Two tablespoons chopped walnuts
- One and a half teaspoons salt
- One and a half teaspoons SAF yeast or two teaspoons bread machine yeast

Instructions

1. Place the ingredients in the pan according to the order in the manufacturer's instructions. Set crust on dark and program for the Whole Wheat cycle; press Start.
2. When the baking cycle ends, immediately remove the pan's bread and place it on a rack. Let cool to room temperature before slicing.

Sourdough Raisin Bread

(Ready in about 3 hours 40 minutes I Servings- One loaf I Difficulty- Moderate)

Ingredients

- One and a half cups raisins
- Half cup sourdough starter Next-Day White Sourdough Starter
- Half cup fat-free milk
- Two large eggs
- Two tablespoons margarine, cut into pieces
- Three cups of bread flour
- Two tablespoons sugar
- One and a half teaspoons salt
- One teaspoon SAF yeast or One and a half teaspoons bread machine yeast

Instructions

1. When the baking cycle ends, immediately remove the pan's bread and place it on a rack. Let cool to room temperature before slicing.
2. Place the ingredients in the pan according to the order in the manufacturer's instructions. Set crust on dark and program for the Basic cycle; press Start.
3. Add the raisins during the first 10 minutes of Knead 2. Gradually sprinkle in the raisins while the machine is kneading. If the dough looks too sticky after the raisins are incorporated, sprinkle another 1 to Two tablespoons of flour around the paddle while the machine is running. Place the raisins in a bowl and cover with hot water. Let stand for One and a half hours at room temperature to soften. Drain the raisins and pat as dry as possible, as any moisture will be incorporated into the dough.

Sourdough Banana Nut Bread

(Ready in about 3 hours 40 minutes I Servings- One loaf I Difficulty- Moderate)

Ingredients

- Half cup sourdough starter Next-Day White Sourdough Starter
- 1/4 cup buttermilk
- Half cup sliced bananas
- One large egg
- Two tablespoons nut oil
- Two and a half cups bread flour
- Half cup whole wheat flour
- Half cup chopped macadamia nuts or pecans
- Three tablespoons chopped dried pineapple or dates
- Two tablespoons light brown sugar
- One and 1/4 teaspoons salt
- One and 3/4 teaspoons SAF yeast or Two and 1/4 teaspoons bread machine yeast

Instructions

1. Place all the ingredients in the pan according to the order in the manufacturer's instructions. Set crust on medium and program for the Basic cycle; press Start.
2. When the baking cycle ends, immediately remove the pan's bread and place it on a rack. Let cool to room temperature before slicing.

Sourdough Bread with Fresh Pears and Walnuts

(Ready in about 3 hours 40 minutes I Servings- One loaf I Difficulty- Moderate)

Ingredients

- 3/4 cup sourdough starter Next-Day White Sourdough Starter
- 1/3 cup buttermilk
- One and a half teaspoons vanilla extract
- Two tablespoons butter, cut into pieces
- Three cups of bread flour
- 1/3 cup rolled oats
- Three tablespoons light brown sugar
- 1/3 cup walnuts
- Two teaspoons apple pie spice
- One and a half teaspoons salt
- One and 1/4teaspoons SAF yeast or one and 3/4 teaspoons bread machine yeast
- One and a half cups peeled, cored, and chopped fresh pear (1 to 2 large Pears)

Instructions

1. Place the ingredients, except the pears, in the pan according to the order in the manufacturer's instructions. Set crust on medium and program for the Basic or Sweet Bread cycle; press Start.
2. About 5 minutes into the kneading, sprinkle the pears into the dough, a few at a time until all the pears are added.
3. When the baking cycle ends, immediately remove the pan's bread and place it on a rack. Let cool to room temperature before slicing.

Orange Sourdough Bread with Cranberries, Pecans, and Golden Raisins

(Ready in about 3 hours 40 minutes I Servings- One loaf I Difficulty- Moderate)

Ingredients

- Half cup French Buttermilk Starter, or any white flour sourdough starter
- 3/4 cup orange juice
- Two tablespoons butter, cut into pieces
- Three and 1/4 cups bread flour
- Three tablespoons sugar
- One teaspoon salt
- One and 3/4 teaspoons SAF yeast or Two and 1/4teaspoons bread machine yeast
- Half cup dried cranberries
- 1/3 cup golden raisins
- 1/3 cup chopped pecans

Instructions

1. Place the ingredients, except the fruit and nuts, in the pan according to the order in the manufacturer's instructions. Set crust on medium and program for the Basic cycle or Fruit and Nut cycle; press Start.
2. When the machine beeps, or between Knead 1 and Knead 2, add the fruits and nuts. If you are using the

Basic cycle, you may also mix all the ingredients at the beginning, if you wish.

3. When the baking cycle ends, immediately remove the pan's bread and place it on a rack. Let cool to room temperature before slicing.

Sourdough Pumpkin Spice Bread

(Ready in about 3 hours 40 minutes I Servings- One loaf I Difficulty- Moderate)

Ingredients

- 3/4 cup sourdough starter Next-Day White Sourdough Starter
- One cup of canned pumpkin puree
- 1/4 cup water
- Two tablespoons vegetable or nut oil
- Three and a Half cups bread flour
- Three tablespoons dark brown sugar
- Two teaspoons apple pie spice
- One and a half teaspoons salt
- One and 1/4teaspoons SAF yeast or 2 1/4 teaspoons bread machine yeast

Instructions

1. Place all the ingredients in the pan according to the order in the manufacturer's instructions. Set crust on dark and program for the Basic cycle; press Start.
2. When the baking cycle ends, immediately remove the pan's bread and place it on a rack. Let cool to room temperature before slicing.

Sourdough Carrot Poppy Seed Bread

(Ready in about 3 hours 40 minutes I Servings- One loaf I Difficulty- Moderate)

Ingredients

- 3/4 cup sourdough starter Next-Day White Sourdough Starter
- Half cup buttermilk
- One and a half tablespoons olive or walnut oil
- Two and a half cups bread flour
- Half cup whole wheat flour
- One and 1/4cups shredded raw carrots
- Two tablespoons minced dried apricots
- One tablespoon poppy seed
- One tablespoon sugar
- One and a half teaspoons salt
- One and 1/4 teaspoons SAF yeast or One and 3/4 teaspoons bread machine yeast

Instructions

1. Place all the ingredients in the pan according to the order in the manufacturer's instructions. Set crust on dark and program for the Basic cycle; press Start.
2. When the baking cycle ends, immediately remove the pan's bread and place it on a rack. Let cool to room temperature before slicing.

Sourdough Cottage Cheese Bread with Fresh Herbs

(Ready in about 3 hours 40 minutes I Servings- One loaf I Difficulty- Moderate)

Ingredients

- 3/4 cup sourdough starter Next-Day White Sourdough Starter
- 3/4 cup cottage cheese
- Two tablespoons olive oil
- Three cups of bread flour
- 1/4 cup chopped fresh watercress leaves, loosely packed
- One tablespoon chopped fresh chives
- One tablespoon chopped fresh basil
- One tablespoon chopped fresh dill
- Two teaspoons chopped fresh marjoram
- 1/4 teaspoon dried lemon rind or Half teaspoon fresh lemon zest
- One and a half teaspoons salt
- One and a half teaspoons SAF yeast or two teaspoons bread machine yeast

Instructions

1. Place all the ingredients in the pan according to the order in the manufacturer's instructions. Set crust on dark and program for the Basic cycle; press Start.
2. When the baking cycle ends, immediately remove the pan's bread and place it on a rack. Let cool to room temperature before slicing.

Sourdough Tomato Bread with Feta

(Ready in about 3 hours 40 minutes I Servings- One loaf I Difficulty- Moderate)

Ingredients

- 3/4 cup sourdough starter Next-Day White Sourdough Starter
- 3/4 cup chopped canned tomatoes with some liquid
- Two tablespoons olive oil
- Three cups of bread flour
- 2/3 cup crumbled feta cheese
- Half teaspoon salt
- One and 1/4 teaspoons SAF yeast or one and 3/4 teaspoons bread machine yeast

Instructions

1. Place all the ingredients in the pan according to the order in the manufacturer's instructions. Set crust on dark and program for the Basic cycle; press Start. The dough will look dry at first but will moisten as the tomatoes break up.
2. When the baking cycle ends, immediately remove the pan's bread and place it on a rack. Let cool to room temperature before slicing.

Sourdough Pesto Bread

(Ready in about 3 hours 40 minutes I Servings- One loaf I Difficulty- Moderate)

Ingredients

- One cup of sourdough starter Next-Day White Sourdough Starter
- 1/3 cup fat-free milk
- Two tablespoons olive oil

- Three tablespoons pesto
- Three cups of bread flour
- One tablespoon sugar
- One and a half teaspoons garlic powder
- One teaspoon dried marjoram
- One teaspoon dried basil
- One teaspoon salt
- One and a half teaspoons SAF yeast or two teaspoons bread machine yeast

Instructions

1. Place all the ingredients in the pan according to the order in the manufacturer's instructions. Set crust on dark and program for the Basic or French Bread cycle; press Start.
2. When the baking cycle ends, immediately remove the pan's bread and place it on a rack. Let cool to room temperature before slicing.

Sourdough English Muffins

(Ready in about 3 hours 40 minutes I Servings- 12 I Difficulty- Moderate)

Ingredients

- One cup of sourdough starter Next-Day White Sourdough Starter
- Half cup fat-free milk
- Two tablespoons unsalted butter, melted
- One large egg
- Three and 3/4 cups bread flour
- One and a half teaspoons salt
- Two teaspoons SAF yeast or Two and a half teaspoons bread machine yeast
- 1/3 cup yellow cornmeal or coarse semolina, for sprinkling

Instructions

1. Place all the ingredients in the pan according to the order in the manufacturer's instructions. Program for the Dough cycle; press Start. The dough ball will be soft and very slightly moist. The softer you leave the dough, the lighter the muffin will be. You can add a bit more flour when you remove the dough from the machine.
2. Lightly sprinkle the work surface with cornmeal. When the machine beeps at the end of the cycle, using a dough card, scrape the dough out onto the work surface and, with a rolling pin, roll it into a rectangle about 1/2-inch thick.
3. Sprinkle the top with cornmeal to prevent sticking. Cut out the muffins with a 3-inch biscuit cutter or the rim of a drinking glass. Roll out the scraps and cut out the remaining muffins. Cover the muffins with a clean tea towel or place them in the refrigerator if they are rising too fast while the others are baking.
4. Preheat an electric griddle to 350° or 375°F, or heat a cast-iron griddle over medium heat until a drop of water sprinkled on the griddle dances across the surface. Lightly oil the surface. Place several muffins on the hot griddle. Cook for about 10 minutes on each side, turning when they are quite brown. Remove the muffins from the griddle with a spatula and cool on a rack.

Chapter 22-Cheese Bread Recipes

Cheese is a universal favorite, and bread without cheese cannot be imagined by the present generation. The following provided are some of the cheese bread recipes that you can easily make in your bread machines.

Cheesy Chipotle Bread

(Ready in about 3 hours 10 minutes I Servings- One loaf I Difficulty- Moderate)

Ingredients

- One and a half teaspoons of salt
- One cup of Shredded Mexican Cheese
- One teaspoon of Chipotle Chili powder
- 1/4 cup of sugar
- One and 1/4 cups of lukewarm water
- One teaspoon of bread machine yeast
- Four cups of bread flour
- Three tablespoons of dry milk

Instructions

1. Add all the ingredients to the bread machine's pan in the suggested order by the manufacturer.
2. Select white bread cycle, light crust. Press the start button.
3. Do not use a delay cycle.
4. Enjoy fresh.

Roasted Garlic Asiago Bread

(Ready in about 3 hours 15 minutes I Servings- One loaf I Difficulty- Moderate)

Ingredients

- One cup of white bread flour
- 1/4 cup of gluten flour
- One and a 3/4 cup of whole wheat flour
- 3/4 cup of grated Asiago cheese
- Two teaspoons of fresh rosemary minced
- Two tablespoons of dry milk
- Three roasted crushed garlic cloves
- One tablespoon of fresh basil minced

- Two teaspoons of fresh oregano minced
- Four teaspoons of active dry yeast
- One and 1/4 cups of water
- One teaspoon of honey
- One teaspoon of salt
- Two tablespoons of olive oil

Instructions

1. Add all the ingredients to the bread machine in the suggested order by the manufacturer.
2. Select whole wheat cycle, crust to your liking.
3. Serve fresh.

Cheddar Cheese Basil Bread

(Ready in about 3 hours 10 minutes I Servings- One loaf I Difficulty- Moderate)

Ingredients

- Four tablespoons of Softened Unsalted Butter
- One and 1/8 Cups of lukewarm Milk
- One cup of Shredded Cheese
- Three cups of Bread Flour
- One tablespoon of Brown Sugar
- One teaspoon of basil
- One and a half teaspoons of Bread Machine Yeast
- One and a half teaspoons of Salt

Instructions

1. Put all ingredients into the bread machine in the suggested order by the manufacturer.
2. Select a basic setting, light crust. Press the start button.
3. Before the baking cycle, add some cheese on top of the bread loaf if you like.
4. Enjoy fresh.

Jalapeño Corn Bread

(Ready in about 2 hours 50 minutes I Servings- One loaf I Difficulty- Moderate)

Ingredients

- 2/3 cup of drained thawed frozen corn
- ¾ cup and two tablespoons of water
- One tablespoon of chopped jalapeño chili
- Two tablespoons of softened butter
- Two tablespoons of sugar
- Three and a ¼ cups of bread flour
- Two and a half teaspoons of bread machine
- 1/3 cup of cornmeal
- One and a half teaspoons of salt

Instructions

1. Put all the required ingredients in the container of the bread machine in the suggested order by the manufacturer.
2. Select White cycle and Light crust—Press the start button. Do not use a delay cycle.
3. Enjoy fresh.

Olive Cheese Bread

(Ready in about 4 hours 10 minutes I Servings- One loaf I Difficulty- Moderate)

Ingredients

- Half cup of small stuffed olives, drained
- One cup of Sharp cheddar cheese, shredded
- Three and ¼ cups of flour
- One and a ¼ teaspoons of yeast
- One cup of water
- One teaspoon of sugar
- One teaspoon of salt

Instructions

1. Place all ingredients in the pan of the bread machine, except for olives. Select basic. Press the start button.
2. Add olives when ten minutes are left in the kneading cycle.
3. Serve fresh.

Blue Cheese Onion Bread

(Ready in about 3 hours 50 minutes I Servings- One loaf I Difficulty- Moderate)

Ingredients

- Three tablespoons of powdered milk
- Two tablespoons of dried onion flakes
- Two tablespoons of sugar
- One and 1/Three cups of water
- A pinch of salt
- Four cups of white flour
- One and a ¼ teaspoons of bread machine yeast
- ¼ cup of shredded blue cheese

Instructions

1. Put all the required ingredients in the container of the bread machine in the suggested order by the manufacturer.

2. Select the sweet bread cycle and dark crust, if you like—Press the start button.
3. Serve fresh

Double Cheese Bread

(Ready in about 3 hours 5 minutes I Servings- One loaf I Difficulty- Moderate)

Ingredients

- Three cups of bread flour
- One teaspoon of salt
- One teaspoon of coarse black pepper
- One and a half cups of shredded sharp cheddar
- Two tablespoons of sugar
- One and a ¼ cup of Luke warm water
- One and a 1/4 teaspoon of bread machine yeast
- One tablespoon of soft butter
- ¼ cup of dry milk powder
- 1/3 cup of finely grated parmesan cheese

Instructions

1. Put all the required ingredients in the container of the bread machine in the suggested order by the manufacturer.
2. Select white bread, medium crust. Press the start button.
3. When 15-20 minutes of the baking cycle is left, sprinkle shredded cheese on top of the loaf.
4. Serve fresh.

Mozzarella & Salami Bread

(Ready in about 3 hours 10 minutes I Servings- One loaf I Difficulty- Moderate)

Ingredients

- 1/3 cup of shredded mozzarella cheese
- One and a half teaspoons of dried oregano
- One cup and Two tablespoons of warm water
- Two tablespoons of sugar
- One and a half teaspoons of garlic salt
- One and a half teaspoons of active dry yeast
- 2/3 cup of diced salami
- Three and a ¼ cup of bread flour

Instructions

1. Put all the required ingredients in the container of the bread machine in the suggested order by the manufacturer except for salami.
2. Select the basic cycle. Do not use the time delay.
3. Add salami before final kneading.
4. Enjoy fresh.

Simple Cottage Cheese Bread

(Ready in about 3 hours 10 minutes I Servings- One loaf I Difficulty- Moderate)

Ingredients

- Three cups of bread flour
- 1/3 cup of water
- Two tablespoons of Butter

- One cup of Cottage Cheese
- One whole Egg
- One tablespoon of Sugar
- Two teaspoons of yeast
- 1/4 teaspoon of Baking Soda
- One teaspoon of salt

Instructions

1. Put all the required ingredients in the container of the bread machine in the suggested order by the manufacturer.
2. Select basic, light crust—Press the start button.
3. Enjoy warm.

Chile Cheese Bacon Bread

(Ready in about 3 hours 20 minutes | Servings- One loaf | Difficulty- Moderate)

Ingredients

- Four cups of bread flour
- Two tablespoons of Vegetable oil
- One and a 1/4 teaspoon of salt
- Two cups of Mexican cheese
- One and 1/3 cups of water
- Three tablespoons of dry milk
- Three tablespoons of bacon bits
- Two tablespoons plus one and a half teaspoon of sugar
- Two teaspoons of active dry yeast

Instructions

1. Put all the required ingredients in the container of the bread machine in the manufacturer's suggested order, except for bacon and cheese.
2. Select basic setting, crust to your liking.
3. Add bacon and cheese at the nut & fruit signal.
4. Serve fresh.

Italian Parmesan Bread

(Ready in about 3 hours 5 minutes | Servings- One loaf | Difficulty- Moderate)

Ingredients

- Four cups of flour
- 1/4 cup parmesan cheese
- One and a half cups of water
- One and a half teaspoons of salt
- Two and a half teaspoons of yeast
- One teaspoon of Garlic powder
- One teaspoon of Italian/pizza seasoning

Instructions

1. Put all the required ingredients in the container of the bread machine in the suggested order by the manufacturer.
2. Select basic or delay cycle—Press the start button.
3. Serve fresh

Rich Cheddar Bread

(Ready in about 3 hours 10 minutes | Servings- One loaf | Difficulty- Moderate)

Ingredients

- Two and a half tablespoons of Parmesan cheese
- One cup of warm water
- Half teaspoon of salt
- Three and a half teaspoons of sugar
- One and a 1/4 cup of freshly grated cheddar cheese
- One teaspoon of Dry mustard
- Two and a half tablespoons of softened butter
- Two and a half cups of bread flour
- One and a half teaspoons of paprika
- Two teaspoons of Active dry yeast
- Two and a half tablespoons of minced onions

Instructions

1. Place all ingredients in the bread machine in the suggested order by the manufacturer.
2. Select the white setting, crust to your liking.
3. Press the start button and assess the dough's consistency if it needs water or more flour.
4. Add one tablespoon of flour or water if required.
5. Serve fresh.

Feta Oregano Bread

(Ready in about 3 hours 10 minutes | Servings- One loaf | Difficulty- Moderate)

Ingredients

- One and a half tablespoons of olive oil
- Three cups of bread flour
- Half cup of crumbled feta cheese
- One cup of water
- Two teaspoons of Active dry yeast
- One tablespoon of Dried leaf oregano
- One teaspoon of Salt
- Three tablespoons of sugar

Instructions

1. Put all ingredients in the bread machine in the suggested order by the manufacturer.
2. Select basic. Press the start button.
3. Serve fresh.

Goat Cheese Bread

(Ready in about 3 hours 10 minutes | Servings- One loaf | Difficulty- Moderate)

Ingredients

- Two cups of bread flour
- 3/4 cup of water
- One and a half teaspoon of active dry yeast
- One tablespoon of granulated sugar
- Half teaspoon of salt
- Three tablespoons of soft goat cheese
- One tablespoon of nonfat dry milk
- One and a half teaspoon of cracked black pepper

Instructions

1. All ingredients must be at room temperature

2. Put all the required ingredients in the container of the bread machine in the suggested order by the manufacturer.
3. Select the normal cycle—Press the start button.
4. Assess dough's consistency; it should not be too dry or too wet.
5. Add one tablespoon of water or flour if required.
6. Serve fresh

Mozzarella-Herb Bread

(Ready in about 3 hours 10 minutes I Servings- One loaf I Difficulty- Moderate)

Ingredients

- One teaspoon of Onion Powder
- Six tablespoons of butter cut into slices
- 1/3 cup lukewarm Milk
- Four cups of Bread Flour
- One and a half teaspoons of Bread Machine Yeast
- Two tablespoons of Sugar
- Two tablespoons of Italian Herb Seasoning
- One and a half Teaspoons of Salt

Instructions

1. Put all the required ingredients in the container of the bread machine in the suggested order by the manufacturer.
2. Select basic, light crust—Press the start button.
3. Before the baking cycle begins, sprinkle Italian seasoning on top.
4. Enjoy fresh.

Ricotta and Fresh Chive Bread

(Ready in about 3 hours 10 minutes I Servings- One loaf I Difficulty- Moderate)

Ingredients

- One cup of water
- 1/3 cup whole or part-skim ricotta cheese
- Three cups of bread flour
- One tablespoon light brown sugar
- One tablespoon gluten
- One and a half teaspoons salt
- Half cup chopped fresh chives
- Dash of ground black pepper
- One tablespoon bread machine yeast

Instructions

1. Place all the ingredients in the pan according to the order in the manufacturer's instructions. Set crust on medium and program for the Basic cycle; press Start.
2. When the baking cycle ends, immediately remove the pan's bread and place it on a rack. Let cool to room temperature before slicing.

Cottage Cheese Dill Bread

(Ready in about 3 hours 10 minutes I Servings- One loaf I Difficulty- Moderate)

Ingredients

- Two tablespoons olive oil
- One medium shallot, chopped
- One cup of cottage cheese
- 1/4 cup fat-free milk
- One large egg plus one egg yolk
- Two and a half cups bread flour
- One tablespoon sugar
- One tablespoon gluten
- Two tablespoons dried dill weed
- One and 1/4 teaspoons salt
- Two and a half teaspoons bread machine yeast

Instructions

1. Heat the oil in a small skillet, and sauté the shallot until translucent. Set aside to cool to warm.
2. Place the ingredients in the pan according to the manufacturer's instructions in the manufacturer's instructions, adding the shallot with the liquid ingredients. Set crust on dark and program for a Basic cycle; press Start.
3. The dough ball will look very dry at first and take a few minutes to come together. Resist the urge to add more liquid.
4. When the baking cycle ends, immediately remove the pan's bread and place it on a rack. Let cool to room temperature before slicing.

Farm-Style Cottage-Cheese Bread

(Ready in about 3 hours 10 minutes I Servings- One loaf I Difficulty- Moderate)

Ingredients

- 3/4 cup water
- 3/4 cup small-curd low-fat cottage cheese
- Two tablespoons olive oil
- Two and a half cups bread flour
- Half cup whole wheat flour
- Two tablespoons sugar
- One tablespoon gluten
- One and a half teaspoons salt
- Two and a half teaspoons bread machine yeast

Instructions

1. Place all the ingredients in the pan according to the order in the manufacturer's instructions. Set crust on medium and program for the Basic cycle; press Start. The dough ball will be slightly moist.
2. When the baking cycle ends, immediately remove the pan's bread and place it on a rack. Let cool to room temperature before slicing.

Buttermilk Cheese Bread

(Ready in about 3 hours 10 minutes I Servings- One loaf I Difficulty- Moderate)

Ingredients

- One cup of buttermilk
- Half cup of water
- Three and a Half cups bread flour
- One cup of shredded Swiss cheese (4 ounces)
- One and a half tablespoons sugar
- One and 1/4 teaspoons baking powder
- One and a half teaspoons salt

- Two and a half teaspoons bread machine yeast

Instructions

1. When the baking cycle ends, immediately remove the pan's bread and place it on a rack. Let cool to room temperature before slicing.
2. Place all the ingredients in the pan according to the order in the manufacturer's instructions. Set crust on medium and program for the Basic cycle; press Start.

Crescia Al Formaggio (Asiago Cheese Bread)

(Ready in about 3 hours 10 minutes I Servings- One loaf I Difficulty- Moderate)

Ingredients

- Half cup plus one tablespoon water
- Three large eggs
- Three tablespoons olive oil
- Three and 1/4 cups bread flour
- 3/4 cup grated Asiago or Locatelli cheese
- One and a half tablespoons nonfat dry milk
- One tablespoon sugar
- Two teaspoons gluten
- Half teaspoon salt
- Two and a half teaspoons bread machine yeast

Instructions

1. Place all the ingredients in the pan according to the order in the manufacturer's instructions. Set crust on medium and program for the Basic or Tender cycle; press Start. The dough ball will be sticky.
2. When the baking cycle ends, immediately remove the pan's bread and place it on a rack. Let cool to room temperature before slicing.

Roquefort Cheese Bread with Walnuts

(Ready in about 3 hours 10 minutes I Servings- One loaf I Difficulty- Moderate)

Ingredients

- One cup of water
- Two tablespoons cream sherry
- 4 ounces Roquefort cheese, crumbled
- One tablespoon walnut oil
- One tablespoon unsalted butter, cut into pieces
- Two and 3/4 cups bread flour
- 1/4 cup medium or dark rye flour
- One tablespoon light brown sugar
- One tablespoon gluten
- Half teaspoon salt
- Half cup chopped walnuts or pecans
- Two and a half teaspoons bread machine yeast

Instructions

1. Place all the ingredients in the pan according to the order in the manufacturer's instructions. Set crust on medium and program for the Basic cycle; press Start.

2. When the baking cycle ends, immediately remove the pan's bread and place it on a rack. Let cool to room temperature before slicing

Parmesan Nut Bread

(Ready in about 3 hours 10 minutes I Servings- One loaf I Difficulty- Moderate)

Ingredients

- One cup of water
- One and a half tablespoons olive oil
- Three cups of bread flour
- 2/3 cup grated Parmesan cheese
- One tablespoon gluten
- Pinch of sugar
- Half teaspoon salt
- Two and a half teaspoon bread machine yeast
- 1/3 cup pine nuts, coarsely chopped
- Half cup walnuts, coarsely chopped

Instructions

1. Place the ingredients, except the nuts, in the pan according to the order in the manufacturer's instructions. Set crust on medium and program for the Basic cycle; press Start. When the machine beeps, or between Knead 1 and Knead 2, add the nuts.
2. When the baking cycle ends, immediately remove the pan's bread and place it on a rack. Let cool to room temperature before slicing.

Roasted Garlic and Dry Jack Bread

(Ready in about 3 hours 10 minutes I Servings- One loaf I Difficulty- Moderate)

Ingredients

- 3 to 4 ounces (1 to 2 heads) garlic
- One and 1/4cups water
- Three cups of bread flour
- Half cup grated dry jack cheese
- Two teaspoons gluten
- One and 3/4 teaspoons salt
- One tablespoon bread machine yeast

Instructions

1. Preheat the oven to 350°F.
2. Place the garlic in a small baking dish and bake until soft when touched with your finger, 40 to 45 minutes. Remove from the oven and let cool to room temperature.
3. Cut the head of roasted garlic in half horizontally. Place all the ingredients in the pan according to the order in the manufacturer's instructions, squeezing out the cloves of garlic and dropping them into the pan along with the water.
4. Set crust on medium and program for the Basic or French Bread cycle; press Start.
5. When the baking cycle ends, immediately remove the pan's bread and place it on a rack. Let cool to room temperature before slicing

Country Pancetta-Cheese Bread

(Ready in about 3 hours 10 minutes I Servings- One loaf I Difficulty- Moderate)

ngredients

- One and 1/8 cups water
- One tablespoon olive oil
- Two cups of bread flour
- Half cup of semolina durum flour
- 1/4 cup whole wheat flour
- 1/4 cup yellow cornmeal or polenta
- One tablespoon gluten
- Pinch of sugar
- One teaspoon salt
- Two and a half teaspoons bread machine yeast
- 2 ounces pancetta, sliced thin
- 4 ounces whole-milk mozzarella, cut into 1/3-inch cubes
- Yellow cornmeal or polenta, for sprinkling

Instructions

1. Place the ingredients, except the pancetta, mozzarella, and cornmeal, in the pan according to the order in the manufacturer's instructions. Program for the Dough cycle; press Start.
2. While the dough is rising, cook the pancetta in a skillet over moderate heat until crisp. Drain on paper towels, cool, and coarsely crumble.
3. Line a baking sheet with parchment paper and sprinkle it with cornmeal. When the machine beeps at the end of the cycle, press Stop and unplug the machine. Turn the dough out onto a lightly floured work surface. Pat the dough into a large, thick oval. Sprinkle the pancetta and the mozzarella over the dough. Fold the dough into thirds and gently knead to distribute the pancetta and cheese evenly. Form into one round loaf and place on the baking sheet. Cover with a clean tea towel and let it rest at room temperature until doubled in bulk, about 40 minutes.
4. Twenty minutes before baking, place a baking stone on the lower third rack of the oven, if desired, and preheat the oven to 425°F.
5. With a small sharp knife, slash the top of the loaf with an X, no more than 1/4 inch deep. Place in the oven, placing the pan on the stone if using one. Bake for 15 minutes. Reduce the oven temperature to 350°F and bake for an additional 30 to 35 minutes, or until the crust is golden brown and the loaf sounds hollow when tapped with your finger. Remove the loaf from the pan and place it on a rack. Let cool to room temperature before slicing.

Hot Jalapeno Bread with Longhorn Cheese

(Ready in about 3 hours 10 minutes I Servings- One loaf I Difficulty- Moderate)

Ingredients

- One cup of water
- Three cups of bread flour
- One cup of shredded longhorn cheddar cheese
- Three tablespoons nonfat dry milk
- Three canned jalapeno chiles, seeded and diced
- One tablespoon sugar
- One teaspoon salt

- Two and a half tablespoon bread machine yeast

Instructions

1. Place all the ingredients in the pan according to the order in the manufacturer's instructions. Set crust on medium and program for the Basic cycle; press Start.
2. When the baking cycle ends, immediately remove the pan's bread and place it on a rack. Let cool to room temperature before slicing.

Beer Bread with Cheddar

(Ready in about 3 hours 10 minutes I Servings- One loaf I Difficulty- Moderate)

Ingredients

- One cup of beer
- Three and a half cups bread flour
- 3/4 cup shredded Colby or mild cheddar cheese
- 1/4 cup sugar
- 3/4 teaspoon salt
- Two and 1/4teaspoons bread machine yeast

Instructions

1. Open the container of beer and let stand at room temperature for a few hours to go flat.
2. Place all the ingredients in the pan according to the order in the manufacturer's instructions. Set crust on medium and program for the Basic cycle; press Start.
3. When the baking cycle ends, immediately remove the pan's bread and place it on a rack. Let cool to room temperature before slicing.

Feta and Spinach Bread

(Ready in about 3 hours 10 minutes I Servings- One loaf I Difficulty- Moderate)

Ingredients

- 7/8 cup water
- 3/4 cup frozen chopped spinach (defrosted and squeezed dry)
- Two tablespoons olive oil
- Three cups of bread flour
- 4 ounces crumbled feta cheese
- One tablespoon sugar
- Half teaspoon salt
- Two and 1/4teaspoons bread machine yeast

Instructions

1. Place all the ingredients in the pan according to the order in the manufacturer's instructions. Set crust on medium and program for the Basic cycle; press Start.
2. When the baking cycle ends, immediately remove the pan's bread and place it on a rack. Let cool to room temperature before slicing.

Cheese and Wholegrain Mustard Loaf

(Ready in about 3 hours 10 minutes I Servings- One loaf I Difficulty- Moderate)

Ingredients

- One teaspoon Easy bake yeast
- One and 5/8 cups of strong white bread flour
- Half cup of strong whole meal flour
- One teaspoon fine sea salt

- Two teaspoons clear honey
- One tablespoon wholegrain mustard
- One and a half cups of water
- Half cup of Cheddar cheese, grated

Instructions

1. Put all the ingredients, except for the cheese, into the pan in the correct order for your machine.
2. Fit the pan into the bread machine and close the lid.
3. Select the basic white raisin setting, medium crust, and the appropriate size. Press Start. When the machine indicates (with a beeping sound), add the cheese and close the lid again.
4. When the program has finished, lift the pan out of the machine, turn the bread out onto a wire rack and leave to cool completely.

Cheddar and Rosemary Loaf

(Ready in about 3 hours 10 minutes I Servings- One loaf I Difficulty- Moderate)

Ingredients

- One teaspoon Easy bake yeast
- One and 5/8 cup of strong white bread flour
- Half cup of strong whole meal flour
- One teaspoon fine sea salt
- One teaspoon golden caster sugar
- One tablespoon finely chopped fresh rosemary leaves
- One and a half cup of water
- Half cup mature Cheddar cheese, grated

Instructions

1. Put all the ingredients, except for the cheese, into the pan in the correct order for your machine.
2. Fit the pan into the bread machine and close the lid.
3. Select the basic white raisin setting, medium crust, and the appropriate size. Press Start. When the machine indicates (with a beeping sound), add the cheese and close the lid again.
4. When the program has finished, lift the pan out of the machine, turn the bread out onto a wire rack and leave to cool completely.

Chapter 23-Stuffed Bread

You can also make stuffed bread in your bread machine. The recipes of some of the stuffed bread you can make in the machine are provided under: -

Fresh Herb and Nut Stuffing Bread

(Ready in about 3 hours 10 minutes I Servings- One loaf I Difficulty- Moderate)

Ingredients

- One cup of plus three tablespoons water
- One and a half tablespoons walnut oil
- Three cups of bread flour
- One tablespoon light brown sugar
- Half cup mixed fresh herbs, minced
- 1/4 cup walnuts
- One tablespoon gluten
- One and a half teaspoons salt
- Two and a half teaspoons bread machine yeast

Instructions

1. Place all the ingredients in the pan according to the order in the manufacturer's instructions. Set crust on dark and program for the Basic cycle; press Start.
2. When the baking cycle ends, immediately remove the pan's bread and place it on a rack. Let cool to room temperature before slicing.

Fresh Herb Stuffing Bread with Fennel Seed and Pepper

(Ready in about 3 hours 10 minutes I Servings- One loaf I Difficulty- Moderate)

Ingredients

- One and 1/8 cups water

- Two tablespoons olive oil
- Two and a half cups bread flour
- Half cup whole wheat flour
- 1/3 cup chopped fresh herbs
- Three tablespoons chopped walnuts or pine nuts
- One and a half tablespoons sugar
- One and a half tablespoons dry buttermilk powder
- Two teaspoons gluten
- One and 1/4 teaspoons salt
- One teaspoon fennel seed
- Half teaspoon grated lemon zest
- Half teaspoon ground black, white, or red peppercorns
- Two and a half teaspoons bread machine yeast

Instructions

1. Place all the ingredients in the pan according to the order in the manufacturer's instructions. Set crust on medium and program for the Basic cycle; press Start.
2. When the baking cycle ends, immediately remove the pan's bread and place it on a rack. Let cool to room temperature before slicing.

Cornmeal Stuffing Bread

(Ready in about 3 hours 10 minutes I Servings- One loaf I Difficulty- Moderate)

Ingredients

- One and 3/8 cup of corn with liquid
- 1/4 cup buttermilk
- Two tablespoons canola or olive oil
- Two tablespoons honey
- Two cups of bread flour
- One cup of yellow cornmeal
- 1/4 cup minced fresh parsley
- One and a half tablespoons poultry seasoning
- Half teaspoon garlic powder
- One tablespoon plus
- One teaspoon gluten
- One and 1/4 teaspoons salt
- Two and a half teaspoons bread machine yeast

Instructions
1. Place all the ingredients in the pan according to the order in the manufacturer's instructions. Set crust on dark and program for the Basic cycle; press Start.
2. When the baking cycle ends, immediately remove the pan's bread and pan's bread and place it on a rack. Let cool to room temperature before slicing.

Prosciutto Stuffing Bread

(Ready in about 3 hours 10 minutes | Servings- One loaf | Difficulty- Moderate)

Ingredients
- 7/8 cup water
- 1/4 cup olive oil
- Three cups of bread flour
- 3/8 cup prosciutto, coarsely chopped
- One tablespoon gluten
- One tablespoon sugar
- One teaspoon ground black pepper
- Half teaspoon salt
- Two teaspoons bread machine yeast

Instructions
1. Place all the ingredients in the pan according to the order in the manufacturer's instructions. Set crust on medium and program for the Basic cycle; press Start.
2. When the baking cycle ends, immediately remove the pan's bread and place the pan's bread and place it on a rack. Let cool to room temperature before slicing.

Khachapuri

(Ready in about 3 hours 10 minutes | Servings- 8 | Difficulty- Moderate)

Ingredients
For the dough:
- One and 1/4 cups plain yogurt
- One tablespoon olive oil
- Three cups of bread flour

- Half teaspoon salt
- One and 3/4 teaspoons bread machine yeast

For the filling:
- One and a half cups shredded Monterey Jack
- 4 ounces feta cheese, crumbled
- 1/4 cup minced Italian flat-leaf parsley
- One large egg
- One tablespoon finely chopped fresh cilantro
- One teaspoon finely chopped fresh mint
- One egg white, beaten with one teaspoon water, for glaze

Instructions
1. To make the dough, place all the dough ingredients in the pan according to the manufacturer's instructions. Program for the Dough cycle; press Start. If the yogurt is very thick, be prepared to add one to two tablespoons of water to the dough. The dough ball should be smooth, slightly soft, and elastic.
2. Meanwhile, make the cheese filling. Combine all of the filling ingredients in a small bowl and toss to combine. Cover and refrigerate until needed.
3. Spray 8 cups of a nonstick standard muffin tin with vegetable cooking spray. At the beep, remove the dough from the pan and turn it out onto a clean work surface. Divide the dough in half, then further divide each half into quarters to make eight pieces.
4. Using a rolling pin, and on a work, surface lightly dusted with flour to prevent sticking, roll out each portion into a 7-to 8-inch round, about 1/4 inch thick. Alternatively, you can press each dough section with your palm and stretch the dough if you don't have a small rolling pin. Fold the dough lightly into quarters and transfer to a muffin cup. Unfold the dough and press to fit into the cup, leaving a dough skirt draped over the sides. Place two heaping tablespoons of the cheese filling into the dough, mounding it higher in the center. Pick up the dough's skirt and pleat in loose folds laying over each other over the filling. You can leave it folded flat or gather up the top ends and twist it into a small knob.
5. Repeat with all the portions of dough. Cover loosely with plastic wrap and let rest at room temperature for 10 minutes.
6. Preheat the oven to 400°F.
7. Brush the tops of the bread with the egg white glaze. Bake for 25 to 30 minutes, or until golden brown. Remove the pan to a rack and cool in the pan for 15 minutes. Remove from the pan and cool for at least 15 minutes before serving. These can be frozen for up to a month in plastic freezer bags. To serve, defrost in the refrigerator in the bag, then warm in a 300°F oven for 8 minutes to soften the cheese. Serve immediately.

Chapter 24-Creative, Special, Country, and International Bread Recipes

The bread recipes are not limited to making classic bread. Bread is a part of a culture, and various communities and countries make the bread of their liking as per their respective traditions and availability of their local produce. Some of those recipes are penned downed for you.

Italian Panettone

(Ready in about 3 hours 40 minutes I Servings- One loaf I Difficulty- Moderate)

Ingredients

- Half teaspoon of rum
- Two tablespoons of butter
- Two whole eggs
- One teaspoon of lemon zest
- 1/4 teaspoon of salt
- 1/4 cup of granulated sugar
- One teaspoon of orange zest
- ¼ cup of Sultana raisins
- Half teaspoon of anise seeds
- Two and a half cups of all-purpose flour
- Half cup of water
- One and a 1/4 teaspoon of bread machine yeast
- Two tablespoons of candied orange, finely diced
- Two tablespoons of citron peel
- ¼ cup of Toasted slivered almonds

Instructions

1. Add all ingredients, except raisins, peel, and nuts, to the bread machine in the manufacturer's suggested order.
2. Select basic bread cycle. Press the start button.
3. Add remaining ingredients at the ingredient signal.
4. Before the baking cycle begins, brush with melted butter and let it bake.
5. Enjoy fresh bread.

Italian Bread

(Ready in about 3 hours 40 minutes I Servings- One loaf I Difficulty- Moderate)

Ingredients

- One and a half cup of water
- One and a half teaspoon of salt
- Four and 1/4 cup of bread flour
- Two teaspoons of bread machine yeast
- Two Tablespoon of olive oil
- Two Tablespoon of sugar

Instructions

1. Put all the required ingredients in the container of the bread machine in the suggested order by the manufacturer.
2. Select the basic cycle. Press the start button.
3. Serve fresh bread.

Bread of the Dead (Pan de Muertos)

(Ready in about 3 hours 40 minutes | Servings- One loaf | Difficulty- Moderate)

Ingredients

- One and 3/4 cups of bread flour
- Three whole eggs
- Three tablespoons of butter
- 1/4 cup of sugar
- Half teaspoon of salt
- 1/4 cup of water
- 1/4 teaspoon of grated orange peel
- One teaspoon of yeast
- 1/8 teaspoon of anise

Instructions

1. Put all the required ingredients in the container of the bread machine in the suggested order by the manufacturer.
2. Select the sweet bread cycle—light crust and Press the start button.
3. Serve fresh bread.

Mexican Sweet Bread

(Ready in about 3 hours 10 minutes | Servings- One loaf | Difficulty- Moderate)

Ingredients

- One cup of milk
- Three cups of bread flour
- One whole egg
- One and a half teaspoons of yeast
- 1/4 cup of sugar
- One teaspoon of salt
- 1/4 cup of butter
- Half teaspoon of cinnamon

Instructions

1. Put all the required ingredients in the container of the bread machine in the suggested order by the manufacturer.
2. Select the sweet bread cycle—light crust and Press the start button.
3. Serve fresh bread.

Challah

(Ready in about 2 hours 30 minutes | Servings- One loaf | Difficulty- Moderate)

Ingredients

- Four and 1/4 cups of all-purpose/bread flour
- One and a half cups of water
- 1 and 1/8 teaspoons of salt
- Half cup of brown sugar
- One tablespoon of active dry yeast
- Sesame or poppy seed
- One whole egg, lightly mixed
- Five egg yolks
- 1/3 cup of oil

Instructions

1. Put all the required ingredients in the container of the bread machine in the suggested order by the manufacturer.
2. Select the dough cycle. Press the start button.
3. Let the oven preheat to 350 F. take the dough out from the machine.
4. Cut the dough into two pieces. Cut each piece into three parts.
5. Braid the three long pieces together. Pinch the bottom and top.
6. Place on an oiled baking sheet. Cover it and let it rise for half an hour.
7. Before baking, brush with egg wash and sprinkle seeds on top.
8. Bake for half an hour.
9. Enjoy fresh bread.

Russian Black Bread

(Ready in about 3 hours 40 minutes | Servings- One loaf | Difficulty- Moderate)

Ingredients

- Two and a half cups of All-Purpose Flour
- One and 1/4 cups of Dark Rye Flour
- Two Tablespoon of Cocoa Powder, Unsweetened
- One Tablespoon of Caraway Seeds
- Half teaspoon of dried onion minced
- One teaspoon of instant crystals coffee
- Half teaspoon of Fennel Seeds
- One and a half Tablespoon of Dark Molasses
- Two teaspoons of Active Dry Yeast
- 1 and 1/3 cups of Water
- One teaspoon of Sea Salt
- Three tablespoons of Vegetable Oil
- One teaspoon of Sugar
- One and a half Tablespoon of Vinegar

Instructions

1. All ingredients should be at room temperature.
2. Put all the required ingredients in the container of the bread machine in the suggested order by the manufacturer.
3. Select the sweet bread cycle—Press the start button.
4. Enjoy fresh bread.

Russian Rye Bread

(Ready in about 3 hours 40 minutes | Servings- One loaf | Difficulty- Moderate)

Ingredients

- Half cup and two tablespoons of warm water
- One and a half tablespoons of melted butter
- Two tablespoons of dark honey
- One teaspoon of salt
- One and 1/4 teaspoons of active dry yeast
- 3/4 cup of rye flour
- One and a half teaspoons of caraway seeds
- One and a half cups of bread flour

Instructions

1. Put all the required ingredients in the container of the bread machine in the suggested order by the manufacturer.
2. Select the basic cycle. Medium crust and Press the start button.
3. Enjoy fresh bread.

Portuguese Corn Bread

(Ready in about 4 hours 10 minutes I Servings- One loaf I Difficulty- Moderate)

Ingredients

- One and a half teaspoons of active dry yeast
- One cup of yellow cornmeal
- One and a half cups of bread flour
- One tablespoon of olive oil
- Two teaspoons of sugar
- One and 1/4 cups of cold water
- 3/4 teaspoon of salt

Instructions

1. Mix half of the cornmeal with cold water until it mixes well.
2. Let it come to room temperature.
3. Put all the required ingredients in the container of the bread machine in the suggested order by the manufacturer.
4. Select the basic cycle. Press the start button.
5. Enjoy fresh bread.

Amish Wheat Bread

(Ready in about 3 hours 40 minutes I Servings- One loaf I Difficulty- Moderate)

Ingredients

- 1/4 cup of Canola Oil
- Two and 3/4 cups of Whole Wheat Flour
- One cup and two tablespoons of warm water
- Half teaspoon of salt
- 1/3 cup of Granulated Sugar
- One package of active yeast
- One whole egg

Instructions

1. Add sugar, yeast, and warm water to a bowl let it rest for 8 minutes.
2. Place all ingredients into the pan of the bread machine in the manufacturer's suggested order.
3. Select basic bread cycle. Light or dark crust. Press the start button.
4. Before the second cycle of kneading starts, switch off the machine. Restart it again. It will give two cycles to bread to raise fully.
5. Enjoy.

British Hot Cross Buns

(Ready in about 3 hours 40 minutes I Servings- One loaf I Difficulty- Moderate)

Ingredients

- 3/4 cup of milk
- One whole egg+ one yolk
- Six tablespoons of sugar
- 3/4 teaspoon of cinnamon
- 1/3 cup of butter

- Half teaspoon of nutmeg
- One tablespoon of yeast
- 1/4 teaspoon of ground cloves
- Half cup of candied fruit
- 3/4 teaspoon of salt
- One and a half teaspoons of grated lemon rind
- Three cups of flour

Glaze

- Half teaspoon of lemon juice
- One tablespoon of milk
- Half cup of icing sugar

Instructions

1. Add all ingredients, except candied fruits, to the bread machine in the manufacturer's suggested order.
2. Select the dough cycle. Press the start button.
3. Add candied fruits at the ingredient signal.
4. Take a 19 by 13 pan, spray with oil generously.
5. Take the dough out from the machine. Slice into 18 to 24 pieces.
6. Make each piece into a ball. Put all dough balls into the pan half-inch apart from each other.
7. Cover them and let them rise in a warm place until they double in size.
8. Make a cross on top of buns with a knife.
9. Bake at 375 F for 12 to 15 minutes.
10. Meanwhile, mix all glaze ingredients.
11. Drizzle over buns and serve.

Hawaiian Bread

(Ready in about 3 hours 10 minutes I Servings- One loaf I Difficulty- Moderate)

Ingredients

- Two tablespoons of vegetable oil
- Two tablespoons of dry milk
- Two and a half tablespoons of honey
- One whole egg
- Two teaspoons of fast-rising yeast
- 3/4 cup of pineapple juice
- 3/4 teaspoon of salt
- Three cups of bread flour

Instructions

1. Put all the required ingredients in the container of the bread machine in the suggested order by the manufacturer.
2. Select the sweet bread cycle—light crust and Press the start button.
3. Enjoy fresh bread.

Greek Easter Bread

(Ready in about 2 hours 40 minutes I Servings- One loaf I Difficulty- Moderate)

Ingredients

- Half cup of caster sugar
- Three whole eggs, lightly mixed
- Two teaspoons of dried yeast
- Four and a half cups of baker's flour
- Two teaspoons of Mallei

- Half cup and one tablespoon of butter melted
- 1/3 cup of milk
- 1/3 cup of lukewarm water
- Juice from half of an orange, grated rinds

Instructions

1. Add one tablespoon of sugar, water, and yeast to the machine's pan. Mix lightly and let it rest for 8 minutes.
2. Add the rest of the ingredients to the pan also. Select dough cycle and Press the start button.
3. Preheat the oven to 338 F. prepare a baking tray by spraying cooking oil and placing parchment paper.
4. Take the dough out and cut it into three pieces. Roll the pieces into sausages shapes and pinch at one end.
5. Braid the dough. Pinch the top and bottom and make a circle.
6. Take three eggs and color them differently. Fit the eggs into the circled dough and let it rest for 20 minutes.
7. Bake in the oven for 20 minutes after glazing with egg wash.
8. Serve.

Fiji Sweet Potato Bread

(Ready in about 2 hours 15 minutes I Servings- One loaf I Difficulty- Moderate)

Ingredients

- Two teaspoons of active dry yeast
- One cup of mashed sweet potatoes (plain)
- Four cups of bread flour
- One and a half teaspoons of salt
- Two tablespoons and a half cup of water
- Two tablespoons of softened butter
- 1/3 cup of dark brown sugar
- chopped pecans
- One teaspoon of vanilla extract
- Two tablespoons of dry milk powder
- 1/4 teaspoon (each) of ground nutmeg & cinnamon

Instructions

1. Add all ingredients, except pecans, to the bread machine in the manufacturer's suggested order.
2. Select white bread cycle—light crust and Press the start button.
3. Add nuts at the ingredient signal.
4. Enjoy fresh bread.

Za'atar Bread

(Ready in about 3 hours 40 minutes I Servings- One loaf I Difficulty- Moderate)

Ingredients

- Three and a half cups of bread flour
- One and 1/3 cups of water
- 1 and 1/4 teaspoons of sugar
- Two and a half tablespoons of olive oil
- Two teaspoons of quick yeast
- One teaspoon of salt
- Two and a half teaspoons of Za'atar

Instructions

1. Put all the required ingredients in the container of the bread machine in the suggested order by the manufacturer.
2. Select the quick bread cycle—medium crust and Press the start button.
3. Let it cool before slicing and serving.

Panettone Bread

(Ready in about 3 hours 10 minutes I Servings- One loaf I Difficulty- Moderate)

Ingredients

- One and a half teaspoons of vanilla extract
- 3/4 cup of water
- Two eggs mixed
- Three and 1/4 cups of flour
- Two tablespoons of sugar
- 1/4 cup of softened butter
- One and a half teaspoons of salt
- Half cup mixed dried fruit, chopped
- Two tablespoons of powdered milk
- Two teaspoons of yeast

Instructions

1. Add all ingredients, except dried fruits, to the bread machine in the manufacturer's suggested order.
2. Select the sweet bread cycle. Light crust. Press the start button.
3. Enjoy fresh bread.

White Chocolate Cranberry Bread

(Ready in about 3 hours 10 minutes I Servings- One loaf I Difficulty- Moderate)

Ingredients

- Four tablespoons of Softened butter
- One cup of milk
- Three tablespoons of water
- One and a half teaspoons vanilla
- One whole egg
- Four cups of bread flour
- Six tablespoons of chopped white baking bar
- Half cup of dried cranberries
- Two tablespoons of sugar
- One and a 1/4 teaspoons of bread machine yeast
- One teaspoon of salt

Instructions

1. Add all ingredients, except cranberries, to the bread machine in the suggested order by the manufacturer.
2. Select white bread cycle. Light crust. Press the start button.
3. Add cranberries at the ingredient signal.
4. Enjoy fresh bread.

Eggnog Bread

(Ready in about 3 hours 10 minutes I Servings- One loaf I Difficulty- Moderate)

Ingredients
- One and a ¼ teaspoon of salt
  Four cups of bread flour
- Half cup of dried cranberries or raisins
- One tablespoon of oil
- Half cup of milk
- Two tablespoons of sugar
- One cup of eggnog
- One and a ¾ teaspoons of active dry yeast
- One teaspoon of cinnamon

Instructions
1. Put all the required ingredients in the container of the bread machine in the suggested order by the manufacturer.
2. Select the basic cycle. Medium crust. Press the start button.
3. Enjoy fresh bread.

Whole-Wheat Challah

(Ready in about 3 hours 10 minutes I Servings- One loaf I Difficulty- Moderate)

Ingredients
- Two whole eggs
- One cup of warm water
- 1/4 or half cup of honey
- Half teaspoon of salt
- 1/4 teaspoon of canola oil
- Two and a half teaspoons of instant yeast
- 4 cups of whole wheat flour
- One cup of white flour

Instructions
1. Put all the required ingredients in the container of the bread machine in the suggested order by the
2. manufacturer.
3. Select the dough cycle. Press the start button.
4. Take the dough out on a floured clean surface. Separate the dough into three long pieces.
5. Bread the dough together. Brush with egg wash and seeds—Bake at 350 F for 30 minutes. It should sound hollow at tapping.
6. Enjoy.

Portuguese Sweet Bread

(Ready in about 3 hours 10 minutes I Servings- One loaf I Difficulty- Moderate)

Ingredients
- One whole egg mixed
- 1/3 cup of sugar
- 3/4 teaspoon of salt
- Two and a half teaspoons of yeast
- One cup of milk
- Two tablespoons of Margarine
- Three cups of bread flour

Instructions
1. Put all the required ingredients in the container of the bread machine in the suggested order by the manufacturer.
2. Select the sweet bread cycle—Press the start button.

3. Serve fresh bread.

Pecan Maple Bread

(Ready in about 3 hours 10 minutes I Servings- One loaf I Difficulty- Moderate)

Ingredients
- One and ¼ cup of whole meal flour
- Three tablespoons maple syrup
- ¾ teaspoon of yeast
- One and ¼ cup white flour
- Half cup of pecan pieces
- One teaspoon of salt
- One cup of and Three tablespoons of water
- One tablespoon of butter

Instructions
1. Add all ingredients, except for pecans, to the bread machine in the manufacturer's suggested order.
2. Select the basic cycle. Light crust. Press the start button.
3. Enjoy fresh bread.

Nana's Gingerbread

(Ready in about 3 hours 10 minutes I Servings- One loaf I Difficulty- Moderate)

Ingredients
- Three tablespoons of melted Butter
- 3/4 cup of Rye flour
- One and a 1/4 cup of milk
- 1/4 teaspoon of grated Nutmeg
- One and a half teaspoon of Salt
- 3/4 teaspoon of ground Cinnamon
- Two and 2/3 cup of bread flour
- 1/4 teaspoon of Ground Cloves
- Two teaspoons of Ground Ginger
- Two and a 1/4 teaspoon of Active dry yeast
- Six tablespoons of Brown sugar

Instructions
1. Add milk to a pot, simmer it and mix with brown sugar and butter.
2. Add the rest of the ingredients to the bread machine in the suggested order by the manufacturer.
3. Select the basic cycle. Press the start button.
4. Serve fresh bread.

Bread Machine Brioche

(Ready in about 3 hours 10 minutes I Servings- One loaf I Difficulty- Moderate)

Ingredients
- Two tablespoons of bread flour
- One and a ¾ teaspoons of active dry yeast
- Three tablespoons of sugar
- One and ¾ cups of bread flour
- Two eggs and one yolk
- ¼ cup of water
- Eight tablespoons of unsalted butter
- ¾ teaspoon of salt

- Two tablespoons of water

Instructions

1. Place all ingredients in the pan of the bread machine, except butter, in the manufacturer's suggested order.
2. Select the basic cycle. Light crust. Press the start button.
3. Dice butter into small pieces.
4. After the end of the kneading cycle or after ten minutes, add butter one tablespoon of worth at a time.
5. Serve fresh bread.

Traditional Pascha

(Ready in about 3 hours 10 minutes I Servings- One loaf I Difficulty- Moderate)
Ingredients

- Half cup of warm water
- Zest of 1⁄4 lemon
- One teaspoon of fresh lemon juice
- Zest of 1⁄4 orange
- Half cup of warm milk
- One teaspoon of fresh orange juice
- Two whole eggs and one yolk
- 1⁄4 teaspoon of Vanilla extract
- One teaspoon of anise seed
- 1⁄3 cup of granulated sugar
- Three and a half cups of flour
- One teaspoon of salt
- One and a half teaspoons of active dry yeast
- Half cup of butter at room temperature

Instructions

1. Add all ingredients, except anise seeds, to the bread machine in the manufacturer's suggested order.
2. Select the sweet bread cycle. Dark crust. Press the start button.
3. Add seeds to the ingredient signal.
4. Enjoy fresh bread.

Raisin & Nut Pascha

(Ready in about 4 hours 5 minutes I Servings- One loaf I Difficulty- Moderate)

Ingredients

- One package of yeast
- Three tablespoons of sugar
- 1⁄4 cup of water
- Four tablespoons of cooled melted butter
- One and a half teaspoons of salt
- 3⁄4 cup of milk
- Two whole eggs
- 1⁄3 cup of golden raisin
- Three cups of bread flour
- 1⁄4 cup of honey
- 3⁄4 cup of mixed nuts
- 1⁄3 cup of regular raisins

Instructions

1. Put all the required ingredients in the container of the bread machine in the suggested order by the manufacturer.
2. Select the basic cycle. Press the start button.
3. Enjoy fresh bread.

Honey Cake

(Ready in about 3 hours 10 minutes I Servings- One loaf I Difficulty- Moderate)

Ingredients

- Two tablespoons of Milk
- Two tablespoons and one teaspoon of Honey
- One and a 1⁄4 cup of Pancake mix
- Two whole eggs mixed
- 1⁄4 cup and Three tablespoons of Unsalted butter at room temperature

Instructions

1. Dice the butter into 1 cm pieces.
2. Put all the required ingredients in the container of the bread machine in the suggested order by the manufacturer.
3. Select cake cycle. Press the start button.
4. At the ingredient signal, with a rubber spatula, scrape the pan. Let the cycle continue
5. Serve fresh bread.

Christmas Fruit Bread

(Ready in about 3 hours 10 minutes I Servings- One loaf I Difficulty- Moderate)

Ingredients

- One and a half tablespoon of sugar
- One whole egg
- One teaspoon of Bread machine yeast
- Half teaspoon of ground cardamom
- One teaspoon of salt
- One cup and two tablespoons of water
- 1/3 cup of mixed candied fruit
- 1/4 cup of softened butter
- Three cups of bread flour
- 1/3 cups of raisins

Instructions

1. Add all ingredients, except the candied fruits and raisins, to the bread machine in the manufacturer's suggested order.
2. Select the basic cycle. Medium crust. Press the start button.
3. Add candied fruits and raisins at the ingredient signal.
4. Enjoy fresh bread.

Stollen Bread

(Ready in about 3 hours 10 minutes I Servings- One loaf I Difficulty- Moderate)

Ingredients

- Two whole eggs
- 1/4 cup of non-fat milk powder
- Two teaspoons of bread machine yeast
- One cup of water
- Three and 3/4 cups of bread flour

- Two tablespoons of sugar
- Two teaspoons of lemon zest
- Two tablespoons of butter
- One and a half teaspoon of salt
- 3/4 teaspoon of ground nutmeg
- 1/4 cup of slivered almonds, cut into slices
- Half-cup of mixed candied fruit
- Half cup of raisins

Instructions

1. Add all ingredients, except for raisins, some almonds slice, and candied fruits, to the bread machine in the manufacturer's suggested order.
2. Select the basic cycle. Light crust. Press the start button.
3. Add raisins and candied fruit at the signal ingredient.
4. Before the baking cycle begins, add the leftover almond slices to the loaf.
5. Enjoy fresh bread.

Tulelake

(Ready in about 3 hours 10 minutes | Servings- One loaf | Difficulty- Moderate)

Ingredients

- One teaspoon Bread machine yeast
- Half teaspoon of ground cardamom
- One teaspoon of salt
- One egg mixed with enough water to make One cup and Two tablespoons of the mixture
- One tablespoon and one teaspoon of sugar
- 1/3 cup of mixed candied fruit
- 1/4 cup of softened butter
- Three cups of bread flour
- 1/3 cup of raisins

Instructions

1. Add all ingredients, except candied fruits and raisins, to the bread machine in the manufacturer's suggested order.
2. Select white bread cycle. Medium or light crust. Press the start button.
3. Add candied fruit and raisins at the nut signal.
4. Enjoy fresh bread.

Spiked Eggnog Bread

(Ready in about 3 hours 10 minutes | Servings- One loaf | Difficulty- Moderate)

Ingredients

- Three cups of bread flour
- One and a 1/4 teaspoons of yeast
- 3/4 teaspoon of salt
- Half cup of eggnog
- 1/4 cup of milk
- One whole egg
- Two tablespoons of sugar
- Half cup of glace cherries, cut into halves
- Two tablespoons of butter, diced
- Half teaspoon of nutmeg

Instructions

1. Place all ingredients in the bread machine, except cherries, in the suggested order by the manufacturer.
2. Select the basic cycle. Medium crust. Press the start button.
3. Add cherries to the ingredient signal.
4. Serve fresh bread.

Hot Buttered Rum Bread

(Ready in about 3 hours 10 minutes | Servings- One loaf | Difficulty- Moderate)

Instructions

- One tablespoon of rum extract
- One whole egg
- Three tablespoons of softened butter
- Three cups of bread flour
- One and a 1/4 teaspoons of salt
- Half teaspoon of ground cinnamon
- One teaspoon of Bread machine
- 1/4 teaspoon of ground nutmeg
- Three tablespoons of brown sugar, packed
- 1/4 teaspoon of ground cardamom

Nuts Topping

- One and a half teaspoons of packed brown sugar
- One and a half teaspoons of pecans, finely chopped
- One egg yolk, beaten

Instructions

1. Mix the whole egg with water to make one cup. Place in the bread machine.
2. Add the rest of the ingredients to the bread machine in the suggested order by the manufacturer.
3. Select a sweet cycle: light or medium crust. Do not use the delay feature.
4. Press the start button.
5. Meanwhile, mix all ingredients of topping in the bowl. Before the baking cycle begins, brush the topping on the loaf.
6. Enjoy fresh bread.

Zucchini Pecan Bread

(Ready in about 1 hour 40 minutes | Servings- One loaf | Difficulty- Moderate)

Ingredients

- 1/3 cup of Vegetable Oil
- Two teaspoons of Baking Powder
- Three whole eggs mixed
- 3/4 cup of sugar
- One teaspoon of Baking Soda
- Half teaspoon of Allspice
- Half teaspoon of salt
- Half cup chopped toasted pecans
- Two cups of all-Purpose Flour
- One teaspoon of cinnamon
- One cup of shredded zucchini

Instructions

1. Add oil and mixed eggs in the bread machine.

2. Add flour, then add the rest of the ingredients, except for zucchini.
3. Select the cake/quick cycle. Dark crust if you like.
4. Press the start button.
5. Add in the zucchini at the ingredient signal. Serve fresh.

Raisin Bran Bread

(Ready in about 3 hours 10 minutes I Servings- One loaf I Difficulty- Moderate)

Ingredients

- Two tablespoons of softened butter
- Two and a 1/4 teaspoons of active dry yeast
- 1/4 cup of packed brown sugar
- One and a half cups of raisin bran
- Half teaspoon of salt
- One cup and one tablespoon of lukewarm water
- 1/4 teaspoon of baking soda
- Half cup of raisins
- Two and 1/4 cups of bread flour

Instructions

1. Add all ingredients to the bread machine, except for raisins, in the manufacturer's suggested order.
2. Select basic bread. Crust color to your liking.
3. Check dough if it needs more water or flour. Add one tablespoon at a time.
4. At the signal, add raisins.
5. Serve fresh bread.

Lemon Poppy Seed Bread

(Ready in about 3 hours 10 minutes I Servings- One loaf I Difficulty- Moderate)

Ingredients

- Three cups of bread flour
- One and a half Tablespoons of dry milk
- ¾ cup of water
- One teaspoon of salt
- One and a half tablespoons of butter
- Two Tablespoons of honey
- Two teaspoons of Lemon extract
- ¾ cup of lemon yogurt
- Half cup of toasted almonds, cut into slices
- One tablespoon of Lemon peel
- Two teaspoons of yeast
- Three tablespoons of Poppy seeds

Instructions

1. Put all the required ingredients in the container of the bread machine in the suggested order by the manufacturer.
2. Select the sweet bread cycle—Press the start button.
3. Enjoy fresh bread.

Mustard Rye Bread

(Ready in about 3 hours 10 minutes I Servings- One loaf I Difficulty- Moderate)

Ingredients

- 1/4 cup of ground mustard
- One tablespoon of Butter
- One and 1/4 cups of water
- Two tablespoons of gluten flour
- Two cups of bread flour
- One and a half cups of rye flour
- 3/4 teaspoon of salt
- One tablespoon of brown sugar
- One teaspoon of dry yeast
- One teaspoon of caraway seed

Instructions

1. Put all the required ingredients in the container of the bread machine in the suggested order by the manufacturer.
2. Select whole wheat/ basic cycle.
3. Serve fresh bread.

Ham & Cheese Bread

(Ready in about 3 hours 10 minutes I Servings- One loaf I Difficulty- Moderate)

Ingredients

- Two tablespoons of softened butter
- One and 1/3 cups of Luke warm water
- One tablespoon of Non-fat dry milk powder
- One tablespoon of Active dry yeast
- Three tablespoons of Mashed potato flakes
- Two tablespoons of Cornmeal
- One and a half teaspoons of salt
- Half cup of Swiss cheese, diced
- Four cups of bread flour
- Half cup of cooked diced ham

Instructions

1. Put all the required ingredients in the container of the bread machine in the suggested order by the manufacturer.
2. Select basic bread cycle. Light crust color. Press the start button.
3. Enjoy fresh bread.

Sausage Herb Bread

(Ready in about 3 hours 10 minutes I Servings- One loaf I Difficulty- Moderate)

Ingredients

- 3/4 teaspoon of Basil leaves
- One and a half tablespoon of Sugar
- One small Onion minced
- Two and a 1/4 teaspoon of yeast
- 3/4 teaspoon of thyme leaves
- 3/4 teaspoon of rosemary leaves
- 3/8 cup of Wheat bran
- Half tablespoon of Salt
- 6 oz. of Italian sausage
- Three cups of bread flour
- 3/4 teaspoon of Oregano leaves
- One and a half tablespoon of grated Parmesan

- One and 1/8 cup of warm water

Instructions

1. Cook crumbled sausage for three minutes on medium flame. Add onion and cook for five minutes, until onion softens.
2. Turn off the heat and let it cool. All the ingredients must be at room temperature.
3. Put all the required ingredients in the container of the bread machine in the suggested order by the manufacturer.
4. Select white bread and Press the start button. In humid, hot weather, use less water.
5. Serve fresh bread.

Wild Rice Hazelnut Bread

(Ready in about 3 hours 10 minutes I Servings- One loaf I Difficulty- Moderate)

Ingredients

- One and a 1/4 cup of water
- Three cups of bread flour
- 1/4 cup of non-fat milk powder
- Two tablespoons of liquid honey
- One and a 1/4 teaspoon of salt
- One tablespoon of olive oil
- ¾ cup of Cooked wild rice
- One teaspoon of Bread machine
- ¼ cup of Pine nuts
- ¾ cup of Celery seeds
- 2/3 cup of Hazelnuts
- 1/8 teaspoon of Black pepper

Instructions

1. Add all ingredients to the bread machine, except cranberries, in the suggested order by the manufacturer.
2. Select basic cycle light crust. Press the start button.
3. Add cranberries at the ingredients signal.

Spinach Feta Bread

(Ready in about 4 hours 10 minutes I Servings- One loaf I Difficulty- Moderate)

Ingredients

- One cup of water
- One cup of fresh spinach leaves, chopped
- Two teaspoons of softened butter
- One teaspoon of sugar
- Three cups of flour
- One teaspoon of salt
- Two teaspoons of minced onion (instant)
- One and a 1/4 teaspoons of instant yeast
- One cup of crumbled feta

Instructions

1. Add all ingredients, except spinach, cheese, and yeast, to the bread machine in the manufacturer's suggested order.
2. Add yeast to yeast hopper. In the kneading cycle (last), add cheese and spinach.
3. Select basic cycle light crust.

4. Enjoy.

Rum Raisin Bread

(Ready in about 3 hours 35 minutes I Servings- One loaf I Difficulty- Moderate)

Ingredients

- Two tablespoons of dark rum
- ¾ cup of room temperature milk
- One teaspoon of salt
- Two tablespoons of packed brown sugar
- One whole egg
- 2 and ¼ cups of bread flour
- One cup of raisins
- Half teaspoon of ground allspice
- One and a ¾ teaspoons of bread machine yeast
- Two tablespoons of softened butter

Instructions

1. Place all ingredients into the pan of the bread machine, except raisins, according to the order suggested by the manufacturer.
2. Use Sweet Cycle. At ingredient signal, add raisins.
3. Serve fresh bread.

Bacon Corn Bread

(Ready in about 2 hours 50 minutes I Servings- One loaf I Difficulty- Moderate)

Ingredients

- Two tablespoons of oil
- One and 1/3 cups of water
- Two teaspoons of active dry yeast
- One and a half teaspoon and two tablespoons of sugar
- Four cups of Bread flour
- Eight slices of bacon
- One and a 1/4 teaspoon of salt
- Three tablespoons of skim dry milk
- Two cups of cheddar cheese

Instructions

1. Add all ingredients, except bacon and cheese, to the bread machine in the manufacturer's suggested order.
2. Add bacon, cheese at the ingredient signal.
3. Select the basic cycle. Press the start button.
4. Enjoy.

Oatmeal Coffee Bread

(Ready in about 3 hours 10 minutes I Servings- One loaf I Difficulty- Moderate)

Ingredients

- One and ¼ cup of Bread flour
- Half cup and two tablespoons of Cake flour
- One and a half tablespoon of Coffee powder
- Two tablespoons and one teaspoon of sugar
- Half cup and two tablespoons of water/milk
- Half cup of oats
- One tablespoon and one teaspoon of Butter

- Three tablespoons and two teaspoons of Milk powder
- One teaspoon of yeast

Instructions

1. Add all ingredients, except butter, to the bread machine in the suggested order by the manufacturer.
2. Select basic cycle, light crust. Add butter after the dough cycle.
3. Serve fresh bread.

Cherry Pistachio Bread

(Ready in about 3 hours 10 minutes | Servings- One loaf | Difficulty- Moderate)

Ingredients

- One whole egg
- Half cup of cherry preserves
- Half cup of water
- 1/4 cup of butter
- One teaspoon of salt
- Two and a 1/4 teaspoons of active dry yeast
- Half teaspoon of almond extract
- Half cup of chopped pistachio
- Three and a half cups of bread flour

Instructions

1. Put all the required ingredients in the container of the bread machine in the suggested order by the manufacturer.
2. Select the basic cycle. Press the start button. Check dough; it should be a smooth ball; add one tablespoon of water or flour if too dry or too sticky, respectively.
3. Serve fresh bread.

Banana Coconut Bread

(Ready in about 3 hours 10 minutes | Servings- One loaf | Difficulty- Moderate)

Ingredients

- Eight tablespoons of sugar
- Three large ripe bananas
- One teaspoon of baking powder
- Two cups of plain flour
- One teaspoon of salt
- Half cup of coconut flakes
- Two whole eggs
- Half teaspoon of vanilla
- Half teaspoon of cinnamon

Instructions

1. Mix the sugar with mashed bananas.
2. Put all the required ingredients in the container of the bread machine in the suggested order by the manufacturer.
3. Select the basic cycle. Press the start button.
4. Enjoy fresh bread.

Easy Honey Beer Bread

(Ready in about 1 hour 45 minutes | Servings- One loaf | Difficulty- Moderate)

Ingredients

- Two tablespoons of olive oil
- 3/4 teaspoon of salt
- Three and a half cups of bread flour
- One and a 3/4 teaspoons of fast-rising yeast
- One and 1/8 cups of flat beer
- 1/4 cup of honey

Instructions

1. Put all the required ingredients in the container of the bread machine in the suggested order by the manufacturer.
2. Select the basic cycle. Press the start button.
3. Enjoy fresh bread.

Coffee Molasses Bread

(Ready in about 2 hours 40 minutes | Servings- One loaf | Difficulty- Moderate)

Ingredients

- Three tablespoons of honey
- Two tablespoons of butter
- One and a half teaspoons of salt
- Three cups of bread flour
- One whole egg mixed
- Instant coffer mixed in One cup of boiling water
- One tablespoon of dark molasses
- Half cup of oats
- Two teaspoons of yeast

Instructions

1. Mix oats with one cup of boiling water and set it aside. Let them come to
2. 110 F or lukewarm temperature.
3. Put all the required ingredients in the container of the bread machine in the suggested order by the manufacturer.
4. Select the basic cycle. Light crust. Press the start button.
5. Serve fresh bread.

Pear Sweet Potato Bread

(Ready in about 2 hours 25 minutes | Servings- One loaf | Difficulty- Moderate)

Ingredients

- Half teaspoon of almond extract
- One can of undrained (15 ounces) pear halves
- Mashed sweet potatoes: half cup
- One and a half teaspoons of salt
- Two tablespoons of softened butter
- Three and a half cups of bread flour
- One teaspoon of ground cinnamon
- Two and a 1/4 teaspoons of active dry yeast
- 1/4 teaspoon of ground nutmeg

Instructions

1. Puree the pear halves and juice in the blender. Add to the bread machine.
2. Add the rest of the ingredients to the bread machine in the suggested order by the manufacturer.
3. Select the basic cycle. Press the start button.

4. Enjoy fresh bread.

Irish Potato Brown Bread

(Ready in about 2 hours 25 minutes I Servings- One loaf I Difficulty- Moderate)

Ingredients

- One and 1/4cups water
- Three tablespoons butter, cut into pieces
- Two tablespoons honey
- Two cups of whole wheat flour
- One cup of bread flour
- 1/4 cup instant potato flakes
- One tablespoon plus two teaspoons gluten
- One and a half teaspoons salt
- Two teaspoons SAF yeast or Two and a half teaspoons bread machine yeast

Instructions

1. Place all the ingredients in the pan according to the order in the manufacturer's instructions. Set crust on medium and program for the Whole Wheat cycle; press Start.
2. When the baking cycle ends, immediately remove the pan's bread and place it on a rack. Let cool to room temperature before slicing.

Harpers' Loaf

(Ready in about 2 hours 25 minutes I Servings- Two loaf I Difficulty- Moderate)

Ingredients

- One and 1/8 cups water
- Two large eggs
- Three tablespoons peanut oil
- Three tablespoons honey
- Three tablespoons unsalted butter, cut into pieces
- Two cups of whole wheat flour
- One and a half cups bread flour
- One and a half teaspoons salt
- Two and a half teaspoons SAF yeast or one tablespoon bread machine yeast
- Two tablespoons rolled oats for sprinkling
- Two tablespoons sunflower seeds for sprinkling

Instructions

1. Place all the ingredients in the pan according to the order in the manufacturer's instructions. Program for the Dough cycle; press Start.
2. Lightly brush the bottom and sides of two 8-by-4-inch loaf pans with peanut oil. Turn the dough out onto a clean work surface; it will naturally deflate. Without working the dough further, use your metal bench scraper or knife to divide the dough into four equal portions. With the palms of your hands, roll into four fat oblong sausages, each about 10 inches long.
3. Place 2 of the pieces side by side. Holding both dough pieces together at one end, wrap one around the other 2 to 3 times to create a fat twist effect. Repeat to form the second loaf. Place in the pans and tuck under the ends. Brush the tops with some peanut oil. Cover loosely with plastic wrap and let rise at room temperature until the dough is almost doubled in bulk, about 1-inch over the pans' rims, 45 minutes to 1 hour.
4. Twenty minutes before baking, set the oven rack to the middle and preheat the oven to 350°F (lower the temperature by 25° if using glass pans).
5. Brush the tops of the loaves with more peanut oil. Sprinkle the tops with the oats and sunflower seeds. Bake for 40 to 45 minutes, or until the loaves are deep golden brown, and the sides are slightly contracted from the pan. Lift one end of a loaf out of the pan to peek underneath to check for even browning on the bottom, and tap on the top and bottom surface with your finger; it should sound hollow. An instant-read thermometer will read 200°F. Immediately remove the loaves from the pans and place them on a rack. Let cool to room temperature before slicing.

Tecate Ranch Whole Wheat Bread

(Ready in about 2 hours 25 minutes I Servings- One loaf I Difficulty- Moderate)

Ingredients

- One and 1/3 cups of water
- Three tablespoons canola oil
- Two tablespoons honey
- Two tablespoons molasses
- Three and 1/4 cups whole wheat flour
- 1/3 cup wheat bran
- Two and a half tablespoons gluten
- One tablespoon poppy seed
- One and a half teaspoons salt
- One tablespoon SAF yeast or one tablespoon plus Half teaspoon bread machine yeast

Instructions

1. Place all the ingredients in the pan according to the order in the manufacturer's instructions. Set crust on dark and program for the Whole Wheat cycle; press Start. After 10 minutes, check the dough ball with your finger. It will be sticky. Add 1 to Two tablespoons more flour. The dough will still be very sticky; don't worry, it will absorb the liquid during the rises. If you add too much flour, the bread will be dense rather than springy. If you don't add the extra flour as needed, the top can collapse.
2. When the baking cycle ends, immediately remove the pan's bread and place it on a rack. Let cool to room temperature before slicing.

Italian Chocolate Bread with Amaretto Icing

(Ready in about 2 hours 25 minutes I Servings- One loaf I Difficulty- Moderate)

Ingredients

For the nuts:

- Two cups of water
- Three tablespoons baking soda
- 2 ounces whole hazelnuts (Half cup)

For the dough:

- 7/8 cup milk

- One large egg
- Two tablespoons amaretto liqueur
- Three tablespoons unsalted butter, cut into pieces
- Two and 7/8 cups bread flour
- 1/3 cup sugar
- Two tablespoons unsweetened Dutch-process cocoa powder
- One tablespoon gluten
- One and 1/4teaspoons salt
- One teaspoon ground cinnamon
- Two teaspoons SAF yeast or Two and a half teaspoons bread machine yeast

For the amaretto icing:
- Half cup sifted confectioners' sugar
- One and 1/4tablespoons amaretto liqueur
- Two teaspoons hot milk

Instructions

1. Preheat the oven to 350oF.
2. To skin the nuts, bring the water to a boil in a saucepan. Add the baking soda and the nuts. Boil for 3 to 5 minutes; the water will turn black. Pour the nuts into a colander and run under a stream of cold water. Using your fingers, slip off each skin, and place the nuts on a clean dish towel. Pat dry and place on a clean baking sheet. Toast the nuts for 10 to 15minutes, stirring twice. Cool on the baking sheet. Coarsely chop the nuts.
3. To make the dough, place all the ingredients in the pan according to the manufacturer's instructions, adding the nuts with the dry ingredients. Set crust on medium and program for the Sweet Bread cycle; press Start.
4. When the baking cycle ends, remove the pan's bread and place it on a rack with a sheet of parchment paper or a large plate underneath.
5. To make the icing, combine the icing ingredients in a small bowl and mix until smooth. Adjust the consistency by adding more milk, a few drops at a time. Using an oversized spoon, drizzle, or pour in a back-and-forth motion over the top of the loaf. As the glaze cools, it will set up.

Cornmeal Honey Bread

(Ready in about 2 hours 25 minutes I Servings- One loaf I Difficulty- Moderate)

Ingredients

- One and 1/8 cups water
- One and a half tablespoons unsalted butter, cut into pieces
- Three tablespoons honey
- Two and 2/3 cups of bread flour
- 1/3 cup yellow cornmeal
- 1/3 cup dry buttermilk powder
- One tablespoon plus one teaspoon gluten
- One teaspoon salt
- One and 3/4 teaspoons SAF yeast or Two and 1/4teaspoons bread machine yeast

Instructions

1. Place all the ingredients in the pan according to the order in the manufacturer's instructions. Set crust on dark and program for the Basic cycle; press Start.
2. When the baking cycle ends, immediately remove the pan's bread and place it on a rack. Let cool to room temperature before slicing.

Polenta-Sunflower-Millet Bread

(Ready in about 2 hours 25 minutes I Servings- One loaf I Difficulty- Moderate)

Ingredients

- One and 1/8 cups water
- Three tablespoons honey
- Two tablespoons sunflower seed oil
- Two and a half cups bread flour
- Half cup whole wheat flour
- 1/4 cup polenta
- Three tablespoons whole raw millet
- Three tablespoons raw sunflower seeds
- One and a half tablespoons gluten
- One and a half teaspoons salt
- One and 3/4 teaspoons SAF yeast or Two and 1/4teaspoons bread machine yeast

Instructions

1. Place all the ingredients in the pan according to the order in the manufacturer's instructions. Set crust on medium and program for the Basic or Whole Wheat cycle; press Start.
2. When the baking cycle ends, immediately remove the pan's bread and place it on a rack. Let cool to room temperature before slicing.

Orange-Buckwheat Bread

(Ready in about 2 hours 25 minutes I Servings- One loaf I Difficulty- Moderate)

Ingredients

- One cup of buttermilk
- One large egg
- Two tablespoons unsalted butter, cut into pieces
- Two cups of bread flour
- 3/4 cup whole wheat flour
- 1/3 cup light buckwheat flour
- Two tablespoons dark brown sugar Grated zest of
- One large orange
- One tablespoon gluten
- One and a half teaspoons salt
- Two and 1/4teaspoons SAF yeast or 23/4 teaspoons bread machine yeast

Instructions

1. Place all the ingredients in the pan according to the order in the manufacturer's instructions. Set crust on dark and program for the Basic cycle; press Start. The dough ball will be moist and springy.
2. When the baking cycle ends, immediately remove the pan's bread and place it on a rack. Let cool to room temperature before slicing

Chestnut Flour Bread

(Ready in about 2 hours 25 minutes | Servings- One loaf | Difficulty- Moderate)

Ingredients

- 7/8 cup fat-free milk
- One large egg
- Three tablespoons butter or margarine, cut into pieces
- Two and a half cups bread flour
- Half cup chestnut flour
- Two tablespoons dark brown sugar
- Two tablespoons minced pecans
- One tablespoon gluten
- One and a half teaspoons salt
- Two teaspoons SAF yeast or Two and a half teaspoons bread machine yeast

Instructions

1. Place all the ingredients in the pan according to the order in the manufacturer's instructions. Set crust on medium or dark and program for the Basic cycle; press Start. The dough ball will be moist and springy.
2. When the baking cycle ends, immediately remove the pan's bread and place it on a rack. Let cool to room temperature before slicing

Polenta-Chestnut Bread

(Ready in about 2 hours 25 minutes | Servings- One loaf | Difficulty- Moderate)

Ingredients

- One cup of plus one tablespoon buttermilk
- Three tablespoons dark honey
- Three tablespoons olive oil
- Two and 1/3 cups of bread flour
- Half cup chestnut flour
- 1/3 cup polenta
- One and a half tablespoons gluten
- One and a half teaspoons salt
- Two and 1/4 teaspoons SAF yeast or two and 3/4 teaspoons bread machine yeast

Instructions

1. Place all the ingredients in the pan according to the order in the manufacturer's instructions. Set crust on dark and program for the Basic cycle; press Start. The dough ball will be firm yet slightly sticky.
2. When the baking cycle ends, immediately remove the pan's bread and place it on a rack. Let cool to room temperature before slicing.

Quinoa Bread

(Ready in about 2 hours 25 minutes | Servings- One loaf | Difficulty- Moderate)

Ingredients

- Half cup of water
- Half cup buttermilk
- Half cup firm-packed cooked quinoa (see cooking information)
- Two tablespoons sesame oil
- Two tablespoons honey

- Three cups of bread flour
- One tablespoon gluten
- One and a half teaspoons salt
- Two teaspoons SAF yeast or Two and a half teaspoons bread machine yeast

Instructions

1. Place all the ingredients in the pan according to the order in the manufacturer's instructions. Set crust on dark and program for the Basic cycle; press Start.
2. When the baking cycle ends, immediately remove the pan's bread and place it on a rack. Let cool to room temperature before slicing.

Teff Honey Bread

(Ready in about 2 hours 25 minutes | Servings- One loaf | Difficulty- Moderate)

Ingredients

- One and 1/8 cups water
- Two tablespoons vegetable oil
- Two tablespoons honey
- Two and 1/4 cups bread flour
- 3/4 cup ivory or dark teff flour
- One tablespoon plus one teaspoon gluten
- One and a half teaspoons salt
- Two and a half teaspoons SAF yeast or one tablespoon bread machine yeast

Instructions

1. Place all the ingredients in the pan according to the order in the manufacturer's instructions. Set crust on dark and program for the Basic cycle; press Start.
2. When the baking cycle ends, immediately remove the pan's bread and place it on a rack. Let cool to room temperature before slicing.

Brown Rice Flour Bread

(Ready in about 2 hours 25 minutes | Servings- One loaf | Difficulty- Moderate)

Ingredients

- One and 1/4 cups water
- Two tablespoons olive oil
- Two tablespoons honey
- One and 1/4 cups whole wheat flour
- One cup of bread flour
- 3/4 cup brown rice flour
- One and a half tablespoons nonfat dry milk
- One and a half tablespoons gluten
- One and a half teaspoons salt
- One tablespoon SAF yeast or one and a half tablespoon bread machine yeast

Instructions

1. Place all the ingredients in the pan according to the order in the manufacturer's instructions. Set crust on dark and program for the Whole Wheat cycle; press Start.
2. When the baking cycle ends, immediately remove the pan's bread and place it on a rack. Let cool to room temperature before slicing.

Wild Rice Bread

(Ready in about 2 hours 25 minutes I Servings- One loaf I Difficulty- Moderate)

Ingredients

- One and 1/8 cups water
- 1/3 cup raw wild rice
- Two and a half tablespoons walnut oil
- Two teaspoons light brown sugar
- Two and 3/4 cups bread flour
- 1/3 cup pumpernickel rye flour
- One tablespoon plus one teaspoon gluten
- One and a half teaspoons salt
- Two teaspoons SAF yeast or Two and a half teaspoons bread machine yeast

Instructions

1. Heat the water to a boil in a medium saucepan. Add the rice. Cover and simmer over low heat for 30 to 45 minutes, until the rice is tender. Strain the remaining cooking liquid into a 2-cup measure and add enough extra water to equal the pan's original amount. Set the liquid and rice aside separately to cool.
2. Place the ingredients, except the rice, in the pan according to the order in the manufacturer's instructions. Set crust on dark and program crust on dark and program for the Basic or Fruit and Nut cycle; press Start.
3. When the machine beeps, or between Knead 1 and Knead 2, add the rice. When the baking cycle ends, immediately remove the pan's bread and place it on a rack. Let cool to room temperature before slicing.

Franskbrod

(Ready in about 2 hours 25 minutes I Servings- One loaf I Difficulty- Moderate)

Ingredients

- One cup of water
- One large egg
- Three cups of bread flour
- One tablespoon sugar
- One tablespoon gluten
- One and 1/4teaspoons salt
- Two teaspoons SAF yeast or Two and a half teaspoons bread machine yeast

Instructions

1. Place all the ingredients in the pan according to the order in the manufacturer's instructions. Set crust on medium and program for the Basic or French Bread cycle; press Start
2. When the baking cycle ends, immediately remove the pan's bread and place it on a rack. Let cool to room temperature before slicing.

Brioche Bread

(Ready in about 2 hours 25 minutes I Servings- One loaf I Difficulty- Moderate)

Ingredients

- 1/3 cup milk
- Two large eggs
- One egg yolk
- Two cups of bread flour
- Two tablespoons sugar
- Two teaspoons gluten
- 3/4 teaspoon salt
- One and 1/4teaspoons SAF yeast or one and 3/4 teaspoons bread machine yeast
- Seven tablespoons unsalted butter, cut into pieces

Instructions

1. Place the ingredients, except the butter, in the pan according to the order in the manufacturer's instructions. Set crust on medium and program for the Basic cycle; press Start. The dough will be soft and sticky.
2. About 10 minutes into Knead 2, open the lid while the machine is running. Add a piece or two of the butter, allowing it to be incorporated before adding more pieces. It will take a full minute or two to add all the butter. Close the lid.
3. When the baking cycle ends, open the lid and let the bread sit in the pan for 15 minutes. Gently remove the loaf from the pan and place it on a rack. Let cool to room temperature before slicing.

Zopf (Swiss Egg Bread)

(Ready in about 2 hours 25 minutes I Servings- One loaf I Difficulty- Moderate)

Ingredients

- Half cup milk
- 1/3 cup water
- One large egg
- Two tablespoons unsalted butter, cut into pieces
- Three cups of bread flour
- One tablespoon sugar
- One tablespoon gluten
- One and a half teaspoons salt
- Two teaspoons SAF yeast or Two and a half teaspoons bread machine yeast

Instructions

1. Place all the ingredients in the pan according to the order in the manufacturer's instructions. Set crust on medium and program for the Basic cycle; press Start.
2. When the baking cycle ends, immediately remove the pan's bread and place it on a rack. Let cool to room temperature before slicing.

Chickpea Flour Bread

Ingredients

- One and 1/8 cups evaporated milk or evaporated goat's milk
- One tablespoon olive oil
- One tablespoon honey
- Two and a half cups bread flour
- Half cup chickpea flour
- One tablespoon plus two teaspoons gluten
- One and a half teaspoons salt
- 1/4 teaspoon ground cinnamon
- 1/4 teaspoon crushed hot pepper flakes

- Two and a half teaspoons SAF yeast or one tablespoon bread machine yeast

Instructions

1. Place all the ingredients in the pan according to the order in the manufacturer's instructions. Set crust on light and program for the Basic cycle; press Start.
2. When the baking cycle ends, immediately remove the pan's bread and place it on a rack. Let cool to room temperature before slicing.

Peasant Bread

(Ready in about 2 hours 25 minutes | Servings- One loaf | Difficulty- Moderate)

Ingredients

- One and 1/8 cups water
- Two tablespoons olive oil
- Three and 1/4 cups bread flour
- Two teaspoons gluten
- Two teaspoons sugar
- One and a half teaspoons salt
- Two teaspoons SAF yeast or Two and a half teaspoons bread machine yeast

Instructions

1. Place all the ingredients in the pan according to the order in the manufacturer's instructions. Set crust on dark and program for the Basic or French Bread cycle; press Start.
2. If using the Basic cycle, after Knead 2, press Stop, reset the machine, and start the cycle again, allowing the dough to be kneaded an extra time. The dough ball will be smooth, slightly moist, and springy.
3. When the baking cycle ends, immediately remove the pan's bread and place it on a rack. Let cool to room temperature before slicing.

Classic Baguettes

(Ready in about 2 hours 25 minutes | Servings- 2 | Difficulty- Moderate)

Ingredients

- One and a half cups water
- Three and 1/4 cups unbleached all-purpose flour
- Two teaspoons gluten with vitamin C
- One and 3/4 teaspoons salt
- Two and a half teaspoons SAF yeast or one tablespoon bread machine yeast

Instructions

1. Place all the ingredients in the pan according to the order in the manufacturer's instructions. Program for the Dough cycle; press Start. The dough ball will be sticky. Do not add any more flour at this point.
2. Oil two baguette trays. When the machine beeps at the end of the cycle, press Stop and unplug the machine. Immediately remove the pan from the machine and turn the wet dough into a floured work surface using a dough card. Knead a few times with your dough card (the dough will be too sticky to knead with your hands) to incorporate just enough flour (no more than 1/4 cup) so that the dough is not in a

puddle, and you can shape the loaves. You want this dough to stay as wet as possible. Divide the dough into two equal portions.

3. Flatten each portion into a thin 10-by-6-inch rectangle with the palm of your hand. Starting with a long side, roll one up, using your thumbs to help roll tightly. With the side of your hand, define a depression lengthwise down the center of the dough. Repeatedly fold the dough over in thirds the long way to make a tight log and pinch the seams to seal. Stretch the log by rolling it back and forth on the table with your palms a few times until about 15 inches long. Gently transfer to the prepared pan seam side down. Stretch the log to fit the 18-inch pan. No dough will hang over the ends of the pan. Repeat with the other piece of dough. Cover loosely with a clean tea towel and let the dough rise at room temperature until two and a half times its size in bulk, about 1 hour.
4. With a small, sharp knife, slash the baguettes' surface 3 or 4 times on the diagonal, no more than One and 1/4inch deep. This must be done gently, as the delicate dough will deflate slightly. Cover again.
5. Place a baking stone or tiles on the center rack and preheat the oven to 450°F.
6. Lightly brush the tops of the loaves with cold water. Place the pans directly on the stone and bake for 20 to 25 minutes, or until the loaves' surfaces are a deep golden brown and sound hollow when tapped with your finger. Immediately remove the bread from the pans and place them on a rack. Eat hot or within 2 hours.

Panino Bruschetta

(Ready in about 2 hours 25 minutes | Servings- 9 | Difficulty- Moderate)

Ingredients

For the dough:
- Half cup of water
- Half cup of milk
- One large egg
- One tablespoon olive oil
- Three and 1/4 cups bread flour
- One tablespoon yellow cornmeal or polenta
- One tablespoon whole wheat flour
- One and a half teaspoons salt
- One teaspoon sugar
- Two and 1/4teaspoons SAF yeast or two and 3/4 teaspoons bread machine yeast

For the garlic oil:
- 1/4 cup olive oil
- Two cloves garlic, pressed
- Coarse sea salt or kosher salt, for sprinkling

Instructions

1. Place all the dough ingredients in the pan according to the order in the manufacturer's instructions. Program for the Dough cycle; press Start.
2. When the machine beeps at the end of the cycle, open the lid and poke the dough with your fingers to deflate.
3. Close the lid, unplug the machine, and let the dough stand in the machine for 45 minutes longer.
4. Line a large baking sheet with parchment paper and dust with flour. Turn the dough out onto a lightly

floured work surface. With a rolling pin, roll the dough out into a 10-by-6-inch rectangle that is 1-inch thick. Cut out circles of dough with a 3-inch biscuit cutter or drinking glass. Reroll scraps and cut out more circles. Place the circles on the baking sheet about 2 inches apart, three across, and four down. Cover loosely with a clean tea towel and let rest for 25 minutes.

5. Twenty minutes before baking, place a baking stone on the lower third rack and preheat the oven to 400°F.
6. To make the garlic oil, combine the olive oil and garlic in a small saucepan or microwave-proof bowl. Heat until just warm.
7. Brush the tops of the rolls with the garlic oil and sprinkle with salt. Bake for 12 to 15 minutes, until golden brown.
8. Remove the rolls from the baking sheet and cool on racks.

Pain De Maison Sur Poolish

(Ready in about 2 hours 25 minutes I Servings- One loaf I Difficulty- Moderate)

Ingredients

For the poolish
- One cup of water
- One and 1/4cups organic bread flour
- 1/4 teaspoon SAF or bread machine yeast

For the dough
- 1/3 cup water
- One and a half teaspoons SAF yeast or two teaspoons bread machine yeast
- Two cups of organic bread flour
- One tablespoon sugar
- One tablespoon gluten
- One and a half teaspoons salt

Instructions

1. To make the poolish starter, place the water, flour, and yeast in the pan. Program for the Dough cycle, and set a kitchen timer for 10 minutes. When the timer rings, press Stop and unplug the machine. Let the starter sit in the machine for about 6 hours.
2. To make the dough, combine the water and the yeast, stirring to dissolve. Pour into the pan with the poolish and add the flour, sugar, gluten, and salt. Set crust on dark and program for the French Bread cycle; press Start. The dough ball will be slightly wet and slack but smooth and elastic.
3. When the baking cycle ends, check the bread. If the crust is still pale and the loaf is not done, reset for Bake Only for 12 minutes longer. When the bread is done, immediately remove it from the pan and place it on a rack. Let cool to room temperature before slicing.

Pain De Paris

(Ready in about 2 hours 25 minutes I Servings- 2 I Difficulty- Moderate)

Ingredients

For the pâte fermentée:
- Half cup of water
- One and 1/4cups bread flour
- Pinch of sea salt
- Half teaspoon SAF or one teaspoon bread machine yeast

For the dough:
- One cup and one tablespoon water
- Two cups of bread flour
- One and a half teaspoons gluten with vitamin C
- 3/4 teaspoon SAF yeast or One and 1/4teaspoons bread machine yeast
- Half cup pâte fermentée
- One teaspoon sea salt

Instructions

1. To make the pâte fermentée starter, place the starter ingredients /in the pan. Program for the Dough cycle; press Start. Set a kitchen timer for 10 minutes. When the timer rings, press Pause and set the timer again for 10 minutes. Let the starter rest for 10 minutes. When the timer rings, press Start to continue and finish the Dough cycle. When the machine beeps at the end of the cycle, press Stop and unplug the machine. Gently deflate the spongy starter, and let it sit in the bread machine for 3 to 12 hours, deflating it every 4 hours. You will have about One and a half cups of starter.
2. With the measuring cup still wet, measure out a half cup of starter and set it aside for the dough. If you have not already stored the pâte fermentée earlier, you can store the rest of the starter.
3. To make the dough, place the water, flour, gluten, and yeast in the pan according to the order in the manufacturer's instructions. Set crust on dark and program for the French Bread cycle; press Start. After Knead 1, press Pause. Add the reserved pâte fermentée and the salt. Press Start to continue. The dough will be moist and smooth.
4. When the baking cycle ends, immediately remove the pan's bread and place it on a rack. Let cool to room temperature before slicing

Pain A L'Ancienne

(Ready in about 2 hours 25 minutes I Servings- One loaf I Difficulty- Moderate)

Ingredients

For the pâte fermentée:
- Half cup of water
- Pinch of sea salt
- One and 1/4cups bread flour
- Half teaspoon SAF or one teaspoon bread machine yeast

For the dough:
- One and 1/4cup plus one tablespoon water
- Two and a half cups bread flour
- 1/3 cup whole wheat flour
- Two teaspoons gluten with vitamin C
- Two teaspoons light brown sugar or malt powder
- One and a half teaspoons SAF yeast or two teaspoons bread machine yeast
- 3/4 cup pâte fermentée
- One and a half teaspoons sea salt
- Yellow cornmeal, for sprinkling

Instructions

1. To make the pâte fermentée starter, place the starter ingredients in the pan. Program for the Dough cycle; press Start. Set a kitchen timer for 10 minutes. When the timer rings, press Pause and set the timer again for 10 minutes. Let the starter rest for 10 minutes. When the timer rings, press Start to continue and finish the Dough cycle. When the machine beeps at the end of the cycle, press Stop and unplug the machine. Gently deflate the spongy starter, and let it sit in the bread machine for 3 to 12 hours, deflating it every 4 hours. You will have about One and a half cups of starter.

2. Rinse out a dry plastic measure with cold water. With the measuring cup still wet, measure out 3/4 cup of starter and set it aside for the dough (it will slide right out of the measuring cup). If you have not already stored the pâte fermentée earlier, you can store the rest of the starter in the refrigerator for up to 48 hours.

3. To make the dough, place the water, flours, gluten, brown sugar, and yeast in the pan according to the order in the manufacturer's instructions

4. Set crust on medium and program for the Dough cycle; press Start.

5. After Knead 1, press Pause. Cut the reserved pâte fermen-tée into pieces, and add it to the machine with the salt.

6. Press Start to continue. The dough will start lumpy but will become a moist and smooth firm dough ball as the kneading continues and the starter is incorporated.

7. When the machine beeps at the end of the Dough cycle, press Stop and unplug the machine. Set a kitchen timer for another hour and leave the dough in the machine to continue to rise in the warm atmosphere.

8. Line a baking sheet with parchment paper and sprinkle with the cornmeal. When the timer rings, using a plastic dough card, turn the dough out onto the work surface; it will naturally deflate. Using as little flour as possible, knead lightly into a round shape with both hands; pull the sides of the dough underneath to make it tighter. Pinch the bottom seam to close the dough. The surface will be smooth and even, with no tears. Dust lightly all over with flour and place, smooth side up, on the baking sheet to leave room for expansion. If you want to use an 8-inch woven reed rising basket or a colander lined with a clean tea towel, dust it with flour and place the dough ball in it, smooth side down. Cover loosely with plastic wrap and let rise at room temperature until doubled in bulk, about 1 hour.

9. Twenty minutes before baking, place a ceramic baking stone or tiles on the lower third oven rack and preheat to 450°F.

10. If using the rising basket, run your hand around the sides to loosen the dough and gently turn it out onto the baking sheet. If you have risen the loaf already on the baking sheet, you will skip this step.

11. Dust the top with flour. Using a sharp knife, slash the top with a triangle, no more than 14 inches deep. Place the baking sheet directly on the baking stone. Bake for 10 minutes. Reduce the oven temperature to 375°F and continue to bake until golden brown and crusty, 25 to 30 minutes longer. The loaf will be dark brown, crusty, and sound hollow when tapped on the top and bottom with your finger. Remove from the pan

and let cool on a rack for at least 1 hour. This bread is best served completely cooled the day it is baked.

Pane Toscana

(Ready in about 2 hours 25 minutes I Servings- 2 I Difficulty-Moderate)

Ingredients

- One and 1/3 cups of water
- Two and 3/4 cups of bread flour
- 1/3 cup whole wheat flour
- One tablespoon gluten
- One and 3/4 teaspoons SAF yeast or Two and 1/4teaspoons bread machine yeast
- Pinch of sugar Pinch of salt

Instructions

1. To make the sponge, place the water, One cup of the bread flour, the whole wheat flour, the gluten, and the yeast in the pan according to the order in the manufacturer's instructions. Program for the Dough cycle, and set a kitchen timer for 10 minutes. When the timer rings, press Stop and unplug the machine. Let the sponge rest in the machine for 1 hour.

2. To make the dough, add the remaining one and a half cups of bread, sugar, and salt to the pan's sponge.

3. Set the crust on dark and program for the French Bread cycle; press Start. The dough ball will be moist and a bit slack.

4. When the baking cycle ends, immediately remove the pan's bread and place it on a rack. Let cool to room temperature before slicing. This bread keeps for three days at room temperature.

Italian Whole Wheat Bread

(Ready in about 2 hours 25 minutes I Servings- one loaf I Difficulty- Moderate)

Ingredients

For the sponge starter:

- One and 1/Three cups of water
- One and 1/8 cups bread flour
- 3/4 cup whole wheat flour
- 1/4 teaspoon SAF yeast or bread machine yeast

For the dough:

- One cup of bread flour
- One tablespoon sugar
- One tablespoon gluten
- One and a half teaspoons salt
- One and 3/4 teaspoons SAF yeast or Two and 1/4teaspoons bread machine yeast
- Yellow cornmeal, for sprinkling

Instructions

1. To make the sponge starter, place the starter ingredients in the pan. Program for the Dough cycle, and set a timer for 10 minutes. When the timer rings, press Stop and unplug the machine. Let the sponge sit in the machine for 4 hours, or as long as overnight. The environment will be nice and warm.

2. To make the dough, place all the dough ingredients in the pan with the sponge. Program for the Dough cycle; press Start. The dough ball will be very moist, tacky, and smooth.

3. Line a baking sheet with parchment paper and sprinkle with cornmeal. When the machine beeps at the end of the cycle, press Stop and unplug the machine. Turn the dough out onto a clean work surface; shape it into a tight round.

4. Place on the baking sheet, cover loosely with plastic wrap, and let it rise at room temperature until almost tripled in bulk, 1 to One and a half hours.

5. Twenty minutes before baking, place a baking stone on a rack in the lower third of the oven and preheat to 450°F.

6. Slash the loaf surface once down the center, no deeper than Half-inch, using a sharp knife. Place the baking sheet directly on the hot stone in the oven. Reduce the oven temperature to 425°F. Bake for 35 to 40 minutes, until golden brown and the top, sounds hollow when tapped. The loaf will not be very dark brown due to the wheat flour and a small amount of sugar. Cool the loaf directly on a rack for at least 20 minutes before slicing and serving.

Ciabatta

(Ready in about 2 hours 25 minutes I Servings- 2 I Difficulty-Moderate)

Ingredients

For the biga starter:

- Half cup of water
- One and a half cups plus 3 to Four tablespoons unbleached all-purpose flour
- 1/4 teaspoon SAF or bread machine yeast

For the dough:

- 7/8 cup warm water
- Two tablespoons milk
- Two teaspoons olive oil or canola oil
- One and a half teaspoons SAF yeast or two teaspoons bread machine yeast
- Two cups of bread flour
- One and a half teaspoons salt

Instructions

1. To make the biga starter, place the water, One and 1/4cups of the flour, and the yeast in the pan. Program for the Dough cycle. After about 5 minutes, scrape down the sides and slowly add another 1/4 cup of flour. When Knead 2 ends, remove the small dough ball from the machine and place it on a work surface. Hand kneads in about three tablespoons more flour. You will have a smooth dough ball firmer and a bit drier than one for bread, stiff yet resilient. Return the dough to the pan and close the lid. The machine will continue with the rise phases of the Dough cycle.

2. When the cycle ends, press Stop and unplug the machine. Let the starter sit in the bread machine for 9 to 12 hours, or overnight. The dough will rise and fall back upon itself, become moist, and smell yeasty.

3. To make the dough, with your fingers, tear the slightly sticky starter into walnut-size pieces and put them back in the machine. Place the water, milk, oil, and yeast in the pan with the biga pieces. Add One and a half cups of the bread flour and the salt. Program for the Dough cycle; press Start. At the start of Knead 2, add the Half remaining cup of flour. The dough will be very wet and sticky like a yeasted savarin batter.

Don't add any more flour; just leave the dough alone except for scraping the sides into the center. The dough will end up elastic and shiny but relaxed and slack, sticking to the sides of the pan. If you tried to mix it by hand, you couldn't knead it on a work surface.

4. When the machine beeps at the end of the cycle, the dough will have almost filled the pan. The top will be smooth, but if you stick your finger in, it will be sticky. Spray a deep 6-quart plastic bucket with olive oil cooking spray or brush with oil. Scrape the risen dough in the container, give the top a light spray or brush with oil, cover, and refrigerate for 6 hours to overnight, but no longer than 24 hours. This long, cool rise is important for the slow fermentation and the finished ciabatta flavor, so don't skimp on it.

5. Line a large, heavy baking sheet with parchment paper (some bakers use aluminum foil) and sprinkle heavily with flour. Turn the chilled dough out onto a lightly floured work surface, sprinkle lots of flour on top, and pat into a long rectangle about 5 inches wide. Divide into two equal rectangles across the middle and place each portion on the baking sheet. Cover with a clean tea towel and let rest at room temperature for 20 minutes to relax the dough.

6. Dust the tops of the loaves with some flour. Using the flat section of your fingers below the fingertips and holding them in an open splayed position, press, push and stretch the dough, making a rectangle about 10-by-5 inches (the width of your hand). Your fingers will not press in some areas, so you will have a dimpling, flattening effect, which will end up producing the characteristic uneven texture in the baked loaf. Cover again and let rest at room temperature until tripled in bulk, about One and a half hours. The loaves will stay flattish looking. Don't worry; they will rise dramatically in the oven.

7. Twenty minutes before baking, place a baking stone on the lower third oven rack and preheat to 425°F.

8. Spray or sprinkle the loaves with some water and place the baking sheet on the hot stone. You can slip the parchment off the baking sheet and bake directly on the stone if you like. Bake for 20 to 25 minutes, until golden brown. Prop open the oven door about 5 inches and let the ciabatta cool in the oven for at least 15 minutes. Remove from the oven and serve. Wrap in plastic to store.

Pagnotta

(Ready in about 2 hours 25 minutes I Servings- 2 I Difficulty-Moderate)

Ingredients

- One and 2/3 cups of warm water
- Half cup Two-Week Biga
- 3/4 teaspoon SAF yeast or One and 1/4teasoons bread machine yeast
- Three and 3/4 cups bread flour
- One and a half teaspoons salt

Instructions

1. Place all the ingredients in the pan, according to the order in the manufacturer's instructions, adding the starter and yeast with the water. Program for the Dough cycle; press Start. The dough will be shiny, very moist to the point of being slightly sticky, and soft. Don't be tempted to add more flour. When the machine beeps at the end of the cycle, press Stop

and unplug the machine. Gently deflate the dough with your finger. Set a kitchen timer and let the dough rest for another hour in the machine's warm environment.

2. Turn the dough out onto a lightly floured work surface. Using your dough card, fold the edges over into the center. You can add another tablespoon or two of flour as you work, just to have the dough hold its shape, but it will still be soft. Work around the loaf in a circular motion, each fold will lay on top of each other, making a tight round with an uneven surface that would normally be on the loaf's bottom. The smooth side will be touching the work surface. Spread a thick layer of flour on the work surface and turn the loaf over to face up the smooth side. Cover with a clean tea towel and let rise at room temperature for about 45 minutes.

3. Twenty minutes before baking, place a baking stone on the lowest rack of the oven, if desired. Place a clean baking sheet in the oven to heat it, and preheat the oven to 425°F.

4. Carefully remove the hot baking sheet from the oven and place it on a rack or top of the stove. Sprinkle with flour. Using a flat surface such as the underside of a sauté pan lid and your dough card, gently slide the loaf off the work surface and turn it over onto the lid so that the bottom is now on top. This is easier than it sounds. Slide the loaf onto the hot baking sheet; it will appear to deflate slightly. This is okay. The rough side of the loaf will be facing up. Immediately place in the oven.

5. Bake for 10 minutes. Reduce the oven temperature to 400°F and bake for an additional 30 to 35 minutes, or until the crust is deep brown, very crisp, and the loaf sounds hollow when tapped with your finger.

6. Remove the bread from the oven and place it on a rack. Let cool completely before slicing.

Saffron and Olive Oil Challah

(Ready in about 2 hours 25 minutes I Servings- 2 I Difficulty-Moderate)

Ingredients

- 2/3 cup water
- Small pinch saffron threads
- 1/3 cup Two-Week Biga
- Half teaspoon SAF yeast or one teaspoon bread machine yeast
- Two large eggs
- 1/4 cup olive oil
- Two and a half cups bread flour
- Two tablespoons sugar
- One and 1/4 teaspoons salt
- One egg beat with one tablespoon of water for glaze
- One tablespoon poppy or sesame seeds, for sprinkling, optional

Instructions

1. Bring the water to a boil in a saucepan or microwave. Add the saffron and let it steep at room temperature for 20 to 30 minutes, until just warm.

2. Place the saffron water and other dough ingredients in the pan according to the manufacturer's instructions, adding the starter and yeast with the liquids. Program for the Dough cycle. The dough ball

will be firm yet smooth and soft. When the machine beeps at the end of the cycle, press Stop and unplug the machine. Set a kitchen timer and let the dough rest for another 30 minutes in the machine's warm environment (no need to deflate).

3. Line a baking sheet with parchment paper or foil a 9-by-5-inch loaf pan. When the timer rings, immediately remove the dough and place it on a lightly floured work surface; divide into three equal portions. Using your palms, roll each portion into a fat cylinder, Half-inches in length and tapered at each end. Be sure the ropes are of equal size and shape. Place the three ropes parallel to each other. Begin braiding like you are braiding hair. Adjust or press the braid to make it look even. If the loaf is to be free-form, taper the ends for a long loaf, or press together to make the braid a compact square. If you are baking it in the loaf pan, tuck the ends to make a rectangle that will fit into the pan. Cover loosely with plastic wrap and let it rise at room temperature until the dough is doubled in bulk, about 1 hour.

4. Twenty minutes before baking, preheat the oven to 350°F.

5. Beat the egg and water glaze with a fork until foamy. Using a pastry brush, brush the top of the loaf with some of the glazes and sprinkle with the seeds, or leave plain. Bake for 40 to 45 minutes, or until the loaf is deep golden brown and the bread sounds hollow when tapped on the top and bottom with your finger. Immediately remove the loaf from the pan or sheet and transfer it to a cooling rack. Let cool to room temperature before slicing.

Red Wine-Walnut Whole Wheat Baguettes

(Ready in about 2 hours 25 minutes I Servings- 2 I Difficulty-Moderate)

Ingredients

- Half cup of water
- 1/4 cup plus one tablespoon dry red wine, such as Merlot
- One 14-ounce or 1-pound box Whole Wheat Bread Machine Mix
- Half cup chopped walnuts
- One yeast packet (included in the mix)

Instructions

1. Place all the ingredients in the pan according to the order in the manufacturer's instructions. Program for the Dough cycle; press Start.

2. Oil an 18-by-2-inch-wide baguette tray. When the machine beeps at the end of the Dough cycle, scrape the wet dough out with a dough card onto a floured work surface. Knead a few times with your dough card. Divide the dough into two equal portions. Flatten each portion into a thin 10-by-6-inch rectangle with the palm of your hand.

3. Starting at a long end, roll up each, using your thumbs to help roll tightly. With the side of your hand, define a depression lengthwise down the center of the dough. Repeatedly fold the dough over in thirds the long way to make a tight log and pinch seams to seal. Stretch each log by rolling it on the table back and forth with your palms a few times to elongate. Gently transfer, seam side down, to the prepared pan. No

dough will hang over the ends of the pans. Cover loosely with a clean tea towel and let rise at room temperature until doubled in bulk, about 40 minutes.

4. Twenty minutes before baking, line the oven's center rack with a baking stone or tiles and preheat the oven to 450oF.

5. With a small, sharp knife, slash the surface 3 or 4 times on the diagonal, no more than 14 inches deep. Place the pan directly on the stone and bake for 20 to 25 minutes, or until the loaves' surfaces are a deep golden brown and sound hollow when tapped with your finger. Remove the loaves from the pans immediately to a cooling rack. Eat hot or within 2 hours.

Green Chile Bread

(Ready in about 2 hours 25 minutes I Servings- One loaf I Difficulty- Moderate)

Ingredients

For the dough:

- One cup of plus Two tablespoons water
- One tablespoon olive oil or walnut oil
- One 14-ounce or 1-pound box white or whole wheat bread machine mix
- One yeast packet (included in the mix)

For the filling:

- 1/4 cup mayonnaise
- Half cup chopped scallions
- Two cups of Monterey Jack cheese, grated
- Half cup canned roasted green chiles, drained and chopped
- Yellow cornmeal, for sprinkling

Instructions

1. Place all the dough ingredients in the pan according to the order in the manufacturer's instructions. Program for the Dough cycle; press Start. Line a baking sheet with parchment paper and sprinkle it with cornmeal. When the machine beeps at the end of the cycle, turn the dough out onto a lightly floured work surface. Pat into a 10-by-16-inch rectangle. Spread with mayonnaise and sprinkle with the scallions. Sprinkle with the cheese and green chiles. Fold the dough's two short ends into the center and bring up the two long ends to encase the filling. Pinch the seams to seal. Place on the baking sheet, seam side down. Cover loosely with plastic wrap and let rise at room temperature for 20 minutes.

2. Preheat the oven to 375oF.

3. With a small sharp knife, slash the tops with three diagonal slashes down the top to expose the filling. Bake until golden brown, 30 to 35 minutes. Cool on the pan and serve at room temperature (let the cheese firm up), sliced with a serrated knife.

Chapter 25-Other Bread Machine Recipes

The bread machine working is not limited to making bread and other doughs, but you can make a lot out of your bread machine. Some of the recipes that you can make in your bread machine other than bread are described as under: -

Strawberry Jam

(Ready in about 3 hours 10 minutes | Servings- one jar | Difficulty- Moderate)

Ingredients

- One cup of sugar
- Half box of pectin
- 4 to 5 cups of fresh or frozen strawberries

Instructions

1. Let the strawberries thaw and mash the berries to make Three cups. Mash as much chunky as you like, but preferably mash well.
2. Add mashed berries, sugar, and pectin to the bread machine.
3. Select the jam cycle. Press the start button.
4. After the jam has been made, let it cool in the machine for 30 to 45 minutes.
5. Take it out into jars. Let it cool completely.
6. Keep in the fridge overnight. Enjoy with freshly baked bread.

Tomato Sauce

(Ready in about 3 hours 40 minutes | Servings- one jar | Difficulty- Moderate)

Ingredients

- One tablespoon of olive oil
- Two and ¾ cups of tomatoes (fresh and canned)
- Half teaspoon of garlic powder
- One teaspoon of sugar
- One tablespoon of onion powder
- A dash of red wine vinegar

Instructions

1. Chop the tomatoes how much chunkier you like.
2. Add all ingredients to the pan of the bread machine in the suggested order by the manufacturer.
3. Select the jam cycle and Press the start button. Do not overfill your pan.
4. Halfway through the process, with the help of a rubber spatula, scrape the sides of the pan.

5. As the machine has completed the jam cycle, please wait for it to cool down.
6. Then blend in a blender to your desired texture.
7. Adjust seasoning by adding any herbs or salt and pepper.
8. Store in a jar.
9. Serve with fresh bread and olive oil.

Apple pie

(Ready in about 3 hours 10 minutes | Servings- One pie | Difficulty- Moderate)

Ingredients

- One and 1/4 cups of apple pie filling
- Half cup of water
- One and a half teaspoons of salt
- One and a half tablespoons of butter
- Three and 1/4 cups of flour
- One and a half teaspoons of yeast
- Three tablespoons of dry buttermilk
- One and a half teaspoons of cinnamon

Instructions

1. Put all the required ingredients in the container of the bread machine in the suggested order by the manufacturer.
2. Select the sweet bread cycle—Press the start button.
3. Enjoy.

Blueberry Jam

(Ready in about 3 hours 40 minutes | Servings- One jar | Difficulty- Moderate)

Ingredients

- One tablespoon of no sugar pectin
- Two and a half cups of granulated sugar
- Five cups of blueberries

Instructions

1. If using frozen blueberries, let them thaw and mash them in a food processor.
2. In a bowl, mix all ingredients and add to the pan of the bread machine.
3. Select the jam cycle and Press the start button.
4. Let it cool for half an hour in the machine. Pour into jars and let it rest for 3 hours.
5. Keep in the fridge for four weeks.

Peach Jam

(Ready in about 3 hours 40 minutes | Servings- One jar | Difficulty- Moderate)

Ingredients

- One tablespoon of no sugar pectin
- Four cups of peeled and halved ripe peaches
- Two cups of granulated sugar

Instructions

1. Mash the ripe peaches with a masher. In a bowl, mix all ingredients and pour into the bread machine.
2. Select the jam or jelly cycle.

3. Let the jam cool in the pan of the bread machine for half an hour.
4. Pour into jars.
5. Serve with fresh bread.

Grape Jelly

(Ready in about 3 hours 40 minutes | Servings- 2 jars | Difficulty- Moderate)

Ingredients

- Two packets of Knox Gelatin
- One tablespoon of lemon juice
- Two cups of 100% grape juice
- One cup of sugar

Instructions

1. Mix all ingredients in a bowl until sugar and gelatin dissolve.
2. Add this into the pan of the bread machine.
3. Select the jam cycle.
4. Let it cool for half an hour in the machine, then take it out.
5. Pour into jars and serve with fresh bread.

Crab Apple Jelly

(Ready in about 3 hours 40 minutes | Servings- 2 jars | Difficulty- Moderate)

Ingredients

- Two packets of Knox Gelatin
- Four cups of Crabapple Juice
- Two cups of sugar

Instructions

1. Juice the apples by a juice or with a blender, add apples and water to blender and pulse and make it 4 cups. Add water to make 4 cups. Strain the juice.
2. In a bowl, add all ingredients until gelatin and sugar dissolves.
3. Select the jam cycle and Press the start button.
4. Let it cool for half an hour in the machine, then take it out.
5. Pour into jars and serve with fresh bread.
6. Keep in the fridge for four weeks.

Milk & Honey Bread

(Ready in about 2 hours 10 minutes | Servings- One loaf | Difficulty- Moderate)

Ingredients

- Three cups of bread flour
- One cup and one tablespoon of milk
- Three tablespoons of melted butter
- Two teaspoons of active dry yeast
- One and a half teaspoons of salt
- Three tablespoons of honey

Instructions

1. Put all the required ingredients in the container of the bread machine in the suggested order by the manufacturer.
2. Select the basic cycle. Medium crust and Press the start button.
3. Enjoy fresh bread.

Soft Pretzels

(Ready in about 3 hours 40 minutes |Servings-8 | Difficulty-Moderate)

Ingredients

- One tablespoon of packed brown sugar
- One and a half cups of water
- Two teaspoons of active dry yeast
- Three and a half cups of flour
- One teaspoon of kosher salt
- Kosher salt
- 1/3 cup of baking soda
- Eight cups of water

Instructions

1. Add the first five ingredients into the bread machine's pan as per the manufacturer's suggested order.
2. Select the dough cycle—Press the start button.
3. Take the dough out on a floured, clean surface.
4. Let the oven preheat to 475 F.
5. Cut dough into 12-14 pieces. Make each piece long into a 15" rope.
6. Make into a pretzel shape. Seal the edges by pinching them.
7. Place these pretzels onto baking sheets.
8. In a large pot, boil the water with baking soda. Let it simmer.
9. Add 2-3 pretzels to the pot and let them boil for 2 minutes.
10. Take out the pretzels and let them cool and sprinkle with salt.
11. Place on baking sheets and bake for 8-12 minutes.
12. Enjoy soft pretzels.

Crispy, chewy breadsticks

(Ready in about one hour and 35 minutes | Servings-32 | Difficulty- Moderate)

Ingredients

Dry ingredients

- Two tablespoons active dry yeast
- Two cups of Light Flour Blend
- 3 /4 cup cornstarch, potato starch (not potato flour), or arrowroot
- 1 /4 cup milk powder or Dari Free
- One tablespoon granulated cane sugar
- Two teaspoons kosher or fine sea salt
- Two teaspoons psyllium husk flakes or powder
- 1 /8 teaspoon ascorbic acid, optional

Wet ingredients

- One cup of water warmed to about 80°F
- Three large egg whites, at room temperature
- One tablespoon vegetable or olive oil
- Two teaspoons champagne vinegar or cider vinegar

Shaping

- 30 ml (Two tablespoons) vegetable or olive oil

Toppings (optional)

- Melted butter or non-dairy butter substitute, milk, olive oil or flavored oil, or beaten egg whites, Coarse sea or pretzel salt, powdered or grated cheese, fresh herbs, sesame seeds, poppy seeds, sunflower seeds

Instructions

1. Set the pan on the counter and insert the beater paddle(s). Unless otherwise directed by your machine's manufacturer, add the liquids first, then the dry ingredients, and finally the yeast.
2. Measure the yeast into a small bowl and set aside. In a large mixing bowl, mix the remaining dry ingredients together.
3. Mix the wet ingredients together in a 2-cup measuring cup and pour into the pan. Use a spatula to spread the dry ingredients over the wet ingredients. Make a shallow well in the center and pour in the yeast.
4. Place the pan in the machine, settle it in the center, and lock it in place. Close the lid and select: Dough cycle, Loaf size, then press Start.
5. While the machine is mixing and kneading the ingredients, open the lid and use a spatula to scrape down the sides of the pan as needed, pushing any flour that has accumulated around the edges, corners, and under the dough into the center to be blended. This dough is drier than other bread, making it heavier and harder for the paddle to blend. The dough tends to be pushed out to the pan's edges, no longer being blended or kneaded. Use a spatula to lift the dough onto the paddle repeatedly to get as much mixing done as possible. Let the machine mix the dough until it is smooth and has no lumps, 4 to 5 minutes. Press the stop button to cancel the cycle, turn off the machine, and remove the pan.
6. For shaping the dough, pour the oil into a large mixing bowl. Use a spatula to scoop the dough into the bowl. Fold the oiled dough parts up and over the top, creating a disk of dough oiled on all sides.
7. Set the racks in the upper and lower thirds of the oven and preheat to 400°F (200°C). Line two baking sheets with parchment paper.
8. Divide the dough in half, divide in half again, and continue halving until you have 32 equal pieces. Working with oiled hands, roll each piece of dough into a slender log by setting it on a very lightly oiled work surface. Using the palms of both hands and starting in the center, gently roll the dough back and forth while moving your hands out to the ends to elongate it into a 10-inch (25 cm) rope. Transfer to the lined baking sheets and continue with the remaining dough, placing 16 pieces on each baking sheet. Please leave a little room between each to allow for some expansion while they bake and get crispy edges.
9. Leave the breadsticks plain or brush them with a little butter, milk, or beaten egg white, and then sprinkle with your choice of topping. For chewier breadsticks, let them rest uncovered for 10 to 15 minutes to rise slightly.
10. Place the sheets in the oven and bake for about 10 minutes, then rotate the pans. This will give you the most even browning. Bake until golden brown and firm to the touch, another 10 to 15 minutes. The darker they are, the crunchier they will be. Use the parchment to transfer the breadsticks to a wire rack, then slide the

parchment out. They will finish crisping as they cool.

11. While these are best and crunchiest on the day they are baked, you can store them in an airtight container on the counter for a couple of days (the longer they sit, the chewier they become). Freezing is not recommended.

Cheesy Soft Breadsticks with Garlic and Herbs

(Ready in about one hour and 35 minutes I Servings-12 I Difficulty- Moderate)

Ingredients

Dry ingredients

- One and a half tablespoons active dry yeast
- Three cups of Light Flour Blend or Whole-Grain Flour Blend
- Half cup cornstarch, potato starch (not potato flour), or arrowroot
- 3 /4 cup cheddar cheese powder, such as Cabot
- Two teaspoons xanthan gum
- Two teaspoons kosher or fine sea salt
- Two teaspoons garlic powder1 teaspoon baking powder
- 1 /8 teaspoon ascorbic acid, optional

Wet ingredients

- One teaspoon honey
- One and 1 /4 cups water, warmed to about 80°F (27°C)
- One egg white, at room temperature
- One tablespoon vegetable or olive oil
- Two teaspoons apple cider vinegar

Topping

- 1 /4 cup shredded Parmesan, Asiago, or other aged cheese
- Two tablespoons minced fresh basil
- Two teaspoons garlic powder
- Four tablespoons unsalted butter, melted

Instructions

1. Line a baking sheet with parchment. Brush lightly with oil.
2. Set the pan on the counter and insert the beater paddle(s). Unless otherwise directed by your machine's manufacturer, add the liquids first, then the dry ingredients, and finally the yeast.
3. Measure the yeast into a small bowl and set aside. In a large mixing bowl, mix the remaining dry ingredients together.
4. In a 2-cup glass measuring cup, mix the honey and water together to dissolve the honey. Add the remaining wet ingredients and mix again. Pour into the pan. Use a spatula to spread the dry ingredients over the wet ingredients, covering completely. Make a shallow well in the center and pour in the yeast.
5. Place the pan in the machine, settle it in the center, and lock it in place. Close the lid and select Dough cycle, Loaf size, and press Start.
6. While the machine is mixing and kneading the ingredients, open the lid and use a spatula to scrape down the sides of the pan as needed,

pushing any flour that has accumulated around the edges and under the dough into the center. Let the machine mix the dough until it is smooth and has no lumps, about 5 minutes. Press the stop button to cancel the cycle, turn off the machine, and remove the pan.

7. Scrape the dough (it will be very soft and sticky) onto the baking sheet. Using oiled hands, press the dough into a 12-inch square—work from the center out, pressing to flatten and spread the dough. Square the edges. Use an oiled bench scraper or knife to cut the dough into 12 equal slices.
8. Mix the shredded Parmesan, minced basil, and garlic powder in a bowl.
9. Gently brush the tops of the breadsticks with the melted butter and sprinkle with the cheesy topping. Cover loosely with a sheet of plastic wrap and set aside to rise in a warm place for 1 hour.
10. While the breadsticks rise, preheat the oven to 400°F (200°C).
11. Remove the plastic wrap and bake until puffed and golden brown and an instant-read thermometer inserted in the center registers 212°F (100°C), 30 to 35 minutes, rotating the baking sheet halfway through.
12. Use the parchment to transfer the breadsticks to a wire rack, then slide the parchment out. Cool for at least 15 minutes. Serve warm or at room temperature.
13. These are best eaten the day they are baked, but you can store them in an airtight container or resealable plastic bag in the refrigerator for up to 2 days. Reheat in a low oven if desired. Freezing is not recommended.

Raspberry Jam

(Ready in about 3 hours 40 minutes I Servings- 2-3 jars I Difficulty- Moderate)

Ingredients

- Three cups of fresh raspberries, rinsed
- ¼ cup of powdered fruit pectin
- One and 3/4 cups sugar, or to taste
- Three tablespoons fresh lemon juice

Instructions

1. Combine all the ingredients in the pan. Let stand for 15 minutes to dissolve the sugar.
2. Program the machine for the Jam cycle and press Start. When the machine beeps at the end of the cycle, carefully remove the pan with heavy oven mitts. You can scrape the jam into heat-resistant jars right away, using a rubber spatula.
3. For other jars, let the jam sit in the pan for 15 minutes before transferring. Let stand until cool. Store, covered, in the refrigerator for up to 2 months, or spoon into small freezer bags and freeze.

Boysenberry Jam

(Ready in about 3 hours 40 minutes I Servings- 2-3 jars I Difficulty- Moderate)

Ingredients

- Two and a half cups fresh boysenberries, rinsed

- One 1.75- or 2-ounce box powdered fruit pectin
- One cup of sugar, or to taste
- Two tablespoons fresh lemon juice

Instructions

1. Combine all the ingredients in the pan. Let stand for 15 minutes to dissolve the sugar.
2. Program the machine for the Jam cycle and press Start. When the machine beeps at the end of the cycle, carefully remove the pan with heavy oven mitts. You can scrape the jam into heat-resistant jars right away, using a rubber spatula.
3. For other jars, let the jam sit in the pan for 15 minutes before transferring. Let stand until cool. Store, covered, in the refrigerator for up to 2 months, or spoon into small freezer bags and freeze.

Fresh Bing Cherry Jam

(Ready in about 3 hours 40 minutes I Servings- 2-3 jars I Difficulty- Moderate)

Ingredients

- Two cups of pitted fresh Bing cherries
- One cup of sugar, or to taste
- One tablespoon fresh lemon juice
- Pinch of salt
- One and a half tablespoons powdered fruit pectin

Instructions

1. Combine the cherries, sugar, lemon juice, and salt in the pan. Let stand for 15 minutes to dissolve the sugar.
2. Sprinkle with the pectin.
3. Program the machine for the Jam cycle and press Start. When the machine beeps at the end of the cycle, carefully remove the pan with heavy oven mitts. You can scrape the jam into heat-resistant jars right away, using a rubber spatula.
4. For other jars, let the jam sit in the pan for 15 minutes before transferring. Let stand until cool. Store, covered, in the refrigerator for up to 2 months, or spoon into small freezer bags and freeze.

Fresh Apricot Jam

(Ready in about 3 hours 40 minutes I Servings- 2-3 jars I Difficulty- Moderate)

Ingredients

- Two cups of pitted and chopped fresh apricots
- One tablespoon fresh lemon juice
- Half of a 1.75- or 2-ounce box powdered fruit pectin
- One and 1/4cups sugar, or to taste

Instructions

1. Place the apricots and the lemon juice in the pan. Sprinkle with the pectin. Let stand for 10 minutes. Add the sugar.
2. Program the machine for the Jam cycle and press Start. When the machine beeps at the end of the cycle, carefully remove the pan with heavy oven

mitts. You can scrape the jam into heat-resistant jars right away, using a rubber spatula.
3. For other jars, let the jam sit in the pan for 15 minutes before transferring. Let stand until cool. Store, covered, in the refrigerator for up to 6 weeks, or spoon into small freezer bags and freeze.

Kiwifruit Jam

(Ready in about 4 hours 40 minutes I Servings- 2-4 jars I Difficulty- Moderate)

Ingredients

- Four large kiwifruits, peeled, sliced, and coarsely chopped
- Two tablespoons finely julienned lemon zest
- Three tablespoons fresh lemon juice
- One and a half tablespoons powdered fruit pectin
- One and a half cups sugar

Instructions

1. Combine all the ingredients in the pan. Let stand for 20 minutes to dissolve the sugar.
2. Program the machine for the Jam cycle and press Start. When the machine beeps at the end of the cycle, carefully remove the pan with heavy oven mitts. You can scrape the jam into heat-resistant jars right away, using a rubber spatula.
3. For other jars, let the jam sit in the pan for 15 minutes before transferring. Let stand until cool. Store, covered, in the refrigerator for up to 2 months, or spoon into small freezer bags and freeze.

Rhubarb Jam

(Ready in about 3 hours 40 minutes I Servings- 2-3 jars I Difficulty- Moderate)

Ingredients

- Two cups of (1 pound) rhubarb stalks, sliced about a Half-inch thick
- One and a half cups sugar
- Half of a 1.75- to 2-ounce box powdered fruit pectin
- 1/4 cup chopped dried apricots

Instructions

1. Mix the rhubarb with the sugar in a glass bowl, cover loosely with plastic wrap, and let stand at room temperature for 12 hours.
2. Combine the rhubarb-sugar mixture, the pectin, and the apricots in the pan.
3. Program the machine for the Jam cycle and press Start. When the machine beeps at the end of the cycle, carefully remove the pan with heavy oven mitts. You can scrape the jam into heat-resistant jars right away, using a rubber spatula.
4. For other jars, let the jam sit in the pan for 15 minutes before transferring. Let stand until cool. Store, covered, in the refrigerator for up to 3 weeks, or spoon into small freezer bags and freeze.

Apple Butter

(Ready in about 3 hours 40 minutes I Servings- 2-3 jars I Difficulty- Moderate)

Ingredients

- Two cups of (1/4 pound) dried apple rings, chopped
- One and 1/4cups unsweetened, unfiltered apple juice
- Two tablespoons apple cider vinegar
- One and a half teaspoons ground cinnamon
- Half teaspoon ground allspice
- Half teaspoon ground cloves

Instructions

1. Combine all the ingredients in the pan. Let stand at room temperature for 1 hour to soften the apples.
2. Program the machine for the Jam cycle and press Start. When the machine beeps at the end of the cycle, carefully remove the pan with heavy oven mitts and let cool until warm.
3. Using a rubber spatula, scrape the mixture into a food processor fitted with the metal blade and process until smooth.
4. Scrape the apple butter into a glass jar. Let stand at room temperature until cool. Store, covered, in the refrigerator for up to 2 months.

Pumpkin Apple Butter

(Ready in about 3 hours 40 minutes I Servings- 3 cups I Difficulty- Moderate)

Ingredients

- One 15-ounce can of pumpkin puree
- 3/4 cup (about one large) peeled, cored, and coarsely grated fresh Pippin, Granny Smith, or other firms, tart cooking apple
- Half cup unsweetened, unfiltered apple juice
- Half cup light brown sugar
- Half teaspoon ground cinnamon
- Half teaspoon ground nutmeg
- Half teaspoon ground cloves
- Three tablespoons unsalted butter

Instructions

1. Combine all the ingredients in the pan.
2. Program the machine for the Jam cycle and press Start. When the machine beeps at the end of the cycle, remove the pan. Stir in the butter until it melts. Let the fruit butter sit in the pan for 15 minutes before transferring.
3. Let stand until cool. Store, covered, in the refrigerator.

Quick and Easy Tomato Ketchup

(Ready in about 3 hours 40 minutes I Servings- 3 jars I Difficulty- Moderate)

Ingredients

- One 28-ounce-can of tomato puree
- One small yellow onion, cut into chunks
- One large shallot, chopped
- One clove garlic, pressed
- Half cup of apple cider vinegar
- 1/3 cup water

- 1/4 cup light brown sugar
- One teaspoon ground allspice
- Pinch of ground cinnamon
- Pinch of ground cloves
- Pinch of ground mace
- Pinch of ground ginger
- Pinch of Coleman's dry mustard
- Pinch of crushed hot red pepper flakes
- Fresh-ground black pepper Sea salt

Instructions

1. In a food processor, preferably, or in batches in a blender, combine the tomato puree, onion, shallot, and garlic. Process until just smooth.
2. Pour the tomato mixture into the pan. Add the vinegar, water, sugar, and spices.
3. Program the machine for the Jam cycle and press Start. When the machine beeps at the end of the cycle, the ketchup will have reduced slightly and thickened. Add salt and pepper to taste. Carefully remove the pan with heavy oven mitts.
4. You can scrape the ketchup into heat-resistant jars right away, using a rubber spatula. For other jars, let the ketchup sit in the pan for 15 minutes before transferring. Serve warm, room temperature, or chilled. Store covered in the refrigerator for up to 2 months.

Mango Chutney

(Ready in about 3 hours 40 minutes I Servings- 2 cups I Difficulty- Moderate)

Ingredients

- Two fresh firm-ripe mangoes (about One and a half pounds)
- 1/4 cup dark or golden raisins, chopped
- One medium shallot, minced
- Half cup dark brown sugar
- A scant tablespoon of minced fresh ginger
- Two teaspoons hot pepper flakes
- Pinch of ground cloves
- 1/8 teaspoon salt
- Half cup of apple cider vinegar
- Two tablespoons fresh lime juice

Instructions

1. Peel the mango by standing the fruit stem (wider) end up. Make four vertical slices through the skin to score the thin, tough skin and divide the fruit into quarters lengthwise. Starting at the top, peel the skin back from each quarter, just like a
2. banana. Slice the flesh away from the flat seed in strips. Coarsely chop.
3. Combine all the ingredients in the pan.
4. Program the machine for the Jam cycle and press start. When the machine beeps at the end of the cycle, carefully remove the pan with heavy oven mitts. You can scrape the chutney into heat-resistant jars right away, using a rubber spatula. For other jars, let the chutney sit in the pan for 15 minutes before transferring. Let stand until cool. Store, covered, in the refrigerator for up to 2 months. Serve at room temperature.

Apple and Dried Fruit Chutney

(Ready in about 3 hours 40 minutes I Servings- 2-3 jars I Difficulty- Moderate)

Ingredients

- Two medium tart cooking apples, peeled, cored, and finely chopped
- 2/3 cup dark brown sugar
- 1/3 cup finely chopped dried apricots
- 1/3 cup finely chopped dried pineapple or dried pears
- 1/3 cup dark or golden raisins
- 1/4 cup finely chopped red bell pepper
- Piece of fresh gingerroot about 1-inch long, peeled and grated
- One large shallot, finely chopped
- One clove garlic, pressed
- 1/4 teaspoon ground cayenne pepper
- Pinch of hot pepper flakes
- Pinch of ground turmeric or curry powder
- Half teaspoon salt
- 2/3 cup apple cider vinegar

Instructions

1. Combine all the ingredients in the pan.
2. Program the machine for the Jam cycle and press Start. When the machine beeps at the end of the cycle, carefully remove the pan with heavy oven mitts. You can scrape the chutney into heat-resistant jars right away, using a rubber spatula. For other jars, let the chutney sit in the pan for 15 minutes before transferring. Let stand until cool. Store, covered, in the refrigerator, for up to 2 months. Serve at room temperature.

Egg Pasta

(Ready in about 3 hours 40 minutes I Servings- 7-8 I Difficulty- Moderate)

Ingredients

- Four large eggs, lightly beaten, at room temperature
- Two tablespoons warm water
- One tablespoon olive oil
- Two cups of unbleached all-purpose or bread flour
- One cup of semolina pasta flour
- One teaspoon salt

Instructions

1. Similar to the order in the manufacturer's orders, put all ingredients in the pan. Dough or Pasta Dough Cycle Program; Press Start. Set a 7-minute kitchen timer. Check the dough ball that has formed on the blade as the timer rings. It is meant to be firm but pliable. Add a couple of drops of water when the unit is kneading if it is too dry. Sprinkle with all-purpose flour, a teaspoon at a time, if it is too sticky. For three more minutes, restart the timer.
2. Click Pause to cancel the loop as the timer rings.
3. From the pan, cut the dough. Shape into a ball, wrap in plastic wrap and allow to rest for 30 minutes at room temperature.

4. As desired, the dough is now able to roll out and cut.
5. To roll the dough by hand: Use all-purpose flour to dust the work surface. To stop drying out, split the dough into three equal parts, leaving the reserved dough balls sealed. Place the dough ball on the working surface, and roll back and forth with the rolling pin. Then start rolling in one direction away from yourself. Make a quarter turn and roll until the dough stretches into a rounded rectangle about 1/8 inch thick in the other direction. To extend the dough farther, roll the dough around the rolling pin and unroll. Keep the dough as thin as possible and as light. Function efficiently as it dries out the pastry.
6. To cut the dough by hand: dust the dough with flour and put together in the middle the two opposite ends of the dough. Repeat two more times before you have a pasta roll of tight double jelly. Keep the roll on one side and slice into 1/8, 1/4- or 1/2-inch-wide narrow, medium, or wide noodles with a sharp chef's knife in the other. Under the middle of the dough, you can slide the knife's rusty edge and raise the noodles; they'll unravel over the knife. Or, with your fingers, raise the noodles.
7. To use a pasta machine to roll the dough: Mound the pasta machine to your counter and place the smooth rollers at the widest opening. With all-purpose flour, dust the work board. Divide the dough into 4 to 6 equivalent parts to avoid drying out, leaving the reserved dough balls sealed. On the work surface, put the dough ball and press to flatten to a diameter no wider than the opening of the unit. Run the unit through the dough. Dust as required with flour. Fold in thirds and cycle once more through the machine. Two more times, run the dough through the machine but don't fold the dough again.
8. To the next smallest setting, set the notch on the machine and run the dough through the rollers. Continue to roll and stretch the dough until the smallest setting is reached, using a smaller setting each time. There are six graded configurations on most computers. Any settings may be skipped. Long and fragile would be the dough strip.
9. Cutting the dough with a pasta machine: Change the machine's cutting mechanism to the appropriate width and run through the dough to cut it. You should directly run the cut pasta onto a baking sheet dusted with some semolina.
10. Move the sliced pasta onto a drying plate, a floured towel, or a floured baking sheet to dry the pasta. When one layer is full, put a sheet of parchment on the baking sheet over the pasta, begin to layer the pasta, and gently sprinkle with flour to avoid sticking. Split with a sharp chef's knife into ideal lengths. Before cooking or freezing, let the paste dry for at least 20 minutes.

Semolina Pasta

(Ready in about 3 hours 40 minutes I Servings- 7-8 I Difficulty- Moderate)

Ingredients

- 7/8 cup warm water

- One tablespoon olive oil
- Two cups of unbleached all-purpose or bread flour
- One cup of semolina pasta flour
- One teaspoon salt

Instructions

1. Similar to the order in the manufacturer's orders, put all ingredients in the pan. Dough or Pasta Dough Cycle Program; Press Start. Set a 7-minute kitchen timer. Check the dough ball that has formed on the blade as the timer rings. It is meant to be firm but pliable. Add a couple of drops of water when the unit is kneading if it is too dry. Sprinkle with all-purpose flour, a teaspoon at a time, if it is too sticky. For three more minutes, restart the timer.

2. Click Pause to cancel the loop as the timer rings.

3. From the pan, cut the dough. Shape into a ball, wrap in plastic wrap and allow to rest for 30 minutes at room temperature.

4. As desired, the dough is now able to roll out and cut.

5. To roll the dough by hand: Use all-purpose flour to dust the work surface. To stop drying out, split the dough into three equal parts, leaving the reserved dough balls sealed. Place the dough ball on the working surface, and roll back and forth with the rolling pin. Then start rolling in one direction away from yourself. Make a quarter turn and roll until the dough stretches into a rounded rectangle about 1/8 inch thick in the other direction. To extend the dough farther, roll the dough around the rolling pin and unroll. Keep the dough as thin as possible and as light. Function efficiently as it dries out the pastry.

6. To cut the dough by hand: dust the dough with flour and put together in the middle the two opposite ends of the dough. Repeat two more times before you have a pasta roll of tight double jelly. Keep the roll on one side and slice into 1/8, 1/4- or 1/2-inch-wide narrow, medium, or wide noodles with a sharp chef's knife in the other. Under the middle of the dough, you can slide the knife's rusty edge and raise the noodles; they'll unravel over the knife. Or, with your fingers, raise the noodles.

7. To use a pasta machine to roll the dough: Mound the pasta machine to your counter and place the smooth rollers at the widest opening. With all-purpose flour, dust the work board. Divide the dough into 4 to 6 equivalent parts to avoid drying out, leaving the reserved dough balls sealed. On the work surface, put the dough ball and press to flatten to a diameter no wider than the opening of the unit. Run the unit through the dough. Dust as required with flour. Fold in thirds and cycle once more through the machine. Two more times, run the dough through the machine but don't fold the dough again.

8. To the next smallest setting, set the notch on the machine and run the dough through the rollers. Continue to roll and stretch the dough until the smallest setting is reached, using a smaller setting each time. There are six graded configurations on most computers. Any settings may be skipped. Long and fragile would be the dough strip.

9. Cutting the dough with a pasta machine: Change the machine's cutting mechanism to the appropriate width and run through the dough to cut it. You should directly run the cut pasta onto a baking sheet dusted with some semolina.

10. Move the sliced pasta onto a drying plate, a floured towel, or a floured baking sheet to dry the pasta. When one layer is full, put a sheet of parchment on the baking sheet over the pasta, begin to layer the pasta, and gently sprinkle with flour to avoid sticking. Split with a sharp chef's knife into ideal lengths. Before cooking or freezing, let the paste dry for at least 20 minutes.

Green Spinach Pasta

(Ready in about 3 hours 40 minutes I Servings- 7-8 I Difficulty- Moderate)

Ingredients

- Half pound fresh spinach washed
- Three large eggs, lightly beaten, at room temperature
- One tablespoon olive oil
- Three cups of unbleached all-purpose flour
- One teaspoon salt

Instructions

1. Similar to the order in the manufacturer's orders, put all ingredients in the pan. Dough or Pasta Dough Cycle Program; Press Start. Set a 7-minute kitchen timer. Check the dough ball that has formed on the blade as the timer rings. It is meant to be firm but pliable. Add a couple of drops of water when the unit is kneading if it is too dry. Sprinkle with all-purpose flour, a teaspoon at a time, if it is too sticky. For three more minutes, restart the timer.

2. Click Pause to cancel the loop as the timer rings.

3. From the pan, cut the dough. Shape into a ball, wrap in plastic wrap and allow to rest for 30 minutes at room temperature.

4. As desired, the dough is now able to roll out and cut.

5. To roll the dough by hand: Use all-purpose flour to dust the work surface. To stop drying out, split the dough into three equal parts, leaving the reserved dough balls sealed. Place the dough ball on the working surface, and roll back and forth with the rolling pin. Then start rolling in one direction away from yourself. Make a quarter turn and roll until the dough stretches into a rounded rectangle about 1/8 inch thick in the other direction. To extend the dough farther, roll the dough around the rolling pin and unroll. Keep the dough as thin as possible and as light. Function efficiently as it dries out the pastry.

6. To cut the dough by hand: dust the dough with flour and put together in the middle the two opposite ends of the dough. Repeat two more times before you have a pasta roll of tight double jelly. Keep the roll on one side and slice into 1/8, 1/4- or 1/2-inch-wide narrow, medium, or wide noodles with a sharp chef's knife in the other. Under the middle of the dough, you can slide the knife's rusty edge and raise the noodles; they'll

unravel over the knife. Or, with your fingers, raise the noodles.

7. To use a pasta machine to roll the dough: Mound the pasta machine to your counter and place the smooth rollers at the widest opening. With all-purpose flour, dust the work board. Divide the dough into 4 to 6 equivalent parts to avoid drying out, leaving the reserved dough balls sealed. On the work surface, put the dough ball and press to flatten to a diameter no wider than the opening of the unit. Run the unit through the dough. Dust as required with flour. Fold in thirds and cycle once more through the machine. Two more times, run the dough through the machine but don't fold the dough again.

8. To the next smallest setting, set the notch on the machine and run the dough through the rollers. Continue to roll and stretch the dough until the smallest setting is reached, using a smaller setting each time. There are six graded configurations on most computers. Any settings may be skipped. Long and fragile would be the dough strip.

9. Cutting the dough with a pasta machine: Change the machine's cutting mechanism to the appropriate width and run through the dough to cut it. You should directly run the cut pasta onto a baking sheet dusted with some semolina.

10. Move the sliced pasta onto a drying plate, a floured towel, or a floured baking sheet to dry the pasta. When one layer is full, put a sheet of parchment on the baking sheet over the pasta, begin to layer the pasta, and gently sprinkle with flour to avoid sticking. Split with a sharp chef's knife into ideal lengths. Before cooking or freezing, let the paste dry for at least 20 minutes.

Grissini (Breadsticks)

(Ready in about 3 hours 40 minutes I Servings- 24 I Difficulty- Moderate)

Ingredients

- One and a half cups water
- 1/4 cup olive oil
- One teaspoon salt
- One and a half cups semolina flour
- Two and a half cups unbleached all-purpose flour
- One tablespoon SAF yeast or one tablespoon plus Half a teaspoon bread machine yeast
- Half cup additional olive oil for dipping
- One and 1/4cups semolina flour, for sprinkling and rolling

Instructions

1. Place all the dough ingredients in the pan according to the order in the manufacturer's instructions. Program for the Dough cycle; press Start.

2. Dust a work surface with semolina flour. When the machine beeps at the end of the cycle, turn the dough out onto the work surface and pat it into a thick 12-by-6-inch rectangle without kneading or overworking the dough.

3. Leave this to rise on the work surface, especially if it is a marble slab, or transfer it to a 17-by-11-inch baking sheet that has been dusted with semolina flour. Brush the top of the dough with olive oil. Cover with plastic wrap and let rise at room temperature until doubled in bulk, about 1 hour.

4. Place a baking stone on the center rack and preheat the oven to 425°F. Brush two heavy 17-by-11-inch baking sheets with olive oil. Place the additional olive oil and semolina flour in two shallow bowls.

5. Press the dough all over to gently deflate it and place it on a floured work surface. Using a pastry or pizza wheel, cut the dough into four equal pieces lengthwise; the dough will deflate a bit more. Cut each piece into six thick strips lengthwise. Pick up each end of each strip and stretch to the desired length or quickly roll out each strip with your palms, stretching from the center out to the ends, to a size that will fit your baking sheet. Dip each strip in the olive oil and then roll it in semolina flour. Place the strips spaced evenly apart on the baking sheets. Each sheet will hold 12 grissini. Bake each sheet separately in the oven center for 15 to 20 minutes, or until the grissini are lightly browned and crisp. Remove the grissini from the baking sheets to cool completely on racks.

Conclusion

I'm very thankful that you took the time to read this book. I hope that all your questions are clear with regards to bread-making in a bread machine.

A bread machine is an easy kitchen tool and is your helping hand while making bread at home. It is easy to use and easy to handle, and you will not regret buying it. This book is a bible for all you bread lovers who like to bake their own bread at home.

The recipes provided in this book are delicious and suits all your preferences. While practicing making them, you would not regret following the directions specified in this book. One piece of suggestion, always read the user's manual and manufacturer's direction before making the recipes because every bread machine is different. Just select the right bread machine and say goodbye to those tiresome kneading and baking.

Buy a bread machine and start baking.Thank you, and good luck!

Printed in Great Britain
by Amazon